A VICEROY'S INDIA

A VICEROY'S INDIA

Leaves From Lord Curzon's Note-Book

BY THE

MARQUESS CURZON OF KEDLESTON

K.G.

VICEROY AND GOVERNOR-GENERAL OF INDIA
1899-1905

EDITED BY

PETER KING

INTRODUCED BY

ELIZABETH LONGFORD

What shall we tell you? Tales, marvellous tales,
Of ships and stars and isles where good men rest,
Where nevermore the rose of sunset pales,
And winds and shadows fall toward the west.
J. ELROY FLECKER,
The Golden Journey to Samarkand

SIDGWICK & JACKSON
LONDON

First published in Great Britain in 1984
by Sidgwick & Jackson Limited
1 Tavistock Chambers, Bloomsbury Way
London WC1A 2SG

Reprinted November 1984

Designed and produced by
Shuckburgh Reynolds Limited
8 Northumberland Place, London W2 5BS

ISBN 0-283-99166-6

Designed by Behram Kapadia
Picture research by Peter King and Jenny de Gex
Maps on endpapers by Bob Chapman

Typesetting by SX Composing Ltd, Rayleigh, Essex
Printed and bound by Purnell & Sons Limited, Bristol

Frontispiece: The Marquess Curzon of Kedleston painted by John Cooke after J. S. Sargent

Contents

Introduction

Elizabeth Longford

In February 1977 I was sitting on the lawn of Flagstaff House at Barrackpore, beneath the twin shadows of a banyan tree and a statue of Lord Curzon, Viceroy of India from 1899 to 1905. At first there seemed nothing unusual about a former viceroy's statue standing on a state lawn against a background of very English-looking rosebeds and the distant Hugli river. True I had learned to call Flagstaff House the 'Raj Bhavan' or Governor's House, and the governor and his wife who so kindly entertained me were Mr and Mrs Diaz, distinguished Indians from Goa. And Curzon – let's face it – would have been horrified to think of *Indians* occupying his delightful little summer residence, just up the river by steam-launch from Calcutta. But there was something else that would have tickled Curzon about that colossal bronze effigy of himself on the lawn. It was the only one.

Of course, all the viceregal and other British statues had been removed after Independence from the Maidan in Calcutta and put out to grass in Barrackpore. But Curzon's alone remained *on the grass*. The rest – admirals, generals, statesmen – were disposed about the shrubberies: here Lord Northbrook, dignified in frock coat and chain but alongside a tall silo; there Lord Montagu of the reformist Montagu-Chelmsford Report, behind a neighbouring hedge, his head bowed as if in sombre thought; even King George V was invisible from the front law. Why Curzon alone in glory?

It was the same in Calcutta itself. As I walked round the vast Victoria Memorial museum, which Curzon initiated, a diminutive boy detached himself from the file of his schoolfellows and boldly asked the curator: 'Why here? Why in Calcutta? Why not in Delhi?' To which the curator replied: 'Because Calcutta was still the capital when Lord Curzon built the Victoria Memorial'; adding in my ear, 'Curzon and Warren Hastings are the only two viceroys or governors they now remember.'

That is part of the answer to the Curzon enigma. He is honoured for the care he gave to India's great monuments. Not only the new ones celebrating the British Raj, but also India's ancient heritage, much of which was in desperate need of conservation. Among other works, he restored the Red Fort at Delhi, the lovely shrine of Fatehpur Sikri which some people consider more perfect even than the Taj Mahal, and the Taj itself, above whose famous tomb Curzon restored the hanging lamp.

If Curzon's work for Indian education, banking and agriculture is added to his concern for India's monuments and culture, and if it is also remembered that his genuine devotion to these causes entailed voluminous reading and exhausting travel, it is not so difficult to understand his honourable position in India even today. 'India had no viceroys of genius after Lord Curzon,' writes A. V. Chaudhuri; there were clever men 'like experienced old foxes' to steal a few marches on the Indian Nationalists, but 'not the grand animals to scatter the pack with a roar and a rush.'

Not that Curzon's popularity must be exaggerated. An Indian official at Barrackpore said to me: 'Curzon did not love India but he loved being viceroy.' Contemporary Indians might think sourly of Curzon's obsession with ceremony and perhaps echo the criticism that emanated from a New York newspaper in 1903, when Curzon organised the greatest durbar of all time, in celebration of the King-Emperor Edward VII's coronation. 'The people asked for bread and he gave them a durbar.' (In fact, the Great Durbar cost £180,000, not the millions that critics alleged, and Curzon worked incessantly for famine relief.) More recently the passionately involved Bombay-born novelist, Salman Rushdie, told me that he did not admire Curzon: in his land assessment and agricultural reforms he had let far too many corrupt landlords through his net. Other critics of Curzon in India would point to his political rigidity and inflexible belief in the eternal British Raj. More than ten years before Curzon's viceroyalty began, his friend Wilfrid Scawen Blunt, an English poet and anti-imperialist, had travelled through India to Calcutta and attended a meeting of Congress. Curzon as viceroy refused even to let the Congress leaders discuss their ideas with him.

If Curzon's lack of political imagination was a grave drawback, we must remember that he suffered from the limitations imposed by the home government and the era in which he lived. Any weakening of British imperialism would have meant the viceroy's prompt dismissal, Britannia being at the height of her imperial self-confidence and sense of mission. The scramble for Africa, the Suez Canal deal, the annexation of Egypt – none of these things would have seemed compatible with a relaxed grip on the Eastern empire. Lord Salisbury once said to Lady Curzon: 'His frontier policy will keep us in India 50 years longer than we should have kept it otherwise.' Strange to think that despite Curzon's policy the passage of 50 years would just about see out the British Raj.

Today we know a great deal more about the Raj than did many Anglo-Indians who were living under its sumptuous shadow. After Rudyard Kipling have come other sensitive Europeans to interpret the country and peoples, like E. M. Forster *(A Passage to India)*, Paul Scott *(The Jewel in the Crown)*, M. M. Kaye *(The Far Pavilions)* and many great Indian writers such as Ruth Prawer Jhabvahla and Ved Mehta. Curzon's own writings, as these most welcome extracts clearly show, are an amazing treasury of information and experience – exotic, funny, curious, illuminating. His memorable account of meeting the Amir of Afghanistan includes not only a superbly comic dialogue between Curzon and the Amir, but also the basis for future prediction. After reading Curzon's many vivid portraits of his wild hosts on India's North-West frontier, it is impossible to foresee permanent success for the Soviets' present adventure.

It was Curzon's relations with the Indian princes that brought out his glowingly romantic side. Their bejewelled splendour and political loyalty made his viceregal visits to their courts an exhausting joy. The floating palace of Udaipur, its strings of lights reflected in the moonlit lake, seemed to the vicereine a marvellous fairyland. Almost the same vision can be enjoyed today – transformed into the Lake Palace Hotel.

A second advantage accrued to Curzon from his princely contacts. They gave him an excuse for indulging his own passion for pageantry. Obviously he could never allow the rulers of Rajisthan, or wherever the princely sway then held, to outshine the living representative of Queen Victoria. The Maharana of Udaipur might be descended from the sun; Queen Victoria ruled an empire on which the sun never set. India was 'the brightest jewel in her crown', and the princes between them possessed virtually all the finest jewels in India. But the viceroy and vicereine at the Great Durbar rode side by side on the biggest elephant in the world.

More is also known today about Curzon the man than anyone knew in the 1890s, probably more than he knew himself. There have been the two-volume official *Life* by Lord Ronaldshay, Kenneth Rose's moving biography of the young Curzon, David Dilke's authoritative *Curzon in India* and two brilliant studies by a father and son, Harold Nicolson on Curzon himself and Nigel Nicolson on Mary Curzon, the viceroy's enchanting American wife. She was born Mary Leiter in 1870, daughter of a Chicago millionaire. They called each other Pappy and Kinkie. The marriage was lyrically happy in essence, crowned by the births of three beautiful daughters who were all to have unusual lives: Irene Baroness Ravensdale; Lady Cynthia Mosley, wife of Sir Oswald ('Tom') Mosley and herself an MP; and Lady Alexandra ('Baba') Metcalfe, wife of Major 'Fruity' Metcalfe, equerry to the Duke of Windsor, and currently vice-president of the Save the Children Fund. Unfortunately Curzon was a workaholic. 'Grind, grind, grind,' he wrote to Mary, '. . . I love it.' His insistence on a second term as viceroy helped to undermine his wife's frail health. She died in 1906. Her Indian diaries (printed in *Mary Curzon*) make a poignant complement to her husband's *Leaves* and *Tales,* so successfully reprinted here.

Modern readers are likely to be most keenly aware of Curzon as an uncompromisingly patrician figure, cold, handsome, arrogant, often too big for his boots, outsize though they were. That image was first modified by Harold Nicolson, who emphasised that Curzon's unbending stance was due to the steel-and-leather corset he wore all his life, after developing curvature of the spine in his last year at Eton. Readers of *A Viceroy's India* will not forget that during the perilous frontier rides, the processions on elephants and the long hours on thrones, he was always in the grip of steel and often of agonising pain. Nevertheless he *was* arrogant; but according to Elinor Glyn, the 'tiger woman' novelist with whom he lived for a time at Montacute in Somerset after his wife's death, arrogance was 'one of his great charms'.

Readers may also be surprised by Curzon's lively sense of humour, sometimes wonderfully sharp and ironic, though occasionally, I must admit, reminding me of *Punch* in the dental waiting-rooms of my youth. However, unlike some of the intellectual stars of the Naughty Nineties, Curzon could be playfully sarcastic about himself and his talents. He was a noted comic versifier at the Crabbet Club weekends, organised in his Sussex home by Wilfrid Scawen Blunt. In 1891 Curzon wrote a parody of the opening of Virgil's *Aeneid* for a prize poem entitled 'Charma Virumque Cano – In Praise of Myself':

> Charms and a man I sing to wit – a most superior person,
> Myself, who bears the fitting name of George Nathaniel Curzon,
> From which 'tis clear that even when in swaddling bands I lay low,
> There floated round my head a sort of apostolic halo.

'Tis also clear that Curzon could himself appreciate and lightly mock the familiar lines written about him when an undergraduate at Balliol College, Oxford:

> My name is George Nathaniel Curzon,
> I am a most superior person.
> My cheek is pink, my hair is sleek,
> I dine at Blenheim once a week.

Curzon, in the role of haughty viceroy, the Hyde-side of his dual nature, was to quarrel with Kitchener, his C-in-C, over power-sharing and resign in 1906. The same Hyde-like aspect of this amazing man refused to receive his successor Lord Minto in state, but stood casually awaiting him in shooting jacket and slippers. He was affronted that he should not be replaced by another intellectual superman, but merely by a 'gentleman' who was good at jumping hedges in the shires. Lady Minto retaliated by writing in her recollections that Curzon had reduced his officials to pulp – 'a young man in a hurry' – and they were relieved to be rid of him.

Curzon was foreign secretary in 1919, but the biggest plum of all, the premiership, eluded him for an appropriately ironic reason. His elevation to the House of Lords – an apotheosis devoutly wished for – enabled plain Mr Baldwin to amble past him into 10 Downing Street in 1923. Curzon was never a so-called realist, and just as he could not grasp that the Jewel in the Crown was not for ever, he had not guessed that a time would come when the Prime Minister would have to be in the House of Commons. He died in 1925 aged sixty-six.

The engaging Jekyll-side of Lord Curzon was prominent in his second marriage, again to a wealthy American, Grace Duggan, a widow. Through her money Lord Curzon was able to restore the derelict remains of Bodiam Castle in East Sussex and bequeath it to the nation. I often think as I visit Bodiam (I live four miles away) how neatly it represents the two sides of its preserver's nature. In some respects a sham – Bodiam Castle has never heard a shot fired in anger – it emerges as a thing of legendary beauty under the spell of *son et lumière*. Curzon the man was not all *son et lumière* by any means. His light produced heat and energy. But he needed *spectacle* to be at his best. He was not above wearing hired theatrical costumier's stars and medals when he met the Amir. These remarkable *Leaves* show what one favoured man could achieve in imperial India under the stimulus of adventure and power.

Editor's Note

Lord Curzon claimed that it gave him greater pleasure to be awarded the Royal Geographical Society's Gold Medal for exploration and research than it did to become a Minister of the Crown – and he was twice Viceroy of India, once Foreign Secretary and very nearly Prime Minister. Yet in our age less than justice has been done to Curzon the traveller or, perhaps more important, to Curzon the writer. My hope is that this new compilation of Curzon's writings will cause him to be revalued as a travel writer of the highest order.

For this volume I have drawn together his writings on India and his period as viceroy from two collections of his essays: *Tales of Travel* (Hodder & Stoughton, 1923) and *Leaves from a Viceroy's Note-book* (published posthumously by Macmillan in 1926). From the former I have extracted: 'The Amir of Afghanistan', 'The Death-bed of Sir Henry Lawrence', 'The Robber of Khagan', 'The Havildar of Sarhad', 'The Maharaja's Adjuration', 'The "Pig and Whistle" at Bunji', 'The Entry into Kabul' and 'The State Entry into Datia'. The remainder of the material comes from *Leaves from a Viceroy's Note-book*.

Those readers who are unfamiliar with the politics of British India should understand that Curzon's viceregal mandate extended in one sense more widely than India itself, allowing him to make significant policy decisions about both Muscat and Kowait (Curzon's spelling), while in another sense his authority over India itself was circumscribed. This was because historically the Punjab government under its own British Lieutenant-Governor acted more or less independently, and because two other important provincial presidencies, Madras and Bombay, were under British governors who seemed to find it unnecessary to inform the viceroy about their policies, much less request his advice. Curzon did not like this arrangement, and did his best to change it, but without success.

Many of the illustrations for this volume are taken from Curzon's own vast collection of photographs now in the possession of the India Office, and I am indebted to that office's Prints and Drawings Department. I am especially grateful to Lord Scarsdale for kindly allowing access to the Curzon collection at Kedleston Hall. The List of Illustrations carries a fuller description of many of the pictures than may be attached to them in the text, where the caption is almost invariably taken from the appropriate chapter of Curzon.

Other illustrations have been supplied by the Royal Geographical Society, the National Army Museum, the *Illustrated London News,* The Royal Botanic Gardens at Kew. The photograph of Roald Amundsen on page 81 was supplied by the Royal Norwegian Embassy in London. The assistance of each of these and of Miss Vivienne Sharp is gratefully acknowledged. Certain photographs have been taken from an album prepared by the official photographers to the Delhi Durbar of 1903. This is now in the possession of Mrs Margaret Soole to whom I am much indebted for permission to reproduce.

I am also much obliged to Mr Simon Bainbridge who suggested the title, and I wish to thank Mr Colin Harris for introducing me to Curzon the travel writer, Mr William Husselby for his generous help to me while editing the book, and Mrs Cherry Carroll for her encouragement throughout.

PETER KING
London 1984

Illustrations

ILLUSTRATIONS

The Installation

O what a fall was there, my countrymen!
SHAKESPEARE, *Julius Caesar*, Act III. Sc.2.

AMONG the duties which the Viceroy is sometimes called upon to perform in India is the installation of a Ruling Chief or Prince on the *gadi*, or, as it is called if he be a Mohammedan, the *musnud*, of his state. I installed three young princes in my time. The occasion is one for the utmost pageantry, and for great rejoicing in the state concerned. The ceremony itself usually takes place in the Durbar Hall of the palace, before an immense concourse of the nobles and ministers of the state and a large assemblage of European officers and guests. Outside are ranged the state elephants, all magnificently caparisoned and with their heads and trunks fantastically painted in every hue of vermilion and saffron and gamboge. The state regalia are plentifully displayed, every servant of the state has a new livery of dress for the occasion, and coloured silks, satins, and velvets provide a sumptuous background to ropes of emeralds, rubies, and pearls. The Viceroy, after being escorted to the dais, delivers a speech or allocution of friendly advice and encouragement to the young man, who duly responds. A good deal of the remainder of the visit is devoted to banquets, entertainments, and visits to institutions, and very likely, if the opportunity offers, to *shikar*. But before any of these functions or amusements can take place, there is always a preliminary exchange of formal visits between the Viceroy and the Chief, at which a consecrated and rigid etiquette is faithfully observed. The Chief calls upon his guest at an early hour after the arrival of the latter. A little later the Viceroy returns the call, and the number of guns, the strength of the escort, the details of the reception, and the offerings made or exchanged are prescribed with the most scrupulous precision.

My 'bearer', not thinking he would be detected, had wrapped it up inside a cooking tin.

As a rule the *bundobust* is magnificent, and the arrangements proceed with clockwork regularity. But occasionally a little grit will get into even the best-oiled machinery, or some unforeseen and laughable incident will occur. On one occasion, just as the Viceroy's procession was about to start for the palace, my solar *topé* could nowhere be found. It was too hot to drive through the streets in a grey top-hat, and my native servant confessed that he had packed up the *topé* and left it at the station. Mounted men were sent galloping down, while I fumed and waited. At length the missing headpiece arrived. But my "bearer", not thinking that he would be detected, had wrapped it up inside a cooking tin, from which it emerged somewhat the worse for its unseemly incarceration.

Outside the Durbar Hall are ranged the state elephants, all magnificently caparisoned and with their heads and trunks fantastically painted in every hue of vermilion and saffron and gamboge.

This, however, was nothing to an experience I once had at a country house in England, when, having entrusted my packing to the footman who was valeting me, I found that, in a meticulous desire to economise space, he had packed my sponge-bag inside my boots and my boots inside my top-hat.

It was my lot to discourse learnedly upon the services which his Camel Transport Corps were capable of rendering to the British Raj.

However, to revert to the Indian installation. The young prince whom I was to install was the Nawab of B——r, and the ceremony took place with due *éclat* in the Durbar Hall of the palace. But the preliminary visits were exchanged in a second palace where I was accommodated, and in a house which was being temporarily occupied by the young ruler. The best state furniture had been moved to the Durbar Hall, and the room in which the Nawab received me was in consequence somewhat sparsely equipped. At the upper end stood the silver chairs of state, upon which my host and I took our seats. Below and lower down were ranged in two confronting rows the seats which were to be occupied by his staff and by mine, the former on the left, and the latter on the right. The procession had entered, the preliminary bows had been made, the Nawab and I had taken our seats. My staff, faultlessly clad in white duck uniforms, stood in a line in front of the chairs upon which they were now expected to sit down. Instead, however, of the customary upright seats, there had been substituted for them, in at least one case, a low English arm-chair upholstered in satin. The ADC for whom this was intended, not realising, when the signal to sit down was given, that his intended seat was a good deal lower than that of his colleagues, made a descent upon it so precipitate that he landed upon the back of the chair instead of on the seat. Over went the chair backwards, and the only spectacle presented to us was the two little white-trousered legs of the Guardsman sticking up in the air, with his spurs protruding from his shining boots, and himself totally unable either to recover his equilibrium or regain his seat. Convulsions of laughter twisted the faces and shook the forms of his comrades. The Indian Sirdars opposite sat immovable, without the flicker of an eyelash, or the symptom of a smile; while on the dais it was my lot, during the extrication of the ADC, to discourse learnedly to the prince on the advantages of the water-works which he was introducing into his capital city, and upon the services which his Camel Transport Corps were capable of rendering, in future imperial campaigns, to the British Raj.

The Abdication

Fortuna saevo laeta negotio et
ludum insolentem ludere pertinax
transmutat incertos honores,
nunc mihi, nunc alii benigna.

Laudo manentem; si celeres quatit
pinnas, resigno quae dedit et mea
virtute me involvo probamque
pauperiem sine dote quaero.

Fortune, her cruel trade quite to my mind,
Persistent still her wanton game to play,
Transfers her favours day by day,
To me, to others, kind.

Stays she, I'm pleased; but if swift wings she shake,
I drop her paltry gifts, wrapping my life
In its own worth; and Want for wife,
Undowered but honest, take.

HORACE, *Odes* iii. 29, 49.

THE relations between the Viceroy and the Ruling Princes of India, based partly on treaty, partly on long usage, partly on considerations of high expediency and honour, are among the most agreeable, but also the most anxious, of his responsibilities. In modern times the standards of administrative efficiency in the Native States have greatly improved, and many of them are ruled over by men who do honour to their exalted order. But in the last resort, in cases of flagrant misdemeanour or crime, the Viceroy retains, on behalf of the Paramount Power, the inalienable prerogative of deposition, though it is only with extreme reluctance and after the fullest inquiry and consultation with the Secretary of State that he would decide to exercise it.

A few such cases occurred in my time. One prince, who was a confirmed drunkard, shot his body-servant dead in a fit of ungovernable temper; another was privy to the poisoning of his uncle; a third, who for nearly twenty years had been guilty of gross maladministration, of shocking barbarity in the treatment of his subjects, and of persistent contumacy to the Government of India, only escaped a similar fate by himself expressing a voluntary desire to abdicate and live henceforward in retirement; although no sooner had this offer been made and accepted than he tried hard to withdraw it and to have the decision of the Government reversed.

This case revealed in so striking a fashion both the weaknesses and the inherent nobility of the Indian nature, that, now the incident is long buried in oblivion, and the principal actors are dead, I can safely tell the story here.

The Maharaja, a man of enormous size.

He bargained for an invitation to attend the impending Delhi Durbar as a faithful feudatory of the King-Emperor.

The prince in question had, I think, a streak of real madness in his composition, which perhaps accounted for his crimes. But he had also an extraordinary sense of humour, no small measure of self-respect, and in the last resort, a feeling of genuine loyalty to the British Crown. In his more violent moods he would heap abuse on the Government of India and its officers, and act as a lunatic towards his own people. Then he would write me a letter saying that he was only a naughty boy who ought to be whipped; although, when frustrated in any of his evil acts, he was more fond of describing himself as a 'rat in a hole' and a 'bison in a cage'. After the acceptance of his abdication, he begged to be allowed to see me – having previously expressed complete indifference to a projected official visit from the Viceroy – and I consented, feeling that if a ruling prince desired, before surrendering his authority, to make any communication to the representative of the Sovereign, he had a right to do so.

I shall never forget the interview. The Maharaja, a man of enormous size, weighing something like twenty-four stone, went down on his knees and touched my feet with his head. Streams of perspiration poured from his face and dropped in big beads from his chin and over his hands. With the utmost difficulty I induced him to resume his seat and to conduct himself with the dignity of a ruler and a prince. When he realised that the decision to accept his retirement was irrevocable, he became more composed, and bargained only for an ample allowance from the state revenues, for permission to reside in future at a country house within the borders of his own state, and for an invitation to attend the impending Delhi Durbar, as a faithful feudatory of the King-Emperor. There was no difficulty in arriving at a suitable arrangement on the first two points. As to the third, I acceded on two conditions – both of which the Prince accepted – viz. that he should comport himself with propriety and decorum while at Delhi, and that he should not announce his abdication (of which nothing was yet known) until after his return. It seemed to me better to trust to his sense of loyalty and self-respect in both matters, although in view of his previous aberrations and explosions I felt that I was incurring some risk.

The Maharaja was true to his word. He appeared at Delhi, where he attended all the functions, said nothing to anyone about his troubles, and enjoyed himself immensely. As I rode off the parade ground, after the great review, I caught sight of a gigantic and bejewelled figure, perched on the top of a charabanc, swaying to and fro, and cheering at the top of his voice. It was he.

After he had returned to his state, the moment for the public announcement of his abdication drew near. The Agent to the Governor-General was rather nervous as to how this would pass off, and consulted me as to the sort of speech that he should make on the occasion. On the other hand, the Maharaja asked my permission to make the announcement in his own language. Here, again, were serious possibilities of danger. But His Highness had already so fully justified my confidence at Delhi that I once more complied, and informed the Prince that I trusted him to make the public declaration in a becoming way. It was not without

Having an ample revenue, he developed a taste for travelling about India in a special train.

some anxiety that I awaited a report of the speech. The Maharaja entered the Durbar Hall with his eldest son, a young boy. The nobles and officials of the state, the Agent to the Governor-General, and the British officers were present, and a considerable crowd.

The Maharaja first announced his own intended retirement, and then placed his son on the *gadi* which he had himself just vacated. Addressing the assemblage he then requested the Government of India to continue to watch with paternal interest over the welfare of the young prince, so that he might prove himself to be an enlightened ruler, beloved by his subjects and worthy of the approval of the King-Emperor. Turning to the boy he then spoke to him as follows:

'On this solemn occasion my earnest injunction to you is to be loyal to the British Government; and if you have any representations to make to the Government, do so in a courteous and respectful manner. Remain always a staunch supporter of the Paramount Power. In your private and public life follow the marriage and other customs of your country, your religion, and your family, and by earnest attention to your education qualify yourself for the exercise of ruling powers as soon as you may be of age to receive them.'

The gadi *which he had himself just vacated.*

Having delivered this admirable and dignified allocution, which was in fact a confession of his own failure, the Maharaja stalked down the Durbar Hall, without another word, entered his carriage outside, and drove away into private life.

There, on the banks of the holy Nerbudda, he speedily recovered his equanimity, and led a very tranquil and happy existence. He even used to invite me to spend a Saturday to Monday in his country retreat. Having an ample revenue, he developed a taste for travelling about India in a special train; but when he reached his destination, his vein of eccentricity would assert itself, and he would decline to emerge from his railway carriage, staying there for some days at a time, and eventually returning without having left it. When I was re-appointed Viceroy for a second term, he wrote to me to express the hope that 'my beneficent sway over the teeming millions of his mother country might be continued with perfect health, peace, and prosperity'.

So we remained friends till I left India; and not many years after, he himself died. The story is a curious one, in its revelation of a very complex and extraordinary character, in which the good and the evil were mixed in puzzling proportions. But it cannot be denied that nothing in his official life became the prince so well as his manner of leaving it, and that by the dignified character of his exit he went far to redeem the undisciplined errors of his earlier career.

Cheers

Oft-times nothing profits more
Than self-esteem, grounded on just and right
Well managed.
MILTON, *Paradise Lost*, Book VIII. 571.

AN incident occurred at a meeting which I attended in India that suggested to me quite a new train of thought, and a possible innovation in public life.

We are familiar with the spectacle of the Guest of Honour at a public banquet in England, who sits, his face suffused with self-conscious blushes, while his health is being proposed, and the most extravagant compliments are paid to his virtues or abilities or career. Then, when the glasses are raised in his honour, he bows in deprecatory response to the salutations of the company. His attitude throughout is one of modest detachment, as though he were gazing from a distance on the spectacle of his own apotheosis.

On the Continent the thing is done in a less exclusive and more convivial way. The guest, when his health is drunk, frequently rises himself, clinks glasses with his neighbours, and joins, in a spirit of effusive good temper, in the general chorus of congratulation.

But why not carry it a step further? If he is conscious of the justice of the plaudits, why should he not take part in them? If he is convinced that he is a 'jolly good fellow', why not join in proclaiming it? If the company insists on shouting 'And so say all of us', why should he be the sole absentee from the chorus?

The late Duke of Devonshire, when Lord Hartington, is reported on one occasion to have paused and yawned in the middle of one of his own speeches in the House of Commons; and, when asked why he had done so, to have replied that he was so bored. But why stop there? If a man may yawn at himself or even laugh at himself – as some people rather enjoy doing – why not applaud himself also? Why leave other people a monopoly of the cheers?

These reflections were suggested to me by the experience in question. One of the most famous incidents of the Indian Mutiny was the heroic conduct of the small party at the Delhi Telegraph Office on the fateful morning of 11th May 1857, when, upon the arrival of the mutinous Sepoys from Meerut, murder and pillage broke out in the imperial city. The scene is thus described in the well-known *History of the Mutiny* by T. Rice Holmes:

> 'In the telegraph office outside the city a young signaller named Brendish was standing, with his hand upon the signalling apparatus. Beside him was his fellow-signaller, Pilkington; and Mrs. Todd, the widow of their chief, who had been murdered a few hours before, was there too with her child. They heard the uproar and the rattle of

musketry; and native messengers brought news of the atrocities that were being enacted in the city. Flashed up the wires to Umballa, to Lahore, to Rawalpindi and to Peshawar, this message warned the authorities of the Punjab. "We must leave office. All the bungalows are on fire, burning down the Sepoys from Meerut. They came in this morning. We are off." More fortunate than their countrymen in the city, the boys, with their helpless charge, were in time to escape the fate which, in the performance of their duty, they had dared.'

Forty-five years later, when I was Viceroy, I was invited to unveil a monument, which had been erected to commemorate this service of the Delhi Telegraphic Staff, on a spot within a few hundred yards of the scene of the original deed. Having ascertained that Brendish, one of the brave trio, was still living – Todd having, as already pointed out, been killed in the early morning of that terrible day and Pilkington having died about ten years later - I wrote to King Edward and asked him if he would authorise me to present the medal of the Victorian Order to Brendish at the ceremonial. The King gladly assented, and accordingly it was my proud privilege to pin the medal upon the veteran's breast.

When I entered the enclosure I saw Brendish, an old man with a flowing grey beard, seated a little below the platform on the right. He was in a state of considerable but legitimate excitement.

In my speech I described the incident of 1857, and made some general observations on the policy of commemorating such events. I had already in my opening remarks referred with satisfaction to the old man as still present among us, and I had noted that this observation was received with loud 'Hear, hears' by him. But when I came to present the medal, and again singled him out as 'the sole survivor of those immortal days', and as 'this old and faithful servant, who had helped to save the British Empire in India nearly half a century ago', the veteran rose in his place and led the enthusiastic cheers of the audience.

It was all very simple and natural and touching. There was no trace of vanity or self-assertion in the action of the old man. He was cheering the memories of the past; his dead companions; the Indian Telegraph Service as a whole; and if incidentally at the same time he was cheering himself, why not? He was the sole survivor and there was no one else left to be cheered.

But I could not help thinking that the precedent, if adopted elsewhere, might lend a new savour to public life. It might even be carried a stage further. For a man might be permitted to cheer not merely the references to himself made in the speeches of other people, but his own speech as well. It would soon become a very popular practice; for the speaker, whether in the House of Commons or on the platform, would be entirely independent of the suffrages of his audience. He would never notice their possible failure to appreciate his efforts, since their silence would be drowned in his own applause. By this simple device every one would be pleased. The speaker would be gratified, for he would get his cheers; the audience would be relieved because there would be no obligation on

The late Duke of Devonshire yawned in the middle of one of his own speeches in the House of Commons; and when asked why replied that he was so bored.

them to define their attitude; and no interest would suffer. I have ever since felt inclined to commend this innovation to the politicians at home.

As a friend of mine, who is very fond of quoting Tennyson, remarked, when I passed on the suggestion to him:

Cheers, idle cheers! I know now what they mean!
Cheers, for which once I craved in deep despair,
Rise in the throat and gather to the tongue
In looking on the happy audience
Who, since I cheer myself, need cheer no more!

Meerut, where the mutinous Sepoys began the insurrection.

A Speech in Portuguese

They have been at a great feast of languages, and stolen the scraps.
SHAKESPEARE, *Love's Labour Lost*, Act v. Sc. 1.

NEVER shall I forget my Viceregal visit to Goa, still the capital of Portuguese possessions in India, as it has been ever since the famous Alfonso de Albuquerque made his triumphal entry into the older city on 17 February 1510. During the succeeding century the name of Goa was a synonym throughout the Eastern world for all that was fastidious in ostentation and refulgent in splendour. The Portugese power, resting on the double basis of a dominant military organisation and a wealthy and proselytising church, presented a gorgeous external façade, though infected with the germs of an early and inevitable decay. Luxury, profligacy, and a complete lack of the colonising and even the commercial spirit sapped the structure which had been so easily and brilliantly reared. With the fall of the Portugese Empire, its outlying possessions dwindled and decayed, the territory was invaded, internal revolutions were frequent, and Goa sank into a swift and irremediable decline.

The old town of Goa, five miles higher up the river than the modern capital, was abandoned, and is now the site only of a few fine churches, in one of which the Apostle of the Indies, St Francis Xavier, is interred in a magnificent tomb. In buildings half as large as St Paul's, services are still kept up by a handful of native Catholic priests for a congregation that is non-existent, and the vestries and chapels are packed with inestimable treasures in vestments, sacramental plate, and other works of art. Otherwise, except when the great church festivals are held, and the body of the saint, at rare intervals, is exposed to view, old Goa is a deserted city, where the relics of bygone splendour are gripped by the encroaching jungle, and the towers of the empty churches spring from a forest of palms. Still, however, at the head of the road leading up from the river stands the great archway under which each new Governor-General on assuming office has to pass on his way to Bom Jesus, where he is inducted into his office with a service during which he holds the staff that at other times is borne by the effigy of St Francis, which stands on the altar before his shrine.

At about the time when George III was ascending the British Throne, the ruin of old Goa was already so far advanced that the capital was moved to a site a few miles lower down the river and in more convenient proximity to its mouth; and there, at Panjim or New Goa, the seat of government of the shrunken Portuguese dominions in India has ever since been placed.

Lord Ripon was the only Viceroy before myself who had ever been to Goa, and that in an unofficial capacity. My visit was official; and my host was the Governor-General of Portuguese India, who extended a lavish hospitality to Lady Curzon and myself.

The relics of bygone splendour are gripped by the encroaching jungle.

The visit was marked by incidents, both rehearsed and unrehearsed, which were not without amusing features. The Portuguese Government had provided a gunboat to take us from the port of Mormugao up the river to the town. But they had not made sufficient allowance – whether it was for the shallowness of the channel or the lack of skilled navigation of the vessel, I never clearly ascertained. Anyhow, we lay for an interminable time in mid-stream immediately off the town, where bands and crowds and guards were to be seen in full view waiting to receive us, while our boat had slowly and laboriously to be warped to the landing-stage. At length we stepped ashore amid every demonstration of enthusiastic welcome from the assembled multitude.

We were presently conducted to a two-horsed equipage in which, preceded by a band and surrounded by a sort of body-guard, we made the slow circuit of the beflagged and crowded streets. I use the word 'circuit' advisedly, for it was not till after a little time that I realised, from the astonishing similarity of the *mise en scène*, that we were going steadily round and round the same streets; in order, I suppose, to sustain the illusion of a more extended city and a larger population. During this procession the salutations of the female portion of the inhabitants who were clustered on the balconies of the houses, whence they threw flowers into the carriage, were appropriated with much gallantry by the Portuguese ADC, who was attached to us, and who occupied a seat in the vehicle. Throwing kisses in bouquets to the feminine beauties of Goa, he was undoubtedly the hero of the hour.

This ceremony over, we drove out to a house, or palace, belonging to the Governor-General on a wooded cape at the mouth of the river, where every effort had been made to entertain us in royal fashion. Baths, of the type favoured by the British in India, being unknown at Goa, a special bath-tub, resembling a wine vat of gargantuan proportions, had been imported for the occasion; and, there being no bathroom in the house, it was placed in the corner of the drawing-room, where the removal of the spigot discharged its contents straight on to the floor.

The heat was suffocating, and when we drove to the state dinner at the Town Palace of the Governor-General, I thought we should almost have expired. Even the staff in their white ducks nearly dissolved under the strain. Afternoon tea with floods of sweet champagne had been a penance; but the sufferings of the banquet, in an immensely long narrow room adorned with full-length portraits of previous Governors-General from the famous Albuquerque downwards, were unimaginable.

The difficulties, or shall I say the humours, of the situation were not diminished by the fact that none of the Portuguese officials spoke a word

We were presently conducted to a two-horsed equipage, in which we made the slow circuit of the beflagged and crowded streets.

either of English or French, while none of my party understood a word of Portuguese. This disability did not, however, prevent an exchange of the liveliest conversation – not the less charming because wholly unintelligible – throughout the repast. At length the Governor-General rose to propose my health, and, in an admirable speech, loudly applauded by the whole of the audience, though unfortunately 'Greek' to us, descanted upon the historical alliance between Portugal and Great Britain, and the compliment of my visit. I rose to reply, and made a speech which was equally unintelligible to the vast majority of my hearers, though warmly cheered by my own staff, who alone had any idea of what I was saying.

But here occurred the unexpected and stupefying finale. In the latter part of my speech, I, who did not know a word of the language, broke suddenly into fluent Portuguese, and, amid a storm of applause, delivered a glowing and impassioned Portuguese peroration. The audience leaped to their feet and shouted themselves hoarse with delight, and I certainly achieved a triumph in an unknown tongue far greater than any I have ever won in my own. What was the explanation? Half-way through the banquet I made the agreeable discovery that the Portuguese lady who sat on my right hand had been educated in an English-speaking school, or convent, in the Portuguese possession of Macao near Canton in China. Realising at once the immense possibilities of the situation, I sought her assistance, and, writing down on a paper, unobserved, the later portions of my intended speech, I prevailed upon her to translate them into Portuguese and to teach me *sotto voce* the correct pronunciation. Nobly did she perform her part, and not inadequately, I am fain to believe, did I accomplish mine. Anyhow it was her fair hand that placed upon my brow the crown of an otherwise imperfect oratorical career.

The Interpreter

Traduttori traditori.
Egad, I think the interpreter is the hardest to be understood of the two.
R.B. SHERIDAN, *The Critic*, Act I. Sc.2.

GREAT are the advantages of being able to speak to a foreigner in his own tongue – maybe only in this way can true comprehension be attained. But of no mean benefit is it sometimes to be so ignorant of the language of the other party to the conversation as to require the aid of an interpreter; never more so than when the ideas and idioms of the two parties differ so radically as to transcend the suasion of a common medium of expression, and when the contributions of each to the dialogue require to be adapted in transmission to the mode of thought or the understanding of the other. In interviews with Eastern potentates and peoples, I have often profited by the interpreter's artful aid. While the other man is speaking, you can watch with curious interest the movement of his lips, the expression of his face, the tone of his voice. You wonder, at times even you correctly guess, what he is saying. Then, while it is being slowly translated, time is given you to meditate the becoming reply. Further, while it is being passed on, you can watch the effect of your answer as it is unfolded word by word. There is also the delicious element of doubt as to whether the interpreter is really reproducing, with anything like fidelity, either what the other man says to you, or what you desire to say to him, with the certainty (at least in Eastern countries, where forms are important and hyperbole abounds) that he is doing nothing of the sort. Rather is he probably clothing your inept or imperfect phraseology with the glowing mantle of Oriental compliment, and quite possibly saying something entirely different from what you had entrusted him to say.

I remember hearing of one Indian Prince who when entertaining, as was his annual wont, a large party of English guests – whom his caste precluded him from joining at table, but to whom he desired through the medium of the British Resident to extend a hospitable welcome before they proceeded to the banquet – said in Hindustani to the latter: 'Tell the ladies I hope they will fill their bellies!' The tactful but unsuspicious officer at once translated this as follows: 'Ladies and gentleman, His Highness hopes very much that you will enjoy your dinner.' But, unhappily, His Highness, who was by nature *méchant*, also knew enough of English to realise that he was not being quite correctly reproduced; whereupon, in tones of thunder, he ejaculated, 'No, I did not say that: I told the ladies to fill their bellies!'

This was an illustration not of employing an interpreter but of the interpreter consenting to be, so to speak, checked and overhauled – a handicap which ought never to be permitted.

The case, however, in my own experience, in which an Oriental Prince to whom I was presented most successfully disposed of the need either of employing an interpreter or of conversing with a foreigner at all, was the

'Tell the ladies I hope they will fill their bellies.'

following: being bored by the prospect of giving an audience to a traveller from a foreign land, he made up his mind to cut the interview as short as possible. Accordingly, French being the diplomatic language of his Court, the potentate would inquire, with apparently great cordiality, of the European traveller: 'Parlez-vous Francais?' If the stranger in reply regretted his ignorance of that tongue, the Prince, with a gesture of disappointment and almost of despair, would close the audience forthwith; leaving it to be inferred that, but for the stupidity of the other party, they might have had a delightful conversation. If, on the other hand, the foreigner replied, 'Mais oui, Monseigneur,' the Prince was equally ready. Like a pistol shot came his rejoinder: 'Mais non,' and a salutation of farewells.

Perhaps he was wise not to indulge in the experiment of conversing in a strange language; anyhow he escaped the fate that befell a worthy prelate of the Church of England who, on the occasion of a visit to the front during the Great War, decided to speak some words of encouragement to the French soldiers. After a moment's meditation he summed up his excellent intentions with the curt benediction: 'Que Dieu vous bless(e).'

A Viceroy's path may conceivably be strewn with similar pitfalls. One of my predecessors, though endowed with many graces, did not include among them either an accurate knowledge or a correct pronunciation of the French tongue. Nevertheless, on the occasion of a visit to the French settlement of Chandernagore, a little higher up the river than Calcutta, he was received with much honour by the then French Governor and the small population; after listening to a flattering address in French from the former, he strove to return the compliment by replying in the same tongue.

His staff listened with due reverence to the efforts of their Chief: but they are alleged to have scarcely retained their gravity when the Governor, after listening with solemnity to the allocution, beckoned to his Hindustani interpreter and asked him to translate His Excellency's remarks!

I once suffered while in India from lack of such timely assistance. In arranging for the Delhi Durbar, I invited a number of Allied and friendly Asiatic states to depute representatives to the Assembly. The Japanese Government sent a very distinguished General, with whom I had two interviews at Viceregal Lodge, one at the outset and the other at the close of the proceedings. The General had sent me a message to say that, being acquainted with English, he did not think it necessary to bring an interpreter with him. Accordingly, I looked forward to the interview without anxiety. The Japanese warrior, clad in a resplendent uniform, his breast ablaze with stars, entered the room, accompanied by a staff equally smart and scarcely less gorgeous. The General, then, after a lengthy clearing of the throat, which appeared to suggest bronchial disorder of a very acute description, gave vent to these words:

'My Imperial Master—'

This was followed by prolonged and guttural mouthing, of which the following is an attempt at a phonetic reproduction:

'G-h-u-r-m-m-m-m!'

This lasted for the best part of half a minute, and was succeeded by complete silence. Three times (like the Chinese *Kowtow*) was this ritual repeated, without the slightest deviation either of form or sound. Realising that the Envoy had exhausted his powers, I bowed him politely out of the room.

Ten days later, he came to thank me for his entertainment and to bid goodbye. There were the same staff, the same uniforms, the same preliminary and sepulchral salute. I waited for the compliments or the congratulations, or even for the farewells of my illustrious guest.

'My Imperial Master – G-h-u-r-m-m-m-m,' – three times repeated, was all that I obtained. Realising that there must be either some esoteric significance in this highly abbreviated formula, or that the General's knowledge of the English language did not admit of more exuberant expression, I cordially shook hands and we parted the best of friends.

But if I had had an interpreter I might perhaps have learned a little more of what 'My Imperial Master' had instructed his faithful lieutenant to say. As it was, the message was buried in eternal oblivion.

Hymns

Psalms and hymns and songs of praise. (Cf. Hymns A. and M. 297).

If I reprehend anything in the world, it is a nice derangement of epitaphs.

R.B. SHERIDAN, *The Rivals*, Act. III. Sc. 3.

THE choice of hymns for any public service or ceremonial is a task of no small importance. For on the one hand we are all apt to choose our favourite hymns, less perhaps because of the words they contain than of the tune to which they are commonly sung; and secondly, many excellent hymns contain some astonishingly bad or foolish lines. Take, for instance, the well-known line in a popular hymn:

Happy birds that sing and fly,

or again, the amazing bathos of the lines:

How the troops of Midian
Prowl and prowl around.

But an even greater snare lurks in the occurrence in a hymn of some allusion that strikes a note of unpremeditated incongruity or innuendo. I remember, for instance, when I was a boy at Eton, and when Dr Warre, afterwards Headmaster and Provost, was a housemaster, how on Sundays in the College Chapel, where he would be seated in a stall, we used to revel in the hymn, two lines of which run:

When comes the promised time
That War(re) shall be no more?

Dr Warre was an exceedingly and deservedly popular master. But no charge either of irrelevance or irreverence could rob the 600 boys of the exquisite delight of allowing the choir to sing in almost inaudible tones the opening words of the above verse, and then shouting themselves hoarse in a full-throated chorus on the second line. This became such a scandal that the hymn had eventually to be barred. On the other hand, it was said that, when the meetings of the Governing Body were going to be held, Mr E.C. Austen Leigh, who had a caustic vein of humour, used, when Lower Master, deliberately to select for the occasion in Lower School Chapel the well-known hymn:

God moves in a mysterious way
His wonders to perform.

When in India I narrowly escaped a serious catastrophe arising out of the incautious selection of a hymn. The Great Durbar was being held at Delhi in January 1903 to celebrate the Coronation of King Edward VII. For the Sunday morning I had arranged a church service to be celebrated on the open polo ground – which was the only space large enough to hold a congregation that included several thousand British troops. The visitors at the Durbar, among whom were the Duke and Duchess of

I had arranged a church service to be celebrated on the open polo ground.

Connaught and the Grand Duke of Hesse, then reigning Prince, were assembled on the ground and in the grand stand. A choir of 500 male voices was massed on a great sloping bank 300 yards away, and sang from there through megaphones, the words being taken up by the troops below and by the congregation, numbering over 15,000 persons.

In making the arrangements I consulted Lord Kitchener, who was Commander-in-Chief, as to the particular hymn which the British Tommy would be most likely to sing with hearty vigour, and he unhesitatingly replied, 'Onward! Christian Soldiers.' This seemed to me an admirable choice, even if it did not accurately reflect the theological attitude of the average British soldier, until in a fortunate moment I remembered that one of the verses begins thus:

Crowns and thrones may perish,
Kingdoms rise and wane.

This couplet depicts not merely a familiar contingency, but also a truth of abundant historical justification. But, as a note of rejoicing at the coronation of a monarch in the presence of his near relatives, it might have been thought inappropriate, if not disrespectful, and I was doubtful how it

I consulted Lord Kitchener as to the particular hymn which the British Tommy would be most likely to sing with hearty vigour.

would be regarded by King Edward when he heard of it. So I passed my pencil through the Commander-in-Chief's choice, and selected some more innocent strophe.

A special danger seems to lurk in this hymn and in this particular verse, the next succeeding lines of which run thus:

Gates of hell can never
'Gainst the Church prevail.

For on one occasion a choir-master, instructing his pupils how to sing the verse, said: "Now, remember; only the trebles sing down to the Gates of Hell – and then you all come in."

But it is not only on occasions of ceremonial that such dangers are likely to arise. When a young lady chooses a hymn which she would like to have sung on the occasion of her marriage, she should be peculiarly careful to look through it in advance, and make sure that it responds fully to the needs of the case. I had a young female relative, who with insufficient caution chose as her favourite for the wedding service the hymn which begins

Days and moments quickly flying
Blend the living with the dead.

All went well till the end of the second line, albeit the choice of hymn seemed not particularly apposite and rather unnecessarily lugubrious. But when the congregation came to the succeeding lines,

Soon shall you and I be lying
Each within our narrow bed,

I am afraid that they broke into titters of irrepressible merriment.

Not even the most exalted are immune from these dangers; for I remember reading that, at the wedding ceremony of King Edward and Queen Alexandra, a discarded funeral march of Handel was played with much effect on the organ.

A less grave but still an untimely pitfall was only avoided at another wedding, when the officiating clergyman, on turning up the hymn which he had been invited by the bridegroom to announce, was confronted with

Thy way, not mine, O Lord,
However dark it be.

A not dissimilar though more auspicious incident occurred while I was in Calcutta. A worthy doctor was about to be espoused to a young lady in the closing days of the year; and the parents of the bride, thinking that it would be both charming and economical to take advantage of the Christmas decoration of the cathedral, sought and received the permission of the Bishop to have the ceremony performed there. The congregation was assembled; the bridegroom was in his place; the bridal procession moved slowly up the nave, when, as the happy couple took their stand below the altar steps, both they and the congregation suddenly realised that emblazoned in front of them in huge frosted white letters on a scarlet background, across the entire width of the cathedral, ran the opening words of Isaiah ix. 6. ['For unto us a child is born, unto us a son is given']. It is true that the original author of these words was a prophet; but no prophecy of even the most gifted of seers could have anticipated this particular connotation.

I was myself the victim of another but quite harmless illustration of the same thesis at Simla. On the hill on which stands Viceregal Lodge there was a very small chapel, the survival of an earlier day, where service was sometimes conducted by the station chaplain on Sunday afternoon. On one occasion, during the monsoon, when the whole place was enveloped in mist and fog, with occasional violent downpours of rain, I attended the service with my ADC, only to find that the sole other occupant of the building was the chaplain. Nevertheless he bravely pursued his task, without omitting a line or even a comma, and we three went through the entire service, including the hymns and canticles, undaunted. At length we came to the sermon, which I fondly hoped we might be spared. Not a bit! The chaplain, who could have had no idea that I was likely to attend, had a favourite address on Dives and Lazarus, which he proceeded to read from a well-thumbed MS. His version was even an improvement upon the original. For he modernised Dives, and depicted him as living in great style in a castle on the top of a hill (Viceregal Lodge was on the highest point of the hill only 200 yards away); as wearing smart clothes (the Viceroy has not infrequently to put on uniform and other gorgeous raiment); and as enjoying good meals every day (the fare at Government House was by no means bad). He then referred to the poor man Lazarus as lying at the gate (the Gurkha Gate to the Viceregal grounds was just below), and as being fed with the crumbs from the rich man's table (I had often seen the native servants taking away the scraps from the Viceregal kitchen, to give to their families). And then he asked the congregation, *i.e.* my ADC and myself, to think seriously of Dives' sins, of his subsequent torment in hell, and of the just reproaches of Father Abraham in heaven. We both bore it quite meekly, and, at the close of the service, my ADC not having a singing voice, the chaplain and I sang with great fervour the concluding hymn, in which I joined with all the greater unction when I found that by a happy coincidence it contained these consolatory words:

> The rich man in his castle,
> The poor man at his gate,
> *God made them, high or lowly,*
> *And ordered their estate.*

Horses

Give me another horse! bind up my wounds!
SHAKESPEARE, *King Richard III*, Act V. Sc. 3.

Better an ass that carries than a horse that throws. – *Proverb.*

ONE of the anxieties inseparable from any office requiring frequent external ceremonial – such as the holding of reviews and parades, street processions, and the like – is lest the animal which is ridden by the chief actor should comport itself in a manner unworthy of the situation and the office.

In London I have seen several catastrophes on such occasions either experienced or but narrowly escaped. I remember how on the occasion of the first Jubilee of Queen Victoria a near relative of the Royal Family, to whom a friend had lent what was reported to be a particularly safe mount, was deposited on the ground with great violence before the procession had passed Constitution Hill, and failed in consequence to appear at the Abbey.

I recall the funeral procession of King Edward, when the corpulent form of Ferdinand of Bulgaria had to be held up on his horse by two men walking on either side of the bridle, lest a similar disaster should befall their royal master. I remember the pictures of King Peter of Serbia, on his coronation day at Belgrade, being similarly sustained on his horse, lest the royal crown and sceptre, together with the royal form, should be mingled with the dust. From my windows in Carlton House Terrace I have often seen the horses ridden by grooms following the troops back from the rehearsals of the trooping of the colour on the Horse Guards Parade, in order that on the actual day these animals might not betray their more eminent riders. Even in distant Korea I recall the spectacle of the chief court dignitaries, on their way to the palace at Söul, propped up by running attendants on small ponies which they bestrode, lest perchance they should slip to the ground.

When I went to India, I was a little disconcerted by terrifying stories of the experiences that had befallen some of my predecessors. One of them, when holding the New Year's parade on the Maidan at Calcutta, was already in his position, mounted, and in full sight of the enormous crowd, when suddenly the rattle of the *feu de joie*, running along the long line of troops, caused his steed to start; off fell his *topé* and was caught by the strap round his neck; and in this absurd plight he was carried at full gallop across the parade ground until arrested by the 'thin red line of 'eroes' on the far side. Another Viceroy narrowly escaped a similar fate; for Lady Canning records in one of her letters that, her husband having mounted her own horse Tortoiseshell for a military parade at Barrackpore, the animal so misbehaved that he had to exchange horses with an ADC in the middle of the royal salute, for fear of a catastrophe. Yet another Viceroy, taking advantage of the option so appositely pointed out

I was a little disconcerted by terrifying stories of the experiences that had befallen some of my predecessors.

by the Psalmist, that 'some put their trust in chariots and some in horses', had solved the difficulty or escaped the peril by not merely eschewing horseback, and attending the parade in a landau, but by having the animals taken out of the vehicle when he arrived on the ground, so that his security was beyond risk.

On one such occasion I had a piece of great good luck myself, for, intending to ride a new horse at the parade, I sent a groom out on him at the rehearsal two days before. The *feu de joie* was too much for the animal, particularly at 7.30 A.M. in the morning, when the air is very crisp and the temperature low, and the rider met his fate on *terra firma*.

The *feu de joie* was indeed looked forward to by the spectators at the annual parade at Calcutta with almost delirious expectation, particularly if the Admiral of the East India Squadron and his staff, who used to come up the river in the flagship at Christmas time, were attending the function, as they were always bidden to do. The scene was apt to be diverting. But I record that on one occasion one of my Admirals and the whole of his staff, on a very 'jumpy' morning, sat their steeds like centaurs when the ordeal came, and covered themselves with an undying renown.

In official entries on horseback into a city or town, the moment of greatest anxiety was when one came opposite the massed schoolchildren, who would suddenly start cheering in the shrillest of staccato voices. It required a very steady animal to stand this sudden shock, and the rider had to be prepared for exceptional capers.

When the preparations were being made for the Great Durbar of 1st January 1903, which was to include a review of 40,000 troops on a sandy plain outside Delhi, at which the Viceroy, accompanied by the Duke of Connaught and the Grand Duke of Hesse, was to take the salute, it was thought desirable that a charger of exceptional distinction should be procured for him. My Acting Commander-in-Chief was nothing loth to serve me in this respect, and magnanimously surrendered to me a magnificent chestnut 'waler', well over seventeen hands in height, and of splendid appearance. Mounted on this noble animal, which was named 'Coronation' in honour of the occasion (we were celebrating the Coronation of King Edward VII), I successfully passed through the ceremonies of the morning, though I remember that 'Coronation', being unused to the experience of standing out alone in the open, kept edging backwards to join the horses with their royal riders standing immediately behind. I used to ride him sometimes afterwards; and, when I left India, I parted with him to a General Officer who commanded one of the principal Indian armies.

The Great Durbar of 1903 included a review of 40,000 troops.

The Viceroy, who was accompanied by the Duke of Connaught (left foreground), was to have a charger of exceptional distinction procured for him.

Some years afterwards, meeting this officer in England, I asked him how he had fared with 'Coronation'. 'Have you never heard?' was his mournful reply. 'The brute laid me on my back on the parade ground in full sight of all the troops at P——r.' 'But how did that come about?' I asked. 'Did you not know', was the reply, 'that he was famous for this performance, which he had successfully executed at the expense of the Acting Commander-in-Chief before he parted with him to you?' 'No, indeed', I said, regretting much that that gallant commander was no longer under my orders, to receive a becoming expression of my gratitude; 'and what was the sequel?' 'I parted with him', said the General, 'without a pang, and he has doubtless treated other Generals in the same manner since. But', he added, 'happening to see the diary of my son, who was my ADC on that fateful occasion, lying open on his desk, I glanced at the entry on that date, in order to see how he had dealt with the parental misfortune:

' "January 1, 19—. – Proclamation Parade – Father came off all right" was the somewhat ambiguous but laconic entry.'

I was shown the scene of a similar catastrophe at Imphal, the capital town of Manipur in the far East of India. The General commanding the forces in Bengal and Assam had come up to that remote spot to inspect the garrison; and the entire population of the town was assembled on the polo ground, which is bounded at the two ends by a broad shallow ditch, across which the goals are struck, and on the low bank above which the native inhabitants sit or stand to watch the show. The gallant General's steed, overcome by the firing of the salute or the cheering of the crowd, retreated steadily backwards and eventually discharged its rider amid great applause into the ditch.

Such incidents are not uncommon in a country where a good deal of the locomotion, apart from ceremonies, requires to be performed on horseback, sometimes by persons who have had no great training or experience in equitation. I recall two such that happened at Simla in my time.

The station chaplain, who was about to take to himself a wife, sought and received my permission to have the ceremony performed at noon in a little chapel of ease that stood on Observatory Hill close to Viceregal Lodge. I was seated at work in my room, when I heard that, just as the reverend gentleman, attired for the ceremony, was riding through the Gurkha Gate that led into the Viceregal grounds, the 12 o'clock gun, which stood under a gun shed hard by, went off – and so did he. He was reported as lying on the ground in a condition that scarcely fitted him for the impending function. The remedy was obvious. Without hesitation I sent down an ADC with a bottle of champagne, a copious libation of which at once restored the prostrate bridegroom to his senses, and enabled the bride within half an hour to change her name.

The other incident befell one of my most esteemed colleagues in Council, a gentleman who, never having bestridden a horse until he came out to India, nevertheless regarded it as an obligation of honour to ride, as did all his colleagues, to the meetings of Council at Viceroy Lodge.

The journey, which was a long one from the other end of the Ridge, was pursued at a snail's pace, a native syce running alongside in order to be prepared for any sudden collapse on the part of the rider. If one met the latter so engaged, it was with the utmost difficulty, and only at great personal risk, that he could raise his left hand to salute. It was reported that on one occasion he was met by a friend who, ignoring his air of concentrated anxiety, asked him a question. 'Don't speak', he said; 'can't you see that I am busy riding?'

At last the inevitable catastrophe occurred. The Members of Council were assembled in the Council Chamber for the weekly Cabinet meeting. I was waiting to go in. Ten minutes, fifteen minutes passed, and our eminent colleague did not appear! I told an ADC to mount and gallop down the hill, searching the roadside as he went. Sure enough, there he found the unlucky equestrian, whom the syce had failed to catch as he made his sudden descent; he was lying on the road, severely battered, while his astonished steed stood patiently at his side. The Government of India had to do without a Member for that particular department for more than three weeks.

The Maharaja's Adjuration

And the driving is like the driving of Jehu, the son of Nimshi; for he driveth furiously.

2 Kings ix. 20

It was a wonderful spectacle. Here Nature had spent upon the land her richest bounties; the sun failed not by day, the rain fell in due season, drought was practically unknown; an eternal summer appeared to gild the scene. In a fairy setting of jungle and backwater and lagoon, properous cities had been founded; and a race of indigenous princes flattered the pride and upheld the traditions of a tranquil and contented people.

This morning from the earliest hour – for it was very hot – was spent in ceremonial duties. State visits had to be paid, formal compliments exchanged, institutions to be inspected or opened, speeches to be made – all this under a cloudless sky and a tropical sun. Even in their white duck uniforms the staff felt and looked hot; even the Maharaja, in all his panoply of silks and jewels, although inured to the climate, was perceptibly warm. The native crowds, however, who lined the streets and packed the public places, in their scantier attire were visibly happy, while not disdaining the use of sunshades of local manufacture. The massed

A fairy setting of jungle and backwater and lagoon.

school children did the requisite amount of shrill cheering at selected sites. The Prince's Body-guard galloped about on quite inferior mounts and attempted a display with which they were evidently unfamiliar. The State landau had been pulled out for the occasion by the Maharaja for the use of the Viceroy and his wife; but neither the horses nor the native coachman on the box appeared to have any clear appreciation of their task or any particular aptitude for performing it.

The State landau had been pulled out for the occasion.

The procession was about to start from one ceremonial scene to another; 'God save the King' was being performed in a somewhat precarious and spasmodic fashion by a native band; the crowds began to cheer, the cavalry escort fell into place; but the carriage and horses seemed reluctant to start, while the native coachman appeared to be so overcome with his responsibilities as to be incapable of anything but futile gesticulation.

Then it was that the Maharaja, whose knowledge of English was limited, but who realised that his reputation as a prince and a host was at stake, rose in his place and ejaculated in tones of thunder two words and two alone:

'D-r-iver! D-r-ive!'

It was felt by every one that the command was adequate to the occasion. The Maharaja sank back into his seat exhausted, but with the air of a great duty solemnly performed; the native coachman ceased gesticulating and with recovered confidence handled the reins; the steeds sprang forward with an unexpected *élan*; the procession fell into line; and the next stage in the morning's performance was securely and triumphantly achieved. The two words of the Maharaja, like the 'Open Sesame' of Ali Baba, had successfully solved the problem.

The State Entry into Datia

Fallen, fallen, fallen, fallen,
Fallen from his high estate.
DRYDEN, "Alexander's Feast."

IT is customary, when the Viceroy of India visits the capital of a Native State, for the Prince whose guest he is to receive him at the railway station – should he arrive by rail – and to conduct him personally to the Palace or camp prepared for his reception.

The Chief on this occasion brings out his State equipages, and ordinarily ushers the Viceroy into a State landau, drawn by four horses with postilions, in which he takes his seat at the side of his guest, the remaining two places, with their backs to the horses, being taken by the Military Secretary and the ADC in waiting.

On the occasion of my visit to the Central Indian State of Datia in 1902 – the native Chief of which was a fine old fellow with henna-dyed beard, a great elephant rider in his day – I observed on arriving at the station that the Prince had paid me the unusual compliment of harnessing no fewer than six horses with three postilions to the State landau. Into this stately equipage we clambered, and proceeded at a smart pace towards the walls

The Chief brings out his state equipages.

of the ancient town of Datia, situated at a slight distance on the crest of a hill, and crowned by the massive and sombre castle of Bir Singh Deo. The State troops lined the road: some were on foot, some on richly caparisoned horses; others were on camels, or in *palkis*, and held obsolete weapons in their hands.

All went well until we approached the city gates, when I realised that the fortifications of the town, which were mediaeval in origin and design, included, not a single barbican or outer gate, often placed for defensive purposes at right angles to the main entrance, but a double barrier of this description, so that any one entering the town had to turn a corner, almost at right angles, not once but twice before penetrating the main entrance walls. I realised the full peril of the situation when I saw the leaders with their postilion disappear altogether from sight, as they turned the first angle – to be followed presently by the middle pair. What was happening or might happen out of sight in the distance it was impossible to conjecture. It was bad enough that the landau itself was lurching heavily and with difficulty escaped impinging upon the sides of the great brick archways. By some unheard-of skill or good fortune the two corners were negotiated without disaster, but as the team pulled itself together and entered the inner gateway of the town, they seemed of one accord to realise that the strain was more than they ought to have been called upon to bear, and they broke into a sharp gallop which the

Others were on camels and held obsolete weapons in their hands.

postilions were powerless to restrain. The street was very narrow, was paved with stone and consequently slippery, and had no pavement – only a sort of gutter or ditch at the side. Moreover, the road presently descended by a rather sharp incline. The welcoming shouts of the good people of Datia, who crowded the galleries and roofs of the houses, added to the fright of the horses, the big landau began to sway dangerously from side to side, and the end was manifestly near.

Suddenly one or other, I daresay more, of the horses slipped up and came with a crash to the ground, the vehicle turned over, and my next sensation was that of finding myself sitting on the top of the old Maharaja, in all his finery of silks and jewels, in the stone gutter. No harm was done: an intelligent ADC sat on the head of the plunging horses; the traces were cut; the carriage was with difficulty dragged on one side; and, changing into a later vehicle in procession, we resumed our State entry unhindered and unhurt. The old Maharaja was very crestfallen; but, being a sportsman, he took the matter in good part, and soon recovered his equanimity.

An amusing sequel occurred when I passed on from Datia to pay my next visit to the neighbouring State of Orcha. In the course of my ceremonial visit to the Maharaja of Orcha, who had heard of the contretemps and was inspired by feelings of amiable rivalry towards his princely colleague, I explained to him what had happened. 'At this stage,' I said, 'I found myself in the melancholy position of sitting upon the head of His Highness the Maharaja of Datia in the ditch.' 'And a very proper position for Your Excellency to occupy,' was the immediate and courtly rejoinder of the old Chief, who, it was suspected, viewed the mishap that had attended his neighbour with some subdued satisfaction.

The Valet

The very pink of perfection. – GOLDSMITH, *She Stoops to Conquer*, Act I.
Quid domini faciant, audent quum talia fures?
(How can we expect the masters to behave, if the lower
orders carry on in such a fashion?)
VIRGIL, *Ecl.*iii.16.

NO man, according to the popular saying, is a hero to his valet. But there may be occasions when the inverse proposition is true, that a valet may be a hero to his master. One such English body-servant did I possess in India, whose performances, spontaneous and unprovoked, were a source to me of incessant surprise, mingled with the most profound admiration. Possessed of a fine appearance, an engaging manner, and unlimited effrontery, beautifully clad and equipped for any emergency, there was no situation with which he was not prepared to cope, and few from which he did not emerge in triumph. He was a little uncertain about his aspirates. But this added to, rather than detracted from, the novelty of his remarks upon men and things in general.

When I went on a visit to the Native States of Cochin and Travancore in Southern India in 1900, arriving at the former by sea, our vessel dropped anchor in the early morning at some distance from the shore. Along this the crested surf could be seen and heard booming in lines of foam, while enormous crowds lined the beach. When I went on deck I saw, dancing on the waves alongside, a boat of wonderful construction with a figurehead in imitation of a gigantic bird, somewhat like the swanboat in Lohengrin, and with two state chairs erected on a platform on its back, under a painted and gilded canopy. I was informed that Lady Curzon and I were expected to go ashore on this fairy barge, propelled by

Lady Curzon and I were expected to go ashore on this fairy barge.

I was visiting the Native State of R——, famous for the excellence of its tiger-shooting, and the hospitality of its chief.

the state rowers who were awaiting our descent from the ship. On the other hand the Resident, with an eye on the surf, strongly dissuaded this form of disembarkation, which he said might precipitate us at a critical moment into the sea. So we decided to wait a little and then land in one of the more ordinary craft that were hovering around.

A little later, happening to look shorewards, I saw the swan-boat, careering gaily towards the beach. On the two state chairs, smiling and self-possessed, sat my valet and the lady's maid, whom he had inveigled into the conspiracy, both exquisitely turned out; and from the shore we heard the loud huzzas that greeted their landing – I am sorry to say without the ducking that ought to have been their lot.

A second and somewhat similar incident occurred when I paid an official visit, with the escort of the East India Squadron, to the Persian Gulf in November 1903. Among the ports at which we called was the little

The result of the shoot was that we killed four tigers and no more.

town of Lingah on the Persian shore of the Gulf. Etiquette prescribed that my military secretary should go ashore to return the visit of the local Governor. Accordingly in the course of the afternoon he went off in the boat attended by several of the staff. Upon landing they were conducted through a street to the house in which the Governor resided, and where the official exchange of courtesies was to take place. This building had an open gallery or reception-room looking over a balcony on to the street. As the military secretary approached, hearing voices overhead, he looked up, and there, in the upper chamber, he saw the valet, comfortably seated in the place of honour, smoking a cigarette and drinking coffee amicably with the Governor, who doubtless thought that the particular angel whom he was entertaining unawares was the military secretary, possibly even the Viceroy himself.

But the valet's greatest achievements were reserved for the field of sport, in which his easy manner and unabashed assurance enabled him to reap many spoils. Perhaps his most conspicuous performance was the following. I was visiting the Native State of R——, famous for the excellence of its tiger-shooting, and the hospitality of its chief. The Viceregal train pulled up at the platform of the station at an early hour in the morning. On these occasions there is usually some little delay in

'Ow many tigers have you got for 'is Hexcellency?'

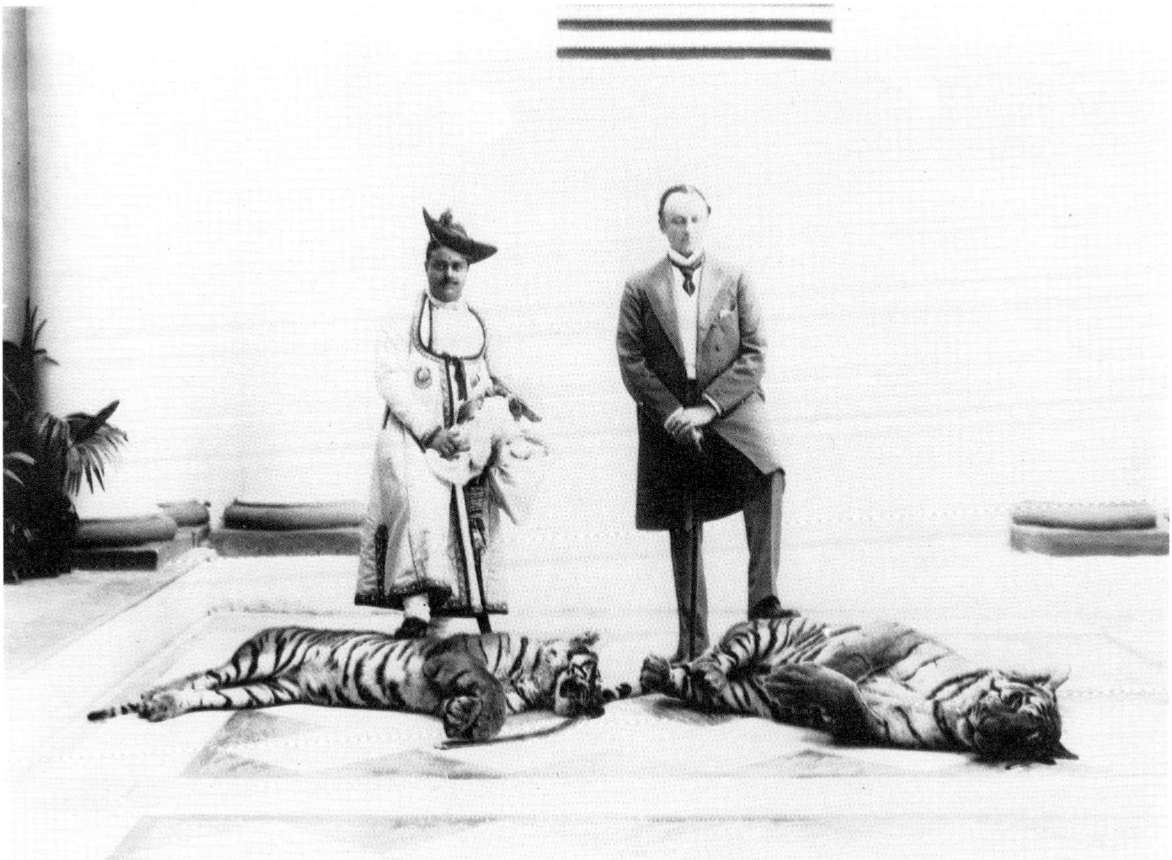

getting everything into order, before the Viceroy is allowed to make his appearance. The prince and his nobles and courtiers have to take up their proper positions; The Guard of Honour must be marshalled; the band must be ready to play; the Viceroy's staff descend and exchange greetings with their host, while the Viceroy from the slats of his carriage window looks out and sees the preparations being made outside.

On this occasion the Maharaja, with his immense turban and dress of pure white, was to be seen moving up and down as the train steamed in. The first to descend from the railway carriage was the valet. His debonair mien and immaculate appearance at once attracted the attention of the prince, who, conceiving him to be some important official of the Vice-regal household, probably the military secretary himself, entered into confidential conversation with him. Then it was that, from the innocent retreat of my compartment, I overheard the following colloquy:

M.R. And how is His Excellency?

V. I am glad to say that 'is Hexcellency is hexceedingly well.

M.R. I hope to give His Excellency a good shoot.

V. 'Ow many tigers, M'raja, have you got for 'is Hexcellency?

M.R. We have marked down no fewer than sixteen.

V. (*with an accurate recollection of the previous failure of similar forecasts, was seen to poke the Maharaja in the ribs, and with a knowing wink replied*) 'Alve it once, M'raja, and 'alve it again, and you'll be nearer the mark!

And the curious thing was that the valet, with his superior acumen, was absolutely right; for the result of the shoot was that we killed four tigers, and no more.

Inscriptions and Petitions

To speak agreeably to him with whom we deal is more than to speak in good words or in good order. – BACON, *Of Discourse*.

THE Indians excel in street decoration, illuminations, and every form of ceremonial observance. When the Viceroy or a Governor proceeds upon tour, still more of course if a member of the Royal House visits India, he passes through streets fantastically adorned, and under triumphal arches, built of the slenderest materials (very often little more than bamboo), but often decorated with the greatest ingenuity and taste. A feature of these arches is the inscriptions with which they are as a rule embellished, and the composition of which affords a much-valued scope for the talents of the local babu or university student, who may possess a smattering of European or even classical knowledge, and who is appealed to for a scholarly composition of words. I recall certain of these inscriptions under which I passed in the course of my official tours.

In some cases there would be a half-conscious reflection of the Prayer Book or the Scriptures. It is true that I was spared the particular welcome that was extended to an unusually ugly Governor, who, on leaving the railway station, read in gigantic characters over the gateway the inscription:

Good Lord! Deliver us!

But at Malda I was welcomed by the words:

Blessed be our Lord;

while at Burdwan the local scholar had even dipped into the Vulgate:

Welcome our Lord
Nisi Dominus frustra.

Elsewhere, an inscription in the vernacular must, I think, have been a quotation from one of the Indian Sacred Books, for it ran when translated:

Rejoice, O Heart, in the advent of Messiah-like being,
representing a nobler one.

At Chittagong, my dress, which so far as I remember was ordinary mufti, received an ambiguous but wholly unmerited compliment:

He cometh as a bridegroom
Clad in the garment of love.

Sometimes the Sovereign would be acclaimed in the same breath as his representative. For instance, Murshedabad thus addressed me:

Vive l'Empereur and Viceroy.
Hail gracious Lord.

The Indians excel in street decoration.

WELCOME THEIR EXCELLENCIES
LORD AND LADY CURZON

On the other hand, at Trichinopoli I drove under the following:

Welcome, our future Emperor.

Any alarm that I might have felt at being regarded as a pretender was, however, removed by the assurance that this particular inscription had been prepared many years before for the Duke of Clarence when he visited Southern India, and that it was pulled out again from time to time, if ever the Viceroy appeared on the scene. At Jeypore an accidental misspacing of the words converted

A Gala Day

into

A Gal a Day

which sounded rather naughty.

But it was when, in deference to my assumed academic reputation, resort was had to the classics, that some of the best efforts were forthcoming. Thus at Azimgunje I was welcomed by:

Vive, Vale.

At Manipur there was a fine combination both of language and sentiment:

Bonjour! Bon Soir!
Vive l'Empereur,
Fidus Achates.

This reminds me of a dinner I once gave in London to an Oriental potentate who knew a little French but no English, and who, as I parted with him at the door, exclaimed: 'Bon Soir, Bien, Merci, Tres fatigué'.

At Sivasamudram a more practical turn was given to the exhortation:

Gloria in excelsis
Be ever healthy.

At Madura, where I was welcomed on one archway to

The Athens of Southern India,

another said:

Adieu the successful Fighter of Famin.

But the salutation which struck the homeliest note and gave me perhaps the greatest pleasure was that of Karachi:

Hail Overworked Viceroy,
Karachi wants more Curzons.

It is, however, in letters, appeals, and petitions, of which the Viceroy receives many scores weekly, that some of the greatest triumphs are achieved. My private secretaries used to paste the best of these into an album, which I still possess, and a few of the gems of which I will here extract. It must not be supposed, if I, or any one else, quote amusing

Triumphal arches are often decorated with the greatest ingenuity and taste.

specimens of what is commonly known as Babu English, that we do it with any idea of deriding the native intelligence, or of poking fun at its errors. On the contrary, one of the most remarkable experiences in India is the astonishing command of the English language – to them a foreign tongue – that is acquired by the better-educated Indians, enabling them not merely to write, but to speak it with an accuracy and a fluency at which I never ceased to wonder. The blunders and absurdities that find a frequent place in the Indian Press are cited both because they strike a note of gaiety in the rather dull routine of Indian official life, and, still more, because they often reveal a sense of humour on the part of the writers that is both quaint and refreshing. It is in this spirit only that I reproduce a number of extracts from my own collection.

The cause of education seemed to spur the inscription writers to their best efforts. The High School at Bikanir thus addressed me in language the sentiment of which was unimpeachable even if the expression was somewhat obscure:

> Fulls wells the fountain of true fealty here
> To hail Your Excellencies' advent dear.
>
> Live I so live I
> To my King faithfully.
>
> Live I so live I
> To my Lord heartily.

On one of the walls at the High Schools at Dhar I read the rather enigmatic gloss on a familiar precept:

> Spare the rod – spoil the child.
> No pains
> No cains.

Sometimes the universal Anglo-Indian custom of condensing composite official titles into initials (for instance 'Agent to the Governor-General' became AGG) operates as a snare, for on one occasion a very popular Political officer, on returning from leave to the state to which he was accredited, found the welcome extended to him on a triumphal arch expressed in the following abbreviated form:

> Let us give a big WC
> To our popular AGG!

I had one correspondent, who claimed to be the legitimate heir to the Native State of which his ancestors had been dispossessed, and to which he apparently expected to be restored. He always addressed me as 'your afflicted and distressed', or as 'your affectionate, humble, and beloved child'. He would always inquire kindly after my own family, who were quite juvenile, but whom he persisted in describing as my 'venerable children'. Perhaps the best among his many productions was one in which he explained his apparent failure to see me when I visited the town in which he resided.

'I wrote to Mr.A—— to procure me interview with your Sublime Lordship. Although he is very aptitude, theological, polite, susceptible, and temporising, yet he did not fulfil the desire of the Royal blood. When your susceptible Lordship was at the Judge's Bungalow, I wrote again. What I heard of your superfine Lordship's conduct, the same I have seen from the balcony of my liberal Highness father. Your inimitable Lordship returned the complements of thousands of people that were standing on the street, but my fortune was such that I could not play before your sumptuous Lordship upon my invaluable lute, which will be very relicious to the ear to hear . . . . I hope that your transident lordship will keep your benevolent golden view on the forlorn royal blood to ennoble and preserve the dignity of His Highness father in sending the blessing letter of the golden hands.'

'I could not play before your sumptous Lordship upon my invaluable lute which will be very relicious to the ear to hear.'

This correspondent had indeed a richer vocabulary than any one I have ever come across, and the epithets with which he honoured me in a correspondence extending over nearly seven years would have surprised even the compilers of the new Oxford Dctionary. I find that in addition to the adjectives already quoted, he described me at one time or another as parental, compassionate, orpulent, predominant, surmountable, merciful, refulgent, alert, sapient, notorious, meritorious, transitory, intrepid, esteemable, prominent, discretional, magnanimous, mellifluous, temperate, abstemious, sagacious, free-willed, intellectual, inimitable, commendable, all-accomplished, delicious-hearted, superfine, ameliorative, impartial, benevolent, complaisant, efficient, progressive, spiritual, prudent, philanthropic, equitable. I could have sworn that he composed with a dictionary at his elbow and dipped into it at random for his adjectives, were it not that several of these no dictionary in the world would be found to contain. He even pursued me to England after my retirement, and described himself as 'anxiously awaiting like a peacock that is longing for drops of rain, to receive his kingdom from the so-called just and benign British Government'.

The commonest circumstances in which the Indian petitioner would appeal to the Viceroy for help were, however, in respect of domestic trouble, or private debt, desire for employment, or failure to pass the University examinations.

One Hindu Matron finally reached this climax, 'You are the Father of my whole family.'

A young Madrasi Brahmin, twenty-four years of age, had become engaged to a girl in Europe, whereupon his family turned him out, and he appealed to me. Writing in the third person, he thus described the attitude of his lady-love:

> 'He has many things to be proud of, but of nothing is he more proud than the love cherished for him by his European bride. She is the only daughter of a gentleman, has two bungalows and some landed property. She loves him too much. She promises to give him some thousands and a living.'

Finally, admitting, in spite of the lady's promises, that he was quite penniless,

> 'he humbly requests Your Excellency to Christianise him and make him the agent of a Mission College for at least a year. After collecting 500 Rupees for his ship fare let him reach Europe. If he gets the sum just now, he is ready to go away to Europe at once. Poor creature, he is passing sleepless nights and shedding midnight tears on his sleepless pillow.'

I am afraid I was unable to give him the narcotic that he desired.

One Hindu matron, I must confess, caused me a little embarrassment; for having appealed to me for succour on every conceivable ground, her destitution, her suffering, her parents, her children, herself, she finally reached this climax:

> 'We have been reduced to such a great poverty and high debt that even we are now spending most of our days by starving. My intention is to meet with you, for *you are the Father of my whole family*. Please write me sharp when, where, and on what date.'

An even more poignant note was struck in the following native petition:

> 'Respectfully sheweth – That your honour's servant is poor man in agricultural behaviour and much depends on season for staff of life, therefore he prays that you will favour upon him and take him into your saintly service that he may have some permanently labour for the support of his soul and his family; wherefore he falls on his family's bended knees and implores to you of this merciful consideration to a damnable miserable like your honour's unfortunate petitioner. That your lordship's honour's servant was too much poorly during the last rains and was resuscitated by much medicines which made magnificent excavations in the coffers of your honourable servant whose means are circumcised by his large family consisting of 5 female women and 3 masculine, the last of which are still taking milk from mother's chest, and are damnably noiseful through pulmonary catastrophe in their interior abdomen. That your honour's damnable servant was officiating in several capacities in past generations but has become too much old for espousing hard labour in this time of his bodily life, but was not drunked, nor thief, nor swindler, nor any of these kind, but was always pious and affectionate to his numerous family consisting of the aforesaid 5 female women and 3 males, the last of whom are still milking the parental mother. That your generous honour's lordship's servant was entreating magistrate for employment in Municipolity to remove filth, etc., but was not granted petition. Therefore your generous lordship will give to me some easy work in the department or something of this sort. For which act of kindness, your noble lordship's poor servant, will as in duty bound, pray for your longevity and procreativeness.'

It will be observed that the usual plea was for immediate and profitable employment, failing which the direst results were prophesied. Thus another letter ran as follows:

> 'I had a very hope from your Royal Majesty's Kingdom of my success. As millions and millions are being fed,by your Royal Majesty and your Royal Majesty is worldly God on the surface of the Earth can make a poor man rich in single stroke of pen. For God's sake pray order my being taken on in any Railway or in any other Dept. for which act of charity I shall ever pray to my Maker may your Royal Majesty bathe in milk and be fruitful in children. Failing all hopes will end my life.'

Sometimes a more purely business tone prevailed. A letter which two brothers at Bombay sent out to their patrons on the death of their father, who had been the head of the firm, came to Government House. It ran as follows:

'We have the pleasure to inform you that our respected father departed this life on the 10th inst. His business will be conducted by his beloved sons whose names are given below. The opium market is quiet at Malwa 1500 rupees per chest. O death, where is thy sting? O grave, where is thy victory? We remain, etc.'

The 'failed' students were, however, the most prolific class of correspondents. One such sought to disarm me by commencing with a quotation:

The greater man, the greater courtesy. – TENNYSON.

'And hence I am writing to you, dearest and most revered Lord, with all the filial love and loyalty that Hindoo subject can bestow on their King. Cause of writing is some greatest grief and sorrow that I have met with. Being a student of the Central Hindoo College I have been most unjustly and cruelly treated and been failed in Physics in the Intermediate examination of the Allahabad University. I have passed in all other subjects, in aggrigate too. I was so very well prepared that the thought of wasting one more year in the same class breaks my heart. My Physics paper too is more than sufficient to secure me pass-marks only if examined ordinarily like other boys of the Government Colleges. Putting aside all these matters we must be shown some favour at the Coronation of King Emperor Edward VII this year. At least all those who have failed in one subject should be called successful. My spirits have, as Cowper says, sunk ten degrees below par. My eyelids are heavy with sorrow. Alas! Can no body remedy. Why do I not find some one who can relieve me. Perhaps because the only remedy is success. I fear I may not take too much of your most valuable time. As a King I appeal to your majesty, as a father I seek for your sympathy.'

One 'insignificant schoolmaster in Bengal'.

Another unsuccessful candidate cherished the same bright idea of turning the Coronation of King Edward VII to good account; for he wrote to me with even more ingenuous candour:

'In the honour of the King-Emperor's Coronation Your Excellency might be pleased to declare all those the Candidates of the different Examinations held by the Indian Universities this time as "passed". In order, however, to keep up the appearance of an examination, *I beg to suggest that the standard of passing be reduced to such a level that nearly all the candidates may get through.*'

Yet another student begged me to relieve him of the moral stigma of deliberate falsehood. An order had been issued that sixteen years should be the minimum age of entry for the Allahabad University entrance examination.

'In my inexperience,' he wrote, 'I do not understand large administrative questions. But this order threatens to be of immense evil to me. I am taught not to tell a lie. But to lose the chance of passing an examination because I shall want a few short months to complete the limit has become the cause of a severe trial to me, presenting a temptation to violate the truth. The mischief is certain. It will determine students oscillating like me towards dishonesty. I have passed months in vain mental struggle, and have not the strength to overcome the temptation. So as a last resource I approach Y.E. to withdraw the order with a hope that I may be spared the moral degradation and may live to bless the rule of the foremost representative of a great nation.'

One 'insignificant schoolmaster in Bengal', describing himself as 'an abandoned and cursed child of alma mater, who in her infantile wrath had refused to admit him into her favour', and 'as having been left in the dark to rot on the same pay these twenty-one years', desired, 'at this fag end of life to have the honour of being a Member of Your Lordship's personal establishment'.

Sometimes an even more exacting request would be put forward. A young man who was employed in a Native Press, finding himself in grave financial straits, thus addressed me:

> 'Evidently I am so tired of my miserable life that on oath I say I most egregiously wish my death. It may perhaps be my foolishness to take undue advantage of Your Most Excellent Majesty's popular philanthroposy, but it is easily to be apprehended that I (a wretch of course) and not in the least way at blame when the unfathomable ways of God and the most astonishing boundaries to which necessity runs are slightly touched.'

The petitioner thereupon asked me, 'just taking him as a son', to 'rescue him on such critical moment by sending, if not more, at least Rs.7000'.

Now and then a different vein would be explored. A correspondent who described himself as a student of Shakespeare, wrote to say that he admired my speeches:

> 'A wandering sinner in search of Solomon the Righteous and Solon the Wise, best identified in Your Excellency, so far as he can fathom Y.E.'s speeches, when they reach him in these untrodden wilds of India, where he reads sermons on stones, books in the running brooks, and Good Gracious God! in everything.'

Another native correspondent, when I was having trouble with the Mahsud Waziris on the north-west frontier, suggested to me a quite original method of dealing with those unruly tribesmen:

> 'If the Waziris knew that he who represents our Queen was the giver of such help as artificial arms and legs to them, it would do more to calm the ruffled waters than any punishment is likely to do.'

On the other hand, when I made inquiries about the status of a very persistent petitioner, I was informed that he was 'addicted to wine and women; he associates himself with loud company, and there is no vice which he is not capable of. *When drunk he spares nobody and even maligns his venerable grand-father-in-law.*'

Frequently my correspondents broke into verse. One who had apparently been unsuccessful in business, wrote:

> Curzon, once I was a Marwar merry.
> Once my sons were mirthful men.
> Lord once I was a prosperous very
> Next to Jeypore in state's ten.

Another gave me a lucid description of pastoral life:

> Then wakes up the husband healthy after a sound sleep.
> And bathing he howls to a believed God,
> Then he milks the mild cows and sheep
> And drenches the milk to children playing on sod.

While I was in India a native paper itself published the following specimen of forensic eloquence in the Mofussil, which was actually delivered by a Hindoo pleader at Barisal:

> 'My learned friend with mere wind from a teapot thinks to brow-beat me from my legs. But this is mere gorilla warfare. I stand under the shoes of my client, and only seek to place my bone of contention clearly in your Honour's eye. My learned friend vainly runs amuck upon the sheet anchors of my case. Your Honour will be pleased enough to observe that my client is a widow, a poor chap with one postmortem son. A widow of this country, your Honour will be pleased to observe, is not like a widow of your Honour's country. A widow of this country is not able to eat more than one meal a day, or to wear clean clothes, or to look after a man. So my poor client had not such physic or mind as to be able to assault the lusty complainant. Yet she has (been) deprived of some of her more valuable leather, the leather of her nose. My learned friend has thrown only an argument *ad hominy* upon my teeth that my client's witneses are only her own relations. But they are not near relations. Their relationship is only homoeopathic. So the misty arguments of my learned friend will not hold water – at least they will not hold good water. Then my learned friend has said that there is on the side of his client a respectable witness, viz., a pleader, and since this witness is independent so he should be believed. But your Honour, with your Honour's vast experience, is pleased enough to observe that truthfulness is not so plentiful as blackberries in this country. And I am sorry to say, though this witness is a man, of my own feathers, that there are in my profession black sheep of every complexion, and some of them do not always speak gospel truth. Until the witness explains what has become of my client's nose leather he cannot be believed. He cannot be allowed to raise a castle in the air by beating upon a bush. So, trusting in that administration of British justice upon which the sun never sits, I close my case.'

There were, of course, many cases in which the native exuberance of fancy and fondness for hyperbole in language found suitable vent, and one of the most pleasing of these was the address from the little Himalayan Hill State of Bushahr, which expatiated with pardonable pride on its own beauties:

> 'Let us first of all thank our Heavenly Father, Whose Grace has to-day enabled us to see Your Honour and Her Ladyship in the Country of Bushahr. O Lord, these beautiful mountains, covered with the lofty trees, clothed in the Aaron's beard, embraced by the lovely

Virginia creepers, bearing the leaves and flowers of the bright green, yellow, pink, and crimson colours, yielding the nourishment to the eyes of the travellers passing by, these fine shrubs, nearly concealed under the air-creepers, bent down by the weight of the small pearl-like flowers of the sweetest fragrance, these huge stones that have gathered abundant velvety moss, situated naturally and beautifully here and there along the valley, these silvery streams and the picturesque waterfalls, that purely flow down to and fro all around the Sutlej Valley, and these invisible Nymphs of the forests, as well as of the eternal snow, do welcome to your Honour and Her Ladyship, by the sweet voice of the warblings of the pretty little birds and hummings of the black bees. O my Lord, the songs of Your Honour's spotless glory, of the impartiality, the love of honesty, the sincerity, and the benevolence to the poor people (which are the real ornaments of the human beings) are cheerfully sung by the celestial maids in heaven.'

Finally, I will conclude with the following veracious summary of the Life of Henry VIII, which was written by the Babu student at about the same time:

'Henry the Eighth was a good looking man, he had a red beard, he was very well proportioned, but he had a hot temper. He was very religious and he pulled down a great deal of churches and monasteries, he built Colleges with them and schools with them too, the school he called the Blue Coat School, and a College called Oxford College. He turned the monks out who were rich once but had to go into the workhouse afterwards, he married Katherine of Arrogant for twenty years. He got to know Anne Beloyn; she waited on Katherine that is how he got to know her. Anne became a Queen and Katherine was sent away. She became religious and became a monk.

Henry got to hear things about Anne, and she had her head cut off – though the things were not true, for she had but a little neck. Henry was left a widow, but he soon got married again – this time it was to Jane Seymour.

He liked Jane Seymour, she had a son a few days after she died. So Henry was a widow again, and he married another Anne; this time Anne Cleves this Anne he did not like, for she was floundering mare, and not Pretty so he sent her away again and gave her some gold to live upon without him, while he got married to another Katherine Howard. She was not a very good wife, and Henry got to hear things again as he did before – so she had her head cut off, and he married Katherine Parr who looked after his bad legs.'

The Mutiny Veterans

DELHI, *1st January 1903*

To-day, across our fathers' graves,
  The astonished years reveal
The remnant of that desperate host
  Which cleansed our East with steel.

Hail and farewell! We greet you here,
  With tears that none will scorn –
O Keepers of the House of old,
  Or ever we were born!
RUDYARD KIPLING, 'The Veterans'.

The Viceroy in brilliant uniform.

BY 11 o'clock, when a bugle sounded, the great arena was cleared. Every seat was occupied in the vast horseshoe amphitheatre, built in imitation of the Moghul style, with Saracenic arches, and light cupolas tipped with gold. Painted a creamy white, it shone like some fairy palace of marble in the fierce light of the Indian sun.

There might be seen the Princes of India, ablaze with jewels and in their most splendid raiment; behind them, a curtained box hid from the public gaze their wives and female relatives. There were the representatives of foreign states, of Japan, Siam, Afghanistan, Muscat and Nepal, of the French and Portuguese possessions in India, and of the British Overseas Dominions of South Africa and Australia. There were picturesque figures from the hill states that skirt the Chinese frontier, from the Persian borderland and the coasts of Arabia, and from the snowy passes of the Hindu Kush. There were the Members of the Governor-General's Council, the Governors of the Presidencies and Provinces, the Commander-in-Chief and his staff, and countless civil and military officers, all in brilliant uniforms. There were the High Court Judges in their state robes and full-bottomed wigs; and there also was a crowd of distinguished guests from all parts of India and from England. Seats were found for 13,500 persons; as many more stood. Out on the plain, through the two points of the horseshoe, could be seen in the near distance the serried ranks of the massed battalions in close formation, 40,000 strong; and behind them was a tall mound, packed from foot to summit with thousands of native spectators. In the centre of the amphitheatre the imperial flag floated at a height of 100 feet in the air. Round its base were massed the bands of twelve regiments that had won glory in the campaigns of the Mutiny, nearly half a century before. The dais, in the inner hollow of the horseshoe, surmounted by a domed pavilion directly copied from a building of Akbar at Agra, awaited its Royal and Viceregal occupants. At the sound of the bugle a sudden hush fell upon the whole assembly.

Then was seen a spectacle that will never be forgotten by those who witnessed it, that brought tears to the eyes of strong men and a choking in every throat. Preceded by a military band, there walked into the arena, in irregular formation, with no attempt at parade or symmetry, a group, a knot, a straggling company, of old or elderly men. Nearly all were grey-headed or white-haired, many were bowed with years, and were with difficulty supported by their comrades or by younger officers who conducted them round. In front marched a little knot of Europeans, headed by a splendid veteran, Colonel A. R. Mackenzie, C.B. Some were in stained and dilapidated uniforms, others in every variety of civil dress; but there was not a bosom that did not glitter with the medals that both explained their presence and bespoke their glory.

Behind them walked, and in some cases tottered, a cluster of Sikh veterans, many with long white beards, clad entirely in white.

The entire procession consisted of between 300 and 400 men, of whom the great majority were Indians, and a small minority of less than 30, Europeans and Eurasians.

They were the veterans of the Mutiny, the survivors of that great drama of mingled tragedy and heroism, the officers and non-commissioned officers who had borne a part in the immortal episodes of Delhi

There might be seen the Princes of India, ablaze with jewels, and in their most splendid raiment.

The Mutiny, that great drama of mingled tragedy and heroism.

and Lucknow, the men but for whom the Imperial Durbar would never have been held.

As they made their way slowly round the broad track of the arena, to which none had hitherto been admitted but themselves, the entire audience, European and Indian, rose to their feet and greeted them with long and tumultuous cheering; but when the proud strains of 'See the Conquering Hero comes', to which the veterans had entered, and in response to which they drew themselves erect and marched with firm step, were succeeded by the wailing pathos of 'Auld Lang Syne', there was audible sobbing both of men and women, and many in that vast audience broke down. One brave old fellow, quite blind, was led by a younger comrade: he turned his sightless orbs towards the cheering, and feebly saluted. It was his last salute; for the excitement was too much for him, and on the morrow he died. At length the old men were all conducted to their seats in the amphitheatre, and the stage was set for the principal scene.

I was gratified at the success of the venture; for when I planned and announced it beforehand, there had been many critics, particularly at a distance, who condemned the proposal as striking a jarring note on a day of rejoicing, and as reviving memories that ought to be forgotten. No such view was entertained by a single person, European or Indian, at Delhi: the Indians themselves regarded the invitation as the greatest of

An elephant salutes His Excellency.

When the veterans had entered, there was audible sobbing both of men and women, and many in that vast audience broke down.

Supreme moments of the Coronation Durbar.

The veterans paraded again in front of my headquarters.

honours; and many, who were present at the scene I have described, declared it to be the supreme moment of the Durbar.

I would gladly have summoned all, of whatever position or rank, from every part of India, who had fought on the British side in the Mutiny. But when it appeared on examination that there were over 1400 of these, many of them living in remote parts of India, distant many days' journey from Delhi, the idea had to be abandoned, and I was obliged to confine the invitation to the list before mentioned.

Two days after the Durbar the veterans paraded again in front of my headquarters in the Central Camp, where, at their own instance, they presented me with an address of thanks, which is one of my most treasured possessions.

The Sikh Way

Well, honour is the subject of my story.
SHAKESPEARE, *Julius Caesar*, Act I. Sc. 2.

Life every man holds dear; but the brave man
Holds honour far more precious-dear than life.
SHAKESPEARE, *Troilus and Cressida*, Act V. Sc. 3.

THE standards of personal or family honour and self-respect that prevail among the Sikh community in India are of a very rigid and uncompromising character. Indeed they recall in some respects the ethical code that even in quite modern times has justified the practice of *hara-kiri* in Japan, and that inspired the immortal tragedy of the Forty-Seven Ronin.

A Sikh will not only take life, but will freely give up his own life, sooner than that an ineffaceable stain should rest upon his family escutcheon. I came across several instances of this remarkable trait while in India, of which I will relate the following.

There were four brothers, Sikhs, who were small landowners in a village in the Native State of Patiala in the Punjab. The two elder were soldiers in the Indian Army, where they both bore exemplary characters as quiet and well-behaved men. The two younger brothers stayed at home, and cultivated the family land, which was not inconsiderable in extent. They were, however, continually harassed by their maternal relatives, who turned beasts into their crops when green, or went in and cut them when ripe, in the hope of driving the brothers out of their holding, and forcing them to leave the village, in which case the land would have devolved upon the usurpers as nearest of kin. The two soldier brothers were being constantly obliged to take leave in order to protect their interests. But endless *makadmas* (lawsuits) brought them no relief, the maternal relatives forming an overwhelmingly strong faction against the brothers, who had no local following.

At length the soldier brothers decided to bring matters to a head; but before doing so they made a final appeal to their persecutors. Attar Singh, one of the two soldiers, laid his turban at the feet of his principal enemies and implored them to desist from further hostility; but in reply he only met with abuse. He then returned to his military station, sent for his brother, obtained four days' leave for both, and collected a revolver and sword and as much ammunition as he could procure.

The brothers arrived at the village, and announced that they had come to fight it out. They then opened fire upon the opposite faction, and in the course of the conflict that ensued, killed seventeen persons and wounded ten, the result being that the entire clique of maternal relatives – women as well as men – were wiped out.

It remained only to complete the work of combined murder and self-sacrifice. The four brothers then mounted to their house-top,

Sikh soldiers in the Indian Army.

whence they sent word to the police station that they wanted to die fighting and would not be taken alive; and accordingly that they were waiting for a *fauj* to come and finish them off. The police having declined the hazardous invitation, the second brother, Attar Singh, saying that his work was done, did public *shinan* (purification), and then sat down and made his elder brother, Ruttan Singh, shoot him through the head.

The latter then remembered that he had a private enemy in the same native regiment, against whom he had to pay off some old score. He accordingly descended, sought out his enemy, and inflicted upon him a severe sword cut and two bullet wounds. He would have killed him if he could.

Having thus satisfied his honour to the full, he returned to the house-top and resumed his seat with his two surviving brothers, the other villagers continuing to supply them with food and water, though not permitted to come near. After two more days Ruttan Singh then did *shinan* for himself, and made one of the two surviving brothers shoot him dead.

The latter, who were not soldiers, and perhaps were allowed to have a less sensitive feeling of honour, then came down and disappeared.

The remarkable feature of the story was that though these men had completely annihilated the whole of their maternal relatives, their conduct was in no sense reprobated by their fellow-countrymen. On the contrary, the entire community looked upon the tragedy as having been conducted in a most seemly manner, *coram publico*. Justice had in fact been satisfied all round.

Perhaps this little anecdote, which is true, will explain to some of the readers of this book why even in the twentieth century it is not always wise or desirable to apply Western criteria to the behaviour of Eastern peoples.

Even in the twentieth century it is not always wise or desirable to apply Western criteria to the behaviour of Eastern peoples.

The Plague Hospital

Which I wish to remark,
  And my language is plain –
That for ways that are dark
  And for tricks that are vain,
The heathen Chinee's *not* peculiar –
  Which the same I would rise to explain.
      BRET HARTE (slightly adapted).

IN the Middle Ages and down to relatively modern times the Plague in one form or another was a familiar and almost a chronic feature in Europe as well as in the East, from which as a rule it came. In recent times it has reappeared with less frequency, and with less devastating consequences. But its most appalling recrudescence occurred during my time in India, when for years it lay like a blight upon the land and was responsible for a mortality that was said to have amounted to over seven and a half millions of people. Brought by rats in the holds of ships from Hongkong in 1896, and transmitted, as subsequent scientific investigation showed, by the rat-flea from rat to rat, and from rats to human beings, it laid hold of the population of great cities whom it swept off with fearful rapidity; it attacked the villages; it cut a swathe as of a mighty death-dealing scythe through the entire country, sparing some districts by a mysterious caprice, but ravaging others. The British authorities began with measures of compulsory inspection, evacuation, disinfection, quarantine, and the like, but were obliged to desist from these by the overpowering ignorance and invincible antagonism of the native population. Literally they would sooner die than be saved against their will. Violent riots occurred, policemen were murdered, even native medical officers were burned alive. Gradually but wisely the Government relaxed the methods employed; persuasion, conciliation, voluntary effort, co-operation, optional inoculation were the agencies that brought the best results. The great thing was to remove the patient at once (for the operation of the disease was extraordinarily rapid) from the infected house or quarter to the nearest plague-camp or hospital, and there to surround him with the conditions – pure air, sound treatment, and stimulating sustenance – that gave the best chance of recovery. Even so 75-80 per cent of those who were stricken died.

In the autumn of 1899, when the visitation was at its height, I went on tour to many of the worst afflicted areas, and was inoculated in advance with the prophylactic serum, which saved so many thousands of lives, and would have saved so many more had not an unfortunate accident, resulting in a number of deaths in a native village from the contamination of a single bottle of fluid there employed, paralysed the scheme, almost in its infancy. The preparations made everywhere by the medical staff were admirable. Plague camps were hurriedly improvised to which the patients were taken from their huts; splendid hospitals were opened. A devoted staff of workers, European and Native, male and female, dedicated themselves to the service of the people. But the conservatism of the latter, their prejudices, their fatalism, were obstacles which the patience not of days or weeks but of months and even years, was required to overcome.

When the Viceroy goes on tour everything is hurriedly prepared for his inspection, hundreds of pounds are spent on projects for which a few rupees could not previously be found, buckets of whitewash are available for the asking, the whole place is swept and garnished, not, as in the Scripture narrative, for the unclean spirits to enter in, but on the opposite assumption that they have been successfully and finally driven out. I used to apply a very critical eye to these spick-and-span demonstrations, of the extemporised and artificial character of which I was more than once made rudely aware.

The most startling revelation occurred at Nagpur. A sharp outbreak of the bubonic plague had attacked that neighbourhood, and people were dying like flies in the surrounding villages. Outside the town a spacious temporary structure had been hastily run up with bamboos and matting, and had been arranged as a hospital for the accommodation of the patients. At an early hour in the morning I was driven out to visit this place. It was a pattern of neatness; the beds stretched in long rows down

I visited the patients, who seemed to me surprisingly few.

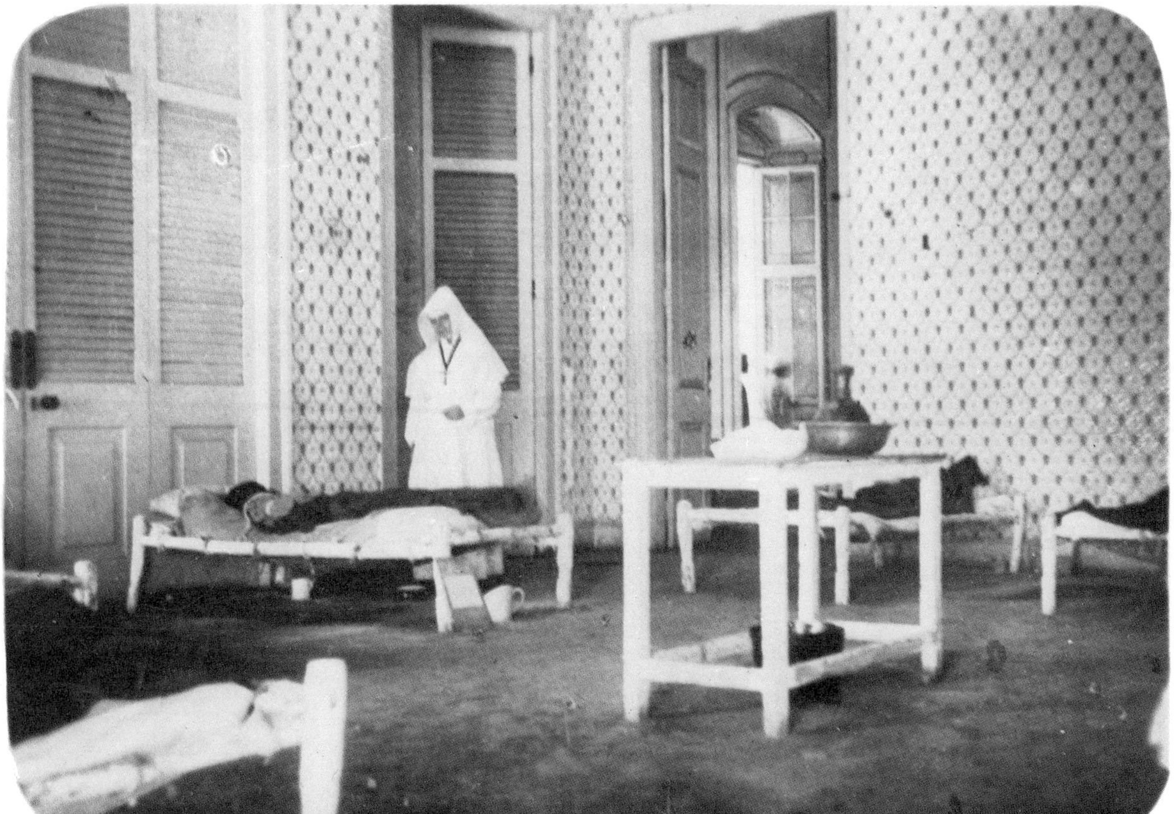

the sides of a central avenue, and above each bed was the chart of the temperature of the occupant. The doctors, European and Native, buzzed around; all the requisite medical appurtenances were there in abundance. Underneath a rough blanket the wretched victims lay, each on his mattress, with a look as of death in their eyes. The morning air percolated with a refreshing coolness through the interstices of the matting.

I visited the patients, who seemed to me surprisingly few, in turn and asked them whence they came, and when they had arrived. Being a little startled at the coincidence by which they all seemed to have come in at 5 or 6 AM on that very morning, I drew a bow at a venture, and said to one man, 'What did they give you to come?' 'One rupee' was his unhesitating reply. The same question to the next invalid elicited a similar reply – there being a slight variation in the figure of the bribe – and so on with the remainder. The whole affair was, I will not say a hoax, because the patients and the plague were both there, but a put-up arrangement for the special edification of the Viceroy. My thoughts were 'too deep for tears'; and, as the same poet says in another place, I also had 'two voices' – one for the innocent victims of the stratagem who had been paid to come in, but who after all may, in the long run, have profited by the experience; the other for the professional authors of the stratagem; and of these two voices, the latter, if my recollection serves me rightly, was the mightier.

'Lest We Forget': The Death-Bed of Sir Henry Lawrence

There is nothing new except what is forgotten.
ANON.

ONE of the most remarkable phenomena in life is the carelessness with which people observe, or rather fail to observe, that which is daily and even hourly under their eyes, either paying no attention to it because it is so familiar, or failing to inquire from sheer lack of interest or curiosity. Of the millions of persons who pass in the year through Trafalgar Square, how many could tell you the number or identity of the bronze heroes who adorn or disfigure its open spaces? Not even the fact that he is riding without stirrups probably induces more than one passer-by in ten thousand to inquire who is the Royal horseman on a pedestal in the top left-hand corner. How many people who daily drive or ride past the nude Achilles in Hyde Park take the trouble to inquire how he came there or what he represents? Take an even stronger case. There are London streets which some of us traverse every day of our lives for years. If we were suddenly challenged to name either the order in which the shops occur for a distance of 100 yards on the side of the street which we affect, or still more the names, is there one in a hundred of us who could survive the ordeal? Familiarity breeds not merely contempt, but in the case of ordinary objects, or objects which we encounter every day, complete forgetfulness if we have ever known, complete indifference if we have not.

In the course of my travels I have come across cases of this indifference or forgetfulness, in circumstances where the very reverse might have been expected by every law of probability, so astonishing that it would have been impossible to believe them had they not actually occurred. In one case I was the accidental means of detecting the lapse; and I owed the discovery to the habit which I have pursued in every one of my travels, and which I believe to be the secret of accurate observation – namely, of acquainting oneself, so far as possible, with the facts of a case or the features of a scene before coming in contact with it. In this way you know what to expect that you will find. But you are also in a position to note what is wanting either in the narratives of your predecessors or in the situation itself.

In December 1899 I paid my first official visit, as Viceroy of India, to Lucknow, and among my earliest proceedings was an inspection of the crumbling ruins and consecrated grounds of the Residency. They bear but slight resemblance now to the aspect they wore at the date of the famous siege; for time and loving care have passed the tender fingers of oblivion over the scars, and have converted a heap of debris into an exquisite garden, from which emerge a few battered walls and skeletons of buildings, embowered amid the luxuriant verdure.

Among my earliest proceedings was an inspection of the Residency at Lucknow.

But the interest lies in them rather than in the pleasaunce, and any Englishman, at all familiar with the history of the Mutiny or the incidents of the siege, wanders eagerly from ruined building to building, or where they exist, from one shattered apartment to another, seeking to identify the actual scenes of so much suffering and so much glory.

So familiar was I from previous reading with the incidents of the siege that I had no difficulty in moving from site to site and identifying the localities, in so far as they survive. After inspecting the Residency, I was conducted into an adjoining and semi-ruined building. On the battered wall inside a great open verandah I saw a white marble tablet fixed, which contained this inscription:

Here Sir H. Lawrence died
4 July 1857

'With all respect,' I said at once, 'here Sir Henry Lawrence did not die.' 'But how,' was the natural retort, 'can that be? This inscription has been on the wall for fifty years – ever since the Residency was consecrated as a national memorial at the end of the Mutiny. Thousands of persons who fought in the Mutiny have passed through the building since. Hundreds who were in the Residency at the time of the siege, and at the moment of Sir Henry's death, have visited the verandah. All of them have seen that tablet on the wall. Not one has ever questioned its accuracy. Can it have been reserved for you in the year 1899 to correct an error that must have existed for half a century and to show that every one has hitherto been wrong?' 'Yes,' I said, 'indeed it has, and I will ask leave to take the party to the inner room in which Sir Henry Lawrence actually did die.'

I then passed through the verandah to the inner room or drawing-room of Sir Joseph Fayrer's house (the building in question), and remarked that that was the spot where Sir Henry Lawrence had breathed his last. There was still general incredulity as to my statement; whereupon, remembering that Sir Joseph Fayrer, who had tended Lawrence in his last hours, was still living at the age of seventy-four in England, I suggested that a plan of the house and its apartments should be sent to him, without any mention of the dispute that had arisen, and that he should be asked to mark upon it the room and the spot where the hero's spirit had fled.

After a time came back the plan with Fayrer's mark on the apartment and upon the place which I had indicated. The mendacious tablet was in due course removed and transferred to the correct site, where it may be seen in the accompanying photograph.

In the following year came out Sir Joseph Fayrer's book: and in it were printed, not merely the details of Lawrence's last hours, but a copy of Lieut. Moorsom's plan of the Residency buildings, made in 1857, and a plan (whether stimulated by my inquiry or not I do not know) of Dr Fayrer's own house.

From these it will be seen that the injured man, mortally wounded by a shell on 2 July 1857, while lying on a couch in an upper room in the Residency, had been carried over and laid down on a bed in the open verandah of Dr Fayrer's house, whence after a time, owing to the severity of the fire, he was moved into the inner room or drawing-room where at 8 AM on the morning of July 4 he expired.

Apart from the interest of historical accuracy, I do not know that any vital importance attaches to the question whether even a great man and a hero breathed his last in this or that exact spot. But I have never ceased to be amazed at the heedlessness which for fifty years had permitted a stream of visitors, some of them eye-witnesses of the tragedy, and many of them intimately acquainted with every detail and incident of the siege, to pass by, without detecting or correcting the error.

Drink

Not the first sparkle of the desert spring,
Nor Burgundy in all its sunset glow,
After long travel, ennui, love, or slaughter,
Vie with the draught of hock and soda water.
BYRON, *Don Juan*, Canto II., st. 180.

MANY poets of diverse nationalities, Horace, Saadi, Omar Khayyám, and, among our own countrymen, Herrick, Congreve, Burns, have sung the praise of liquor, and have commended its timely use as a factor in good fellowship or enjoyment. An interesting anthology might be, perhaps has been, composed of the glorification of wine in verse. But I have often been struck by the paucity of such references in works of travel; albeit in that sphere the occasional stimulus of drink, spirituous, alcoholic, or otherwise, is apt to be not merely a source of pleasure but an element in success. As a traveller – not the modern traveller, whose progress is punctuated by a meteoric succession of motors, trains, steamboats, and hotels – but the old-time traveller, who covered great distances on horse or mule or camelback, or maybe on foot, pushed ahead through long and exciting marches, carrying with him whatever he must eat or drink, how much turned on the resources of the commissariat or the contents of the canteen! When at the end of the day he sat down or lay down to take his hard-earned, and perhaps self-cooked, meal, with what beverage was he to wash it down?

If a man is marching with a caravan, where his impedimenta are carried either on the backs of animals or, as in Africa, on the heads of native porters, or, as in many parts of the East, slung on poles or from the shoulders of men; still more, if there is no limit but that of expense or supplies to the size of the party, we may be sure that the cases of wine or spirits will be there in sufficient quantity: that these will be broached at the end of the day, and that, after an exceptional spell of exertion, the corks will fly and the day's toil will be rehearsed to this merry tune. I have noticed that the French in particular, who are admirable travellers, never travel without champagne; and when I was marching in their company, in the interior of Annam and Cambodia, either tramping on foot or carried in a litter through the soaking rain, it was always a compensation to know that the Moët would be forthcoming when the day's labour was over and the halt was called. And even in older records of sport and adventure, when comfort was less diffused and the standard of relaxation more strict, we find that the veteran explorer, a Stanley or a Baker, was never without these resources, to be used on rare occasions either to celebrate achievement, or for medicinal purposes, or to overcome fatigue.

I incline, however, to the belief that the reason for which so little mention is made of this legitimate solace in travel pages is that the traveller likes to credit himself with an endurance even more Spartan than is justified by the facts. But supposing he is either moving too quickly or with too small a following to be able to indulge in such luxuries; supposing, for instance – to take two opposite extremes – he is either riding *chapar* in Persia, seventy miles or more a day on hired horses, or is climbing Everest or making a dash for the Pole, what is he to do? He has, of course, his flask of brandy or whisky, or whatever spirit he may prefer. But beyond that, he must live in anticipation of the good time that is to come. For him are the joys, not of fruition, but of hope.

But how great these are, and what varied forms they may assume! One man will dream of one type of future enjoyment for his thirsting gullet, another of another. I once asked Roald Amundsen, the Norwegian explorer, who cut in ahead of our brave Scott and his companions and got first to the South Pole, what was the particular food or drink that filled his imagination during that fearful ordeal, or would have pleased him most had he suddenly been able to conjure it into existence. He replied that all the while he was longing for a cup of hot coffee and a plate of bread and butter.

Lord Byron, whom I have quoted at the head of this chapter, would apparently have called for hock and soda (I believe, by the way, the above

All the while he was longing for a cup of hot coffee and a plate of bread and butter.

to be the first mention of soda water in English verse) – and there is something to be said for his selection. But for the traveller in remote parts, who cannot be burdened with over-heavy loads, the double ingredients may be too bulky to carry, while they suggest, even in imagination, rather too dilettante a drink.

If I may relate my own humble experience, when I was galloping for nine long days from Meshed to Teheran, getting up in the darkness of the night long before sunrise, and riding through the heat of the day, with no more liquid than the contents of a flask in one of my holsters, I used to think fondly of the prospective amenities of the British Legation, and to murmur to myself the magic incantation: 'Wolff's Champagne.' (Sir H. Drummond Wolff, whose guest I was to be, was at that time the British Minister at Teheran.) When at length I rode exhausted into the Legation Compound, and a friendly secretary asked me what I would like, I answered without the slightest hesitation, 'Wolff's Champagne.' And I got it!

During my travels in the Pamirs in 1894, I had run out of liquor altogether, and sometimes felt the want of some stimulant in face of the cruel cold at night and in the early dawn, and of the scorching sun at noontide. Finally I turned back towards India, crossed the shallow trough of the Baroghil Pass, and came down on the upper waters of the Yarkhun River, which in its later course is variously known as the Mastuj, Chitral, and Kunar River, and eventually flows into the Kabul River at Jellalabad. Opposite me gleamed the frozen cataract of the Great Chatiboi glacier, just as though some vast Niagara, pouring down from the skies, had suddenly been congealed in its descent, and converted into pinnacles and towers of ice. I was expecting to join my friend Younghusband, and to march with him to Chitral. But I felt sure that as soon as I crossed the frontier and entered the territory of British India, he would send out some one to meet me and guide me to his camp.

Sure enough, as I rode down the grassy slopes, I saw coming towards me in the distance the figure of a solitary horseman. It was Younghusband's native servant. At that moment I would have given a kingdom, not for champagne or hock and soda, or hot coffee, but for a glass of beer! He approached and salaamed. I uttered but one word, 'Beer.' Without a moment's hesitation, he put his hand in the fold of his tunic and drew therefrom a bottle of Bass. Happy forethought! O Prince of hosts! Most glorious moment! Even now, at this distance of time, it shines like a ruddy beacon in the retrospect of thirty years gone by.

Furthermore, in this belated tribute have I not done something to remove the stigma of another British poet?

O Beer, O Hodgson, Guinness, Allsop, Bass!
  Names that should be on every infant's tongue,
Shall days and months and years and centuries pass,
  And still your merits be unrecked, unsung?

No, Calverley, no! Let me, at any rate, be innocent of your hitherto well-merited reproach! My withers shall remain for ever unwrung!

The 'Pig and Whistle' at Bunji

I will fetch you a toothpicker now from the furthest inch of Asia.
SHAKESPEARE, *Much Ado about Nothing*, Act II. Sc. I.

NOTHING is more remarkable than the character and spirit of the young men, British Subalterns as a rule, who on the outskirts of our Indian Dominions are upholding the fabric and sustaining the prestige of the British Raj.

In remote mountain fastnesses, amid wild tribes, far from civilisation, in a climate sometimes savagely hot, at others piercingly cold, with no comforts or luxuries, often amid cruel hardships, they face their task with unflinching and patriotic ardour, dispensing justice among alien populations, training and disciplining native forces, and setting a model of manly and uncomplaining devotion to duty, which reflects undying credit on the British name.

Scattered as they may be over wide areas, it will be rarely that they can meet together to enjoy society or to exchange experiences. When they do, warm is the hospitality and high are the spirits that prevail. On my march from Kashmir to the Pamirs, in the autumn of 1894, I came across such a place, and I was lucky in joining such a gathering at a spot known as

Others whose names I cannot now recall.

Bunji, not far from the Indus on the mountain road to Gilgit. It is a forlorn and melancholy spot, destitute either of amenities or attraction. Here, however, stood a humble single-storied bungalow, consisting, as far as I remember, of three small rooms, one of which was used as a mess-room, where the young officers from time to time foregathered as they went up and down the road. With a somewhat forced jocularity, seeking to invest this dingy meeting-place with the simulacrum of a tavern, its frequenters had christened it the 'Pig and Whistle.'

On this occasion, hearing of my visit, they had collected from far and near. I was accorded the sleeping-place of honour in a flea-haunted bedroom, where I spent a night of horror. But the real entertainment was in the so-called mess-room, where was dispensed whatever of hospitality the limited local resources might permit.

As we sat down to dinner, however, I noticed that on the bespattered walls of this primitive hostelry were pinned a series of portraits of famous English beauties, cut from the pages of illustrated newspapers. There I saw the likenesses of a number of great ladies whom I knew well in England – Georgina Countess of Dudley, Millicent Duchess of Sutherland, Lady Warwick, and others whose names I cannot now recall. Each visitor, as he journeyed to and fro and enjoyed the modest hospitality of the 'Pig and Whistle,' had written his name in pencil against the portrait which he thought the most beautiful, thus offering his humble and innocuous tribute at the shrine of Venus. Such was the solitary recreation of these gallant but futile lovers.

When I arrived, the result was a tie between the three principal competitors; and upon my revealing that I knew the subjects of all the portraits, I was invited with uproarious enthusiasm to append my name to the most lovely, and so to award the apple. I did so, but to whom I gave the prize I have never revealed, nor would wild horses now induce me to disclose. It remains a secret buried for ever in the unwritten records of the 'Pig and Whistle' at Bunji in the Himalayan Mountains.

The Havildar of Sarhad

The poet, wandering on
Over the aerial mountains which pour down
Indus and Oxus from their icy caves,
In joy and exultation held his way.
SHELLEY, 'Alastor.'

IN the course of my visit to the Pamirs in the early autumn of 1894 in order to determine the true source of the Amu-Daria or Oxus

In her high mountain cradle of Pamere,

I descended from the lofty passes where the Hindu Kush and Mustagh ranges join and are merged, into the valley of Wakhan. This narrow valley, down which the Oxus flows, had just been assigned by the Pamir Boundary Commission to the Amir of Afghanistan, as a buffer state between British and Russian territories and ambitions, and it was believed to be sparsely occupied by Afghan troops. I camped for one night at Bozai Gumbaz, the place where Sir Francis (then Captain) Younghusband had been arrested by Colonel Yonoff in August 1891 – a bleak and cheerless spot – and from there my companion and I made our way down stream, over *paris* or cliff tracks of appalling steepness, to a spot where the river, released from its long mountain imprisonment, spread itself out in countless fibres over a wide watery plain, closed on either hand by magnificent snow peaks. Below us lay the terraced fields of Wakhan. Oxen, goats, and sheep were being driven in at the sunset hour, and thin curls of smoke arose from the settled habitations of men. My companion and I were a good deal in advance of our caravan, which we had left struggling on the mountain tracks, and we arrived alone at a group of Wakhi villages in the valley bottom, to all of which the Afghans apply the collective title of Sarhad. This spot is 10,400 feet above the sea. It was a place of somewhat evil reputation for English travellers: for there in 1890 Mr and Mrs St G. Littledale, the well-known explorers, had been stopped for twelve days by the officiousness or discourtesy of the Afghan captain from Kila Panja, 50 miles farther down the river.

To guard against any such contretemps, I had written in advance to the Amir of Afghanistan, whose guest I was going later to be at Kabul, asking him to send word to his officials in Wakhan of my intended arrival. This he had done, and the petty officer at Sarhad was well aware of my identity. Nevertheless, the opportunity of swaggering a little at the expense of a Great Power before the inhabitants of this remote spot was too good to be lost, and, the local officer having presently been joined by his superior officer, a *havildar* from the little Afghan fort of Chehilkand, lower down the valley, these worthies, who wore a nondescript combination of uniform and ordinary dress, informed my companion and me that we were Russian spies and must consider ourselves under arrest until their commanding officer could arrive from Kila Panja. In the course of

Captain Younghusband (left front row) who had been arrested by Colonel Yonoff.

It was a happy novelty to be suspected of being a Russian spy.

Two of the Lord Sahib's servants had already passed through with an insignificant following.

my travels I have, on different occasions, been mistaken for a good many things and persons, but it was a happy novelty to be suspected of being a Russian spy!

Retaining our equanimity as best we could, we watched with anxious eyes the mountain defile from which our camp and escort must presently emerge, the while we palavered with the intractable and insolent Afghans. Presently, as the welcome caravan debouched upon the plain, the relative strengths of the two parties were reversed; we found ourselves in a very decided numerical majority, and, promptly turning the tables, I informed the two Afghans that if they and their seedy sepoys took the smallest step to impede our progress, they should themselves be placed under immediate arrest. This was sufficient; and after a warning of my sincere intention to inform the Amir at Kabul of the hospitable reception accorded at Sarhad to his impending guest, we packed our loads and marched away.

Two months later at Kabul the Amir himself raised the matter in my first audience with him, having received my letter of complaint and made inquiries. The reply of the *havildar*, however, had been of such a character as to excite my reluctant admiration. 'He was still awaiting,' he said, 'the arrival of the great English Lord *sahib*, who would no doubt presently appear in uniform with an escort of 1000 men. In the meantime two of the Lord *sahib*'s servants (i.e. my companion and myself) had already passed through with an insignificant following. He himself would continue diligently to await the great Lord.'

I heard later that this estimable intention on the part of the polite *havildar* had been frustrated by an imperative summons to Kabul. What happened there I do not know, though from my knowledge of the Amir I should fear the worst. For my own part, I could not help feeling a sneaking admiration for the ingenuity of my two inhospitable friends of Sarhad in Wakhan.

The Robber of Khagan

A territory
Wherein were bandit earls, and caitiff knights,
Assassins, and all flyers from the hand
Of justice, and whatever loathes a law.
TENNYSON, 'Geraint and Enid' (*Idylls of the King*).

WHEN I came back again into India from the Pamirs in October 1894, after leaving Chilas, I crossed by the Babusar Pass (13,400 feet) into the Khagan Valley and descended by that route at Abbottabad, where I was to stay with my friend, that eminent soldier and charming man, Sir William Lockhart. Four years later he was to be my first Commander-in-Chief in India, though his tenure of that high office was lamentably brief, being terminated by his death in Calcutta in March 1900.

Lockhart had told me that the Khagan Valley, which, though inside the borders of British India, was left pretty much to itself, had an evil reputation for its bad characters, who escaped easily across the border into the Alsatia of Kohistan. He had accordingly insisted on sending out a detachment of Gurkhas who were to help me over the pass, which was likely to be deep in snow, and to guard me during my transit through Khagan.

These sturdy little fellows, though brave as lions in warfare, and belonging to a race of natural mountaineers, were strangely upset by the ordeal of crossing the pass in deep snow, and had themselves to receive, instead of rendering, assistance. One of them turned sick and burst out

A detachment of Ghurkas to guard me during my transit through Khagan.

crying, and I had to lift and hold him on to a pony. The difficulty of the pass, however, once surmounted, we then rode for two days down the exquisite valley of Khagan through lovely woods of pine and cedar, crossing repeatedly, by cantilever bridges of rude timbers, the rushing Kunhar river that foamed and roared below. I was escorted by the head of the friendly family of Seyids, who are the principal land-owners and (under the British Raj) the practical rulers of the valley, and by his brothers and cousins.

The farther we descended the more beautiful was the scenery, which became Swiss in its tone and beauty. Tall plumy pines clothed the sides of the ravine to the water's edge, and even sprang in the bed of the stream. This sometimes widened into crystal-clear pools, anon roared hilariously in rapids and cascades. I rode over ground littered with pine-needles and cones. The villages or hamlets consisted of log-huts built on the steep slope of the hill, so that the back of the house sprang straight from the hill-side, or at most was raised above it by two horizontal rows of logs, while the façade was sometimes two storeys in elevation, with verandahs. The side walls were built of big logs and stones, but the front, as a rule, consisted of upright timbers. Outside the villages were great stacks of grass and other herbs.

Nearing Khagan the timber and scenery acquired a more English character. Chestnuts and sycamores, yellow with the autumn, abounded. Many of the trees were pollarded, and bundles of dry leaves on sticks were trussed up in the forks for winter use. From every village emerged numbers of tall, spider-waisted, big-turbaned, handsome Seyids, every one apparently a brother or a cousin of the chief. Each as he came up stretched out his right hand, in the palm of which were two rupees, to be politely touched and returned. The dress of the men was very different from that with which I had so long been familiar among the dark communities of the Hindu Kush. The Khaganis wore a big turban, white, or of a dark blue tartan, with long ends hanging down behind. An overcoat reached nearly to the knee, and was tightly drawn in by a waist-band at the waist. Below this were loose *puttee* or cotton knickerbockers; white *puttees* were bound round the legs with black fastenings, and on the feet were leather shoes turned up at the point. All manner of leather straps and belts were distributed about the person. The men's faces were very yellow in colour, and the majority wore a beard and moustache which was shaven bare over the middle of the lip. The beard of my host, Ahmed Ali Shah, was stained a brilliant red, and his manners were those of a Renaissance courtier. The hair was worn long, and turned up at the ends upon the back of the neck. The entire appearance of the Khagan Seyids suggested in fact some human vanity and no small taste.

On the second night we camped on a grassy slope just outside the principal village of Khagan. My own little Kabul tent was placed on the left side of the miniature terrace, and just above it was pitched the large tent of the Gurkha escort, four of whom were to be on duty by day and the remainder by night.

Tired out by my long day's ride, I ate my simple dinner in the little

Sir William Lockhart, my first Commander-in-Chief in India, though his tenure of that high office was lamentably brief.

tent, and after writing my diary, went to bed between ten and eleven. The bed consisted of a leather roll stretched on rings between the two *yakdans* or leather trunks, which are the most serviceable form of travelling baggage in those regions. Slung on mule-back in the daytime, they serve both as packing-cases, seat, and bedstead in the tent at night. I had placed the bed against the left-hand canvas of the tent, the open space in the centre and on the right being occupied with my saddle and holsters and the whole of my kit, lying in a litter on the floor. The Gurkha guards were presumably posted outside the tent.

Soon after midnight I woke, not with a start, but with the consciousness of which I had often read, though I had never before experienced it, that I was not alone in the tent. The darkness was black as pitch and thick as velvet; and though I listened intently without moving a muscle, I heard no sound. Half unconsciously I put out my left hand and dropped it between the bed and the canvas wall of the tent which the bed all but touched. It fell plumb, as though my fingers had alighted upon a billiard ball, on the shaven head of a man. I could feel the prickle of the sprouting hair against my palm. But in the same moment the object slid out of my grasp and a rustle indicated the stealthy withdrawal of the intruder. By this time I was wide awake. Springing up, I struck a match, seized my revolver, and dashed in my pyjamas out of the tent, shouting to the Gurkhas as I emerged. Not a man was to be seen. I rushed up the short slope to the guard-tent and tore aside the flap. The eight guards were all lying fast asleep on the ground.

In a few moments the whole camp was astir, the guilty Gurkhas were flying in every direction in pursuit of the intruder, and the place resounded with shouts and yells. But neither then, nor on the next morning, nor at any time afterwards was any trace of him found. The polite Seyids were visibly disturbed at this reproach upon their hospitality and the good character of their village. But they protested that the evildoer could not possibly be a Khagan man; no Khagani could be guilty of so outrageous and criminal an act; he was a *budmash* from across the border who had fled back incontinently to his own people.

I do not suppose that the *budmash* in question had come to kill me, unless indeed he was a Ghazi who wished to reduce by one the number of unbelievers in the world. He was much more probably a local thief who expected to find in my tent money or some other valuables, or who was ready to steal anything upon which he could lay his hands.

But I have always been grateful for the chance that led him to crawl under the left rather than the right canvas of my tent, and that led me to drop my hand upon his unsuspecting cranium at the very moment when he was just lifting his head to find out where he was. Had he effected his entry on the other side of the tent, he might either have absconded with some of my belongings or, had I interrupted him in the act, have dealt with me in a manner which would have prevented this anecdote from ever being written.

The Entry into Kabul

Fortes Fortuna iuvat
PLINY.

Blesses his stars and thinks it luxury.
ADDISON, *Cato*, Act I. Sc. IV.

WHEN in the autumn of 1894 I received an invitation from Amir Abdur Rahman Khan to visit him in his country, I had to consider the dress in which I should present myself at the Afghan capital. As I was the first private visitor for many years to Kabul, and as the Amir had paid me an exceptional compliment in the invitation, knowing that I was a Member of Parliament and had been Under-Secretary for India, it was desirable that my appearance should be adequate to the occasion. So many incorrect versions of my visit have appeared in print that I will here set down the facts. If I practised a slight measure of deception I trust that it was as innocent as it was successful.

The only official uniform that I possessed, apart from the pseudo-military outfit of a Deputy-Lieutenant, was that which is worn by an English Under-Secretary of State (I was not at that time a Privy Councillor); and I remembered the mediocre impression which this exceedingly plain and unattractive garb had produced at the Court of Korea. Moreover, I was not the owner of a star or cross or medal of any description. I also remembered that in conversation with Mr Ney Elias, the famous explorer and member of the Indian Political Department, a few years before, he had told me that the main reason for the excellent

I recall the anxiety when I drew near to Kabul.

impression he had produced when engaged upon a Boundary Commission in Afghan Turkestan, was the extreme width of the gold stripe which he had taken the precaution to have sewn upon his trousers, and the size of the sword with which he had girt his thigh. Acting upon this prudent hint I decided that, if I were to produce the desired effect at the Afghan capital, I must not be too strict in my observance of the rules laid down by the Lord Chamberlain at the Court of St James. After all, while in Afghanistan as the guest of the Amir, I should be regarded not merely as an ex-Minister of Great Britain, but also for the time being as a representative of my own nation: and it behoved me therefore to represent this double personality with becoming dignity.

Accordingly I devised a costume which, made up as it was, partly in London, partly at Bombay, and partly in the Punjab, was certainly composite, but would, I thought, be appropriate to the occasion. In London, before starting, I called upon Messrs Nathan, the well-known theatrical costumiers, and there I found a number of stars of foreign orders, which had no doubt once adorned the bosoms of foreign diplomats, and been purchased by Messrs Nathan for the purpose of their business. I negotiated the hire of three of the most gorgeous of these for the space of six months, for a very moderate sum. What they were exactly, I do not remember; but I think that they belonged to some of the smaller states of Eastern Europe, and I fancy from its splendour that one was Russian. I also discovered and hired by far the biggest pair of gold epaulettes that I have ever seen. They must have decorated the shoulders of some eighteenth-century Admiral of vast proportions, about the time of the French wars; and they reposed in a beautiful tin case, which was almost the size of a hat-box.

A special tent had been pitched for me, by order of the Amir, where I might change into something more becoming to the occasion.

This was the English contribution to my equipment. Then, while I was in India, it struck me that, for the purpose of an entry on horseback, the blue trousers and the boots of the ordinary levee dress were hardly sufficiently business-like or imposing. I accordingly ordered from a well-known Bombay bootmaker a gorgeous pair of patent leather Wellington top-boots, which I still possess, and which certainly lent a much needed elegance to the lower extremities of my person. Finally, while staying at Abbottabad with my friend Sir William Lockhart, then Commander-in-Chief in India, before I entered Afghanistan, I consulted him as to procuring a cavalry sword of suitable dimensions and splendour, in preference to the miserable skewer that is an appendage of the English Court dress. He replied that he had the very thing, and forthwith produced a gigantic curved weapon with an ivory hilt and a magnificent chased and engraved scabbard, which had been presented to him in honour of some successful campaign, and the blade of which was covered with a lordly inscription. The clatter made by this weapon when hung loosely from the belt was of the most approved and awe-inspiring description. Such was the get-up with which I approached my fateful journey.

Well do I recall the anxiety with which, when I drew near to Kabul, I extracted these objects from their resting-place and proceeded to don my variegated apparel! A special tent had been pitched for me, by order of the Amir, a mile or more from the city walls, in order that I might halt and exchange my travel-stained riding dress for something more becoming to the occasion. I was very near to a fiasco, for I had completely forgotten that epaulettes (which I had never worn) require a special attachment to the shoulders of the particular uniform of which they form a part. Still more was this the case with appendages of the titanic proportions of my purchase. At the last moment it was only possible to correct this unfortunate oversight by a liberal use of needle and thread, and I had over an hour's hard work with both in the endeavour to sew the epaulettes into a position of becoming stability on my shoulders. Even so, at any sudden jolt or movement of the body they were liable to jump forward with a leap that sent my heart into my mouth and nearly tore asunder their frail attachments. However, all was at length adjusted. The patent leather boots with a pair of handsome spurs shone upon my legs; Sir W. Lockhart's presentation sword rattled at my side; my breast was ablaze with the insignia of unknown diplomats of the past; and a cocked hat nodded on my head.

Thus attired I entered the town, and was escorted to the Palace. I flattered myself, as I was conducted into the Durbar Hall of the Amir, that I created the desired impression, though I was a little perplexed when His Highness betrayed an admiring interest in my trophies, and wished to know exactly what services or exploits they commemorated, or the favour of what monarch they testified. To these inconvenient queries I could only return the most general and deprecatory replies. But for the gilded epaulettes, with their ample bullion, hanging in rich festoons, there was reserved the greatest triumph. For the Amir, sending for the Court tailor, pointedly called his attention to these glittering appendages as of a character necessitating serious notice and even reproduction at the Court of Afghanistan; and for all I know, they may have left a permanent mark upon the sartorial equipment of the God-granted Government.

Little more than four years later I had as many genuine orders on my bosom (though not drawn from quite so wide a range) as it could conveniently hold; and I was corresponding with my friend the Amir as the authorised representative of my Sovereign. But I still cherish the fond belief that my improvised entry into the Afghan capital was not altogether without *éclat* and even distinction.

Somewhat later, in the course of my reading, I came across a passage which showed that I was by no means the first English traveller to find it desirable to pay special deference in respect of costume to the ideas or etiquette of an Asiatic Court. When W. Hawkins went out in command of the newly-founded East India Company to India in 1607, to proceed to the Court of the Great Mogul (Jehangir), 'in order that he might appear with becoming splendour, he was furnished with scarlet apparel, his cloak being lined with taffeta, and embroidered with silver lace.' (W. Foster, *Early Travels in India*, p. 62.)

Hawkins, it is clear, easily beat me in point of raiment, but I flatter myself that he had not my unique collection of stars.

The Amir of Afghanistan

He civilised his people and himself remained a savage.
VOLTAIRE.

One still strong man in a blatant land
Who can rule and dare to lie.
TENNYSON, 'Maud' (slightly adapted).

I HAVE never before narrated the circumstances in which I came to visit the Capital and Court of the famous Afghan ruler, Amir Abdur Rahman Khan. I had devoted so many years to the study of the Central Asian problem – the security of the Indian frontier; the policy of Russia, then in the full tide of her career of Asiatic aggression and conquest; the part that was being played in the drama by all the countries lying on the glacis of the Indian fortress, Persia, Baluchistan, Afghanistan, Tibet, China – and I had explored so many of these regions myself, that I was beyond measure desirous to visit that one of their number which, though perhaps the most important, was also the least accessible, and to converse with the stormy and inscrutable figure who occupied the Afghan throne, and was a source of such incessant anxiety, suspicion, and even alarm to successive Governments of India as well as to the India Office in London.

I knew that the Amir was intensely mistrustful of the Calcutta Government, and I thought it not impossible that he might be willing to converse with an Englishman who had been the Minister responsible for the Government of India in the House of Commons in London, who was still, though no longer in office, a member of that House, and who had for some years written and spoken widely, though always in a friendly spirit, about the defence of the Indian frontier, and the importance of intimate relations with Afghanistan. Accordingly in the spring of 1894 I wrote a personal letter to the Amir, in which I confessed these desires, explained to him my impending programme of travel in the Himalayas and the Pamirs, and sought his permission to visit him at Kabul in the latter part of the year.

After expatiating with more than Oriental hyperbole upon all these considerations, I added a passage in which I felt a modest pride:

> 'Khorasan I have seen and visited; I have been in Bokhara and Samarkand; I have ridden to Chaman, and I have sojourned at Peshawur. But the dominions of Your Highness, which are situated in the middle of all these territories, like unto a rich stone in the middle of a ring, I have never been permitted to enter, and the person of Your Highness, which is in your own dominions like unto the sparkle in the heart of the diamond, I have not been fortunate enough to see. Many books and writings have I studied, and have talked to many men; but I would fain converse with Your Highness who knows more about these questions than do other men, and who will perhaps be willing to throw upon my imperfect understanding the full ray of truth.'

The Amir at the time of my visit in 1894.

Apart, however, from the hoped-for invitation from the Amir – never before extended to any Englishman except to those in his personal employ, or to an official Mission from the Government of India, such as that of their Foreign Secretary, Sir Mortimer Durand – there were other and formidable difficulties to be overcome. The Home Government (Lord Kimberley was then Secretary of State for India) viewed my project with some anxiety; the attitude of the Government of India was veiled in a chilly obscurity, which was not dissipated until I arrived at Simla in the early autumn to plead my own case. Sir Henry Brackenbury, then Military Member, and a man of great ability and much imagination, was my one friend; the Commander-in-Chief, Sir George White, was non-committal; the Viceroy, Lord Elgin, hesitated. At a meeting of the Executive Council, however, it was decided to let me cross the frontier (on my return from the Pamirs), provided that a direct invitation from the Amir arrived in the interim; but I was told that I must go as a private individual (which was exactly what I desired), and that the Government of India would assume no responsibility for my safety.

It was while I was in camp in the Gurais Valley in Kashmir, on my way to the Gilgit frontier, that I received a telegram from Kabul announcing the invitation of the Amir. From that moment all my anxieties were at an end, and it remained only for me to get through my Pamir explorations in safety in order to realise my supreme ambition in the later autumn. Nearly three months later, on 13 November 1894, I rode alone across the Afghan frontier at Torkham beyond Lundi Khana, and consigned myself to the care of the God-Granted Government, and to the hospitality of its Sovereign.

And now let me say something about the personality and career of that remarkable man, so that my readers, to whom his name is perhaps now little more than a memory, may know what sort of being it was with whom I was about to spend long days in friendly intercourse, and who was to reveal to me, with an astonishing candour, his innermost thoughts and ideas.

Born in 1844, Abdur Rahman Khan was the eldest son of Dost Mohammed, the celebrated Afghan ruler who had been alternately the foe and the protégé of the British Government. He was therefore by birth and inheritance the direct and legal heir of his grandfather, and the recognised head of the Barukzai clan. It may be a consolation to reluctant students and to naughty boys at large to know, as the Amir himself told me, that up till the age of twenty he declined to learn either to read or write, and that at a time when most European lads have their knees under a desk he was engaged in manufacturing rifled gun-barrels and in casting guns. It was in 1864, the year following upon the death of the Dost, that he first appeared in public life, being appointed to a Governorship in Afghan Turkestan; and after that date there were few elements of romance or adventure that his career did not contain. Here victorious in battle (for he was a born soldier); there defeated; now a king-maker in his own country, anon a fugitive from its borders; for a time the powerful Governor of the Cis-Oxian provinces, and presently an exile in the courts of Meshed, Khiva, and Bokhara; later on a pensioner of the Russians at Samarkand, and, finally, the British nominee upon the throne of a recovered Afghanistan, for nearly forty years, whether in the forefront or the background, he presented the single strong figure whose masculine individuality emerged with distinctness from the obscure and internecine and often miserable drama of Afghan politics.

It was he who placed, first his father Afzul, and afterwards his uncle Azim, on the throne; and when, Afzul having died and Azim having been defeated by a younger brother, Shere Ali, he was obliged to flee from his country into a ten years' exile, it was with the conviction, which he never abandoned, that his services would again be called for and that he would assuredly return.

For this purpose he accepted a Russian pension (the greater part of which was, he told me, systematically filched from him by peculation) and resided at Samarkand, in order that he might be near to the Afghan frontier whenever the emergency should arise. The Russians never quite recovered from their astonishment that one who had been a recipient of their hospitality and their pay should, in later years, after recovering the throne, have pursued a policy so little in accord with Russian aspirations; and for a while they consoled themselves with the reflection that this was a mere ruse, and that the true Russophil would appear later on. These expectations were sadly disappointed; for although he did not care for the British much, Abdur Rahman disliked the Russians far more, and had a very shrewd idea of the fate that a Russo-Afghan alliance would bring upon his country. Incidentally, he told me that while a refugee in Russia he secretly learned the language, and never enjoyed himself more than when he heard the Russian officers discussing their real policy in the presence of the seemingly simple-minded and unsophisticated Afghan.

In 1878 his opportunity came, when Shere Ali, inveigled by Russian promises to his doom, threw off the British alliance, and brought a British army into his country, thereby forfeiting first his throne, and, a little later, his life. Crossing the frontier, Abdur Rahman overran the whole country, and by 1880 had acquired so commanding a position that when, after the treachery of Yakub Khan and the open hostility of Ayub, the Indian Government were looking out for a suitable candidate for the throne, they had no alternative but to take the single strong man in the country, whom they forthwith installed as ruler, and then retired.

In the thirteen years that elapsed before my visit the Amir had consolidated his rule over one of the most turbulent peoples in the world by force alike of character and of arms, and by a relentless savagery that ended by crushing all opposition out of existence, and leaving him the undisputed but dreaded master of the entire country. No previous Sovereign had ever ridden the wild Afghan steed with so cruel a bit, none had given so large a measure of unity to the kingdom; there was not in Asia or in the world a more fierce or uncompromising despot. Such was the remarkable man whose guest I was for more than a fortnight at Kabul, living in the Salam Khana or Guest House, immediately overlooking the moat of the Ark or Citadel. The Amir was residing in a neighbouring two-storied house or villa, surrounded by a high wall, and known as the Bostan Serai. In the grounds of this place he now lies buried. Our meetings and conversations took place in a large room in that building. They usually commenced at noon or 1 PM and lasted for some hours.

I do not propose to narrate here the long conversations, mainly of a political character, in which the Amir indulged, because, as I have before said, I do not wish this volume to become a political treatise, and because much of what he said was intended to be confidential. Later on, however, I shall narrate one of his most characteristic harangues about his impending visit to England, the invitation to which he accepted through me, since it reveals many of the most interesting traits of his shrewd but untutored intellect. In the intervals, however, of these quasi-political conversations the Amir would talk discursively about almost every topic under heaven; while, during my stay, I heard many anecdotes of his curious character and amazing career.

Perhaps before I come to these I may say a few words about his external appearance and mien. A man of big stature though not of great height, of colossal personal strength, and of corresponding stoutness of frame when in his prime, he was much altered by sickness when I saw him from the appearance presented, for instance, by the photographs taken at the Rawal Pindi Durbar in 1885. The photograph that I reproduce represents him as he was at the time of my visit in 1894. He suffered greatly from gout, and one of the favourite amusements or jests of the native compositor in the Indian Press was to convert 'gout' into 'government' and to say, not without truth, that the Amir was suffering from 'a bad attack of government.'

A large, but in no wise unwieldy figure sitting upright upon silken quilts, outspread over a low *charpoy* or bedstead, the limbs encased in close-fitting lamb's wool garments; a fur-lined pelisse hanging over the shoulders, and a spotless white silk turban wound round the conical Afghan skull-cap of cloth of silver, or of gold, and coming low down on to the forehead; a broad and massive countenance with regular features, but complexion visibly sallow from recent illness; brows that contracted somewhat as he reflected or argued; luminous black eyes that looked out very straightly and fixedly without the slightest movement or wavering, a black moustache close clipped upon the upper lip, and a carefully trimmed and dyed black beard, neither so long nor so luxuriant as of yore, framing a mouth that responded to every expression, and which, when it opened, as it not unfrequently did, to loud laughter, widened at the corners and disclosed the full line of teeth in both jaws; a voice resonant but not harsh, and an articulation of surprising emphasis and clearness; above all, a manner of unchallengeable dignity and command – this was the outward guise and bearing of my kingly host. I may add that for stating his own case in an argument or controversy the Amir would not easily find a match on the front benches in the House of Commons; whilst if he began to talk of his own experiences and to relate stories of his adventures in warfare or exile, the organised minuteness and deliberation with which each stage of the narrative proceeded in due order was only equalled by the triumphant crash of the climax, and only exceeded by the roar of laughter which the *dénouement* almost invariably provoked from the audience, and in which the author as heartily joined. Like most men trained in the Persian literary school (Persian being the language of the upper classes in Afghanistan), the Amir was a constant quoter of saws and wise sayings from that inexhaustible well of sapient philosophy, that Iranian Pope, the Sheikh Saadi.

The Amir's appearance, like that of most Orientals, was greatly enhanced by his turban. I never saw him in the sheepskin *kolah* or *kalpak* of his military uniform. On one occasion when we were talking about his visit to England he removed his turban and began to scratch his head, which was shaved quite bald. In a moment he was transformed from the formidable despot to a commonplace and elderly man. I implored him when he came to London never to remove his turban or scratch his head; and, when I told him my reason, his vanity was at once piqued, and he promised faithfully to show himself at his best.

His characteristics were in some respects even more remarkable than his features. This terribly cruel man could be affable, gracious, and considerate to a degree. This man of blood loved scents and colours and gardens and singing birds and flowers. This intensely practical being was a prey to mysticism, for he thought that he saw dreams and visions, and was convinced (although this was probably only a symptom of his vanity) that he possessed supernatural gifts. Generous to those who were useful to him, he was merciless to any whose day was past or who had lost his favour. But even in the most unpropitious circumstances his humour never deserted him. At one of his country *durbars* certain tax-gatherers were disputing with the local landowners as to the taxes to be paid. As they all insisted on speaking at once, he placed a soldier behind each of them with orders to box the ears of any man who spoke out of his turn.

On one occasion he put a man to death unjustly, i.e. on false evidence. Thereupon he fined himself 6000 rupees, and paid this sum to the widow, who for her part was delighted at being simultaneously relieved of her husband and started again in life.

On another occasion his humour took a more gruesome turn. It was pointed out to him by one of his courtiers that he had ordered an innocent man to be hanged. 'Innocent!' cried the Amir. 'Well, if he is not guilty this time, he has done something else at another. Away with him.'

In this strange and almost incredible amalgam of the jester and the cynic, the statesman and the savage, I think that a passion for cruelty was one of his most inveterate instincts. The Amir often exerted himself to deny the charge or claimed that it was the only method of dealing with a race so treacherous and criminally inclined. For instance, as I rode to Kabul, I passed on the top of the Lataband Pass an iron cage swinging from a tall pole in which rattled the bleaching bones of a robber whom he had caught and shut up alive in this construction, as a warning to other disturbers of the peace of the King's highway. He revelled in these grim demonstrations of executive authority. Nevertheless, the recorded stories – as to the truth of which I satisfied myself – were sufficient to show that a love of violence and an ingrained ferocity were deeply rooted in his nature. He confided to an Englishman at Kabul that he had put to death 120,000 of his own people. After one unsuccessful rebellion he had many thousands of the guilty tribesmen blinded with quicklime, and spoke to me of the punishment without a trace of compunction. Crimes such as robbery or rape were punished with fiendish severity. Men were blown from guns, or thrown down a dark well, or beaten to death, or flayed alive, or tortured in the offending member. For instance, one of the favourite penalties for petty larceny was to amputate the hand at the wrist, the raw stump being then plunged in boiling oil. One official who had outraged a woman was stripped naked and placed in a hole dug for the purpose on the top of a high hill outside Kabul. It was in midwinter; and water was then poured upon him until he was converted into an icicle and frozen alive. As the Amir sardonically remarked, 'He would never be too hot again.'

A woman of his harem being found in the family way, he had her tied up in a sack and brought into the Durbar hall, where he ran her through with his own sword. Two men having been heard to talk about some forbidden subject, he ordered their upper and lower lips to be stitched together so that they should never offend again. A man came into the Durbar one day and openly accused the Amir of depravity and crime. 'Tear out his tongue,' said the Amir. In a moment he was seized and his tongue torn out by the roots. The poor wretch died. One day an old beggar threw himself in the way of the Amir as he was riding through the streets. The following dialogue then ensued: 'What are you?' 'A beggar.' 'But how do you get your living?' 'By alms.' 'What? Do you mean to say that you do no work?' 'None.' 'And you have never done any?' 'Never.' 'Then it is time that we were relieved of your presence.' And the Amir nodded to the executioner.

His cruelty even extended to punishing acts, however innocent, which had not been authorised by himself or which seemed to trench upon his prerogative. Though I was his guest and he sincerely desired to do me honour, and did so, he could not tolerate that any of his subjects should show spontaneous courtesy to the stranger. A man who spoke to me while I was on the road to Kabul was seized and thrown into prison. A man who offered me a pomegranate as I rode into Kandahar was severely beaten and imprisoned and deprived of his property.

Nevertheless, this monarch, at once a patriot and a monster, a great man and almost a fiend, laboured hard and unceasingly for the good of his country. He sought to raise his people from the squalor and apathy and blood-shedding of their normal lives and to convert them into a nation. He welded the Afghan tribes into a unity which they had never previously enjoyed, and he paved the way for the complete independence which his successors have achieved. He and he alone was the Government of Afghanistan. There was nothing from the command of an army or the government of a province to the cut of a uniform or the fabrication of furniture that he did not personally superintend and control. He was the brain and eyes and ears of all Afghanistan. But it is questionable whether in the later part of his life he was more detested or admired. He ceased to move abroad from fear of assassination, and six horses, saddled and laden with coin, were always kept ready for a sudden escape.

I should describe him, on the whole, in spite of his uncertain temper and insolent language, as a consistent friend of the British alliance. Though he often had differences with the Government of India, whom he loved to snub and annoy, though there were moments when the relations between them were very strained, though, when I became Viceroy, he did not spare me these conventional amenities and we were sometimes on the verge of a serious quarrel, I did not and do not doubt that on the broad issues of Imperial policy his fidelity was assured. But he acted in this respect, as in all others, from expediency alone. He knew that the British neither coveted nor desired to annex his country. As an independent Sovereign he was compelled, for the sake of appearances with his own people, to exhibit a truculence that was often offensive and at times insupportable. But at a crisis it was to British advice and British arms that he invariably turned. His name will always deserve to rank high in the annals of his own country as well as in the history of the Indian Empire.

Among the devices that he adopted in order to stimulate the patriotism and ensure the due subordination of his people and incidentally to render them more amenable to military conscription, was the issue of a map, accompanied by a Proclamation which was read out in the bazaars and mosques of all the principal towns and posted in every village. As this map, however viewed, is quite unlike any other map that I have ever seen, I give a small-scale reproduction of it here. My original copy, printed on canvas, measures 5 feet by 4½ feet.

The Proclamation was even more remarkable than the map, which indeed stands in some need of explanation. It was in the nature of a lecture, invested with all the authority of a royal *firman* or decree. I will quote a few passages from it.

> 'I have now prepared for you a kind of map, which shows the condition of Afghanistan as compared with that of its surrounding countries. This I have done in order to enable you to study the matter attentively and to make out a path for yourselves in such a way that good may accrue both to your country and to your religion. I am hopeful that a careful study of this map will suffice for your prosperity and happiness both in this world and the next.
>
> In entering into the details of this map, I hereby declare that whatever has been predestined by the Almighty for each one of you, the same has been put into the heart of your King, and he is thus enabled to find suitable appointments for all. Some of you have attained to the rank of a Commander-in-Chief, while others are still in the position of a sepoy. It is, however, fitting for you all to offer thanks to God and to your King, and to be contented with your lot. You should not be envious of those who hold higher rank than yourselves, but you should rather look to those who are inferior. By doing so you will gain three benefits – first, the favour and blessing of God, for it is

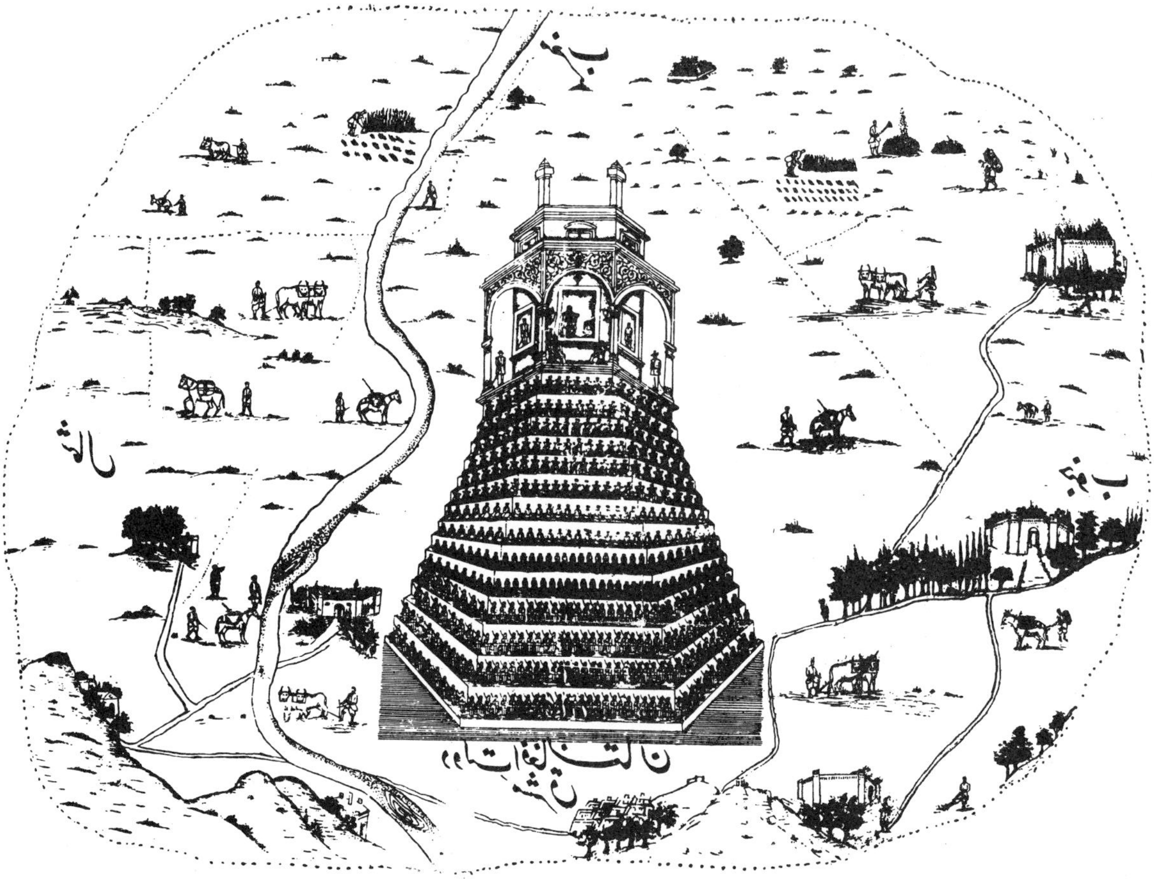

'I have now prepared for you a kind of map, a careful study of which will suffice for your prosperity and happiness both in this world and the next.'

written that "if you express your gratitude for the blessings poured forth upon you, the same shall be increased"; secondly, the approbation and good will of your ruler; and thirdly, you will thus be enabled to hold your present position in the sure hope of obtaining advancement. For God has said, that if you offer thanks for His blessings He will increase them. The increase of blessings signifies the exaltation of rank. All blessings in this world depend upon the exaltation of position, and when a man's rank is increased he can then only be said to have obtained the blessings of this world. But if you are not contented with your present state and neglect to offer your thanks to God, and do not look to those who are inferior to you in position, but rather envy those who are above you, and ask in your hearts why such and such persons are superior to yourselves, you lay the foundation of envy and hatred, and cause many calamities to fall upon you.

Therefore, take care and listen to me, who am your King, with all your heart, and weigh well what I say, for it is of no use to make lamentations for that which has passed and gone. This advice is for all, from the Commander-in-Chief down to the sepoy, and also for the subjects, who are inferior to all, and for those who carry guns on their shoulders. A sepoy should look upon the subjects, who are inferior to him, as members of his own society, for it is with the help of God and by the kindness of the King that he has obtained his rank. You should sympathise with the subjects, who are your own tribesmen and who are continually employed in cultivating their lands, in cutting their crops, in thrashing their corn, in gathering in the harvests and in winnowing the wheat from the chaff. They are also occupied in trade and undergo hardships and troubles by night and by day, and only enjoy a portion of the produce themselves after they have paid in the taxes which are necessary for the expenses of the State. I, who am your King, spend all this money on the army. It therefore behoves you all, whether you are men in high places or sepoys or subjects, to be grateful, because all that you pay is given back to your brothers, sons and tribesmen. By this God is pleased, religion flourishes and honour is preserved. In a like manner, the subjects should also be grateful, so that God's blessings may increase day by day, for it is written, that on him who is grateful He increases his bounties. It is therefore incumbent on you to be grateful both to God and to your King.

The real object of my teaching is that the kindness and compassion of the King towards his subjects resembles the feelings of a father towards his son; and as it is natural that a father should be kind to his son, so it is also natural that the King should be kind to his subjects. These are also the orders of God to the King. But when the father sees the errors of his son, he admonishes and punishes him. Now this punishment is not due to ill-feeling, but rather to the excessive love which the father bears towards his son, so that he cannot even bear the sight of any wrong-doing on the part of his son; in the same way the King has the same feelings towards his subjects as a father has towards his son. The King only wishes to spread the blessings of tranquillity and peace among his subjects and to gain a good name thereby. When a boy is young and ignorant, he hates and despises the advice of his father, but when he becomes of age and becomes endued with wisdom and intellect, he considers that there is none so kind and affectionate as his father, and it is the whole purport and desire of his life to obey the orders of his father. In the same way, I, the ruler of you Afghans, have the same desire of being kind and generous to you, even as a father is kind and generous to his son. If you are wise enough to understand and benefit by my advice, I am confident that you will see that your religion will flourish and your country will be prosperous. May it so please God.'

Considering the manner, as already described, in which Abdur Rahman Khan was in the habit of demonstrating his paternal love for his subjects, the latter, if they had one-thousandth part of the sense of humour of their sovereign, must have smiled somewhat grimly as they listened to this sermon.

One of the subjects that interested the Amir most was his claim, on behalf of himself and of his people, to a descent from the Lost Tribes of Israel. I had heard of this theory; and I had noted the distinct resemblance of many Afghan features to the Semitic type. But when I interrogated him about it, he unhesitatingly proclaimed his acceptance of the legend. He declared that the Afghans took their name from Afghana, who was Commander-in-Chief to King Solomon; some were descended from him, and others from Jeremiah the son of Saul. On another occasion the Amir's eldest son Habibulla, whose ethnology was a little hazy, told me that the Afghans were Jews who had been conquered by Babu-Nassar (i.e. Nebuchadnezzar) in the time of Yezdigird, and deported to Persia, where they lived a long time. Later on they migrated to Afghanistan, where they settled in the region of the Suleiman (Solomon) Mountains, to which, in reference to their origin, they gave that name. As a matter of fact, the Hebrew descent of the Afghans has been the subject of prolonged dispute, great authorities having argued on either side. The champions of the theory point to the marked Jewish features of so many Afghans, to the great number of Jewish Christian names (*e.g.* Ibrahim = Abraham, Ayub=Job, Ismail=Ishmael, Ishak=Isaac, Yahia=John, Yakub=Jacob, Yusuf=Joseph, Isa=Jesus, Daoud=David, Suleiman= Solomon, and many others), to the fact that the Feast of the Passover is still observed by the Pathan border tribe of the Yusufzai; and to the occurrence of the name Kabul in the Old Testament (*e.g.* 1 Kings ix. 13), where Solomon, having given King Hiram twenty cities of Galilee in return for the timber and gold presented to him for the Temple, Hiram went out to see them and was very much disgusted, 'calling them the land of Cabul (*i.e.* dirty or disgusting) unto this day.' I believe that this reasoning is quite fallacious, the Biblical names employed by the Afghans being all in their Arabic form, *i.e.* post-Mohammedan in origin; and the Hebrew word Kabúl in the Old Testament having no connection, except in spelling, with the Afghan Kābul. The theory of a Semitic origin is now generally discredited, but there is nothing inherently improbable in the belief that some of the Afghan tribes may have entered the country from Persia (of which language they speak a patois) and may have come at an earlier date into Persia from Syria or Assyria (the land of the captivity). There I will leave the matter, to which I have only alluded here in order to record the opinions of the Amir.

And now, having given a general picture of the man, his personality and his acts, let me pass on to narrate a few of the more interesting conversations, other than on political subjects, with which he overflowed. He spoke in Persian through an interpreter; and while at times he would indulge in short and staccato phrases, at others he would pour forth a torrent of declamation that lasted for six or seven minutes without a pause.

Never was the mixture of shrewdness, vanity, and ignorance, which were so strangely blended in Abdur Rahman's character, more patently shown than in the conversation which he held with me one day in open Durbar with regard to his contemplated visit to England. He had already received an official invitation from Her Majesty's Government, tendered through the Viceroy (Lord Elgin) to pay such a visit, and to this invitation, with calculated rudeness, he had declined for months to return a reply. I had good reason for thinking that he was postponing his answer until I arrived at Kabul, and he could hear from me personally what sort of reception he would be likely to meet with in London. From the start, accordingly, this formed a constant topic of our conversation; and I very soon realised that, while appearing to hang back, the Amir was in reality intensely anxious to come, provided, on the one hand, that he could be assured of a welcome in England compatible with his own exalted conception of the dignity and prestige of the Afghan Sovereign, and, on the other, that he could safely be absent from his country for several months of time. He would discuss these subjects with me interminably in all their bearings, being in reality much more concerned about the former than the latter. At length, towards the end of my visit, his mind was made up; the decision to pay the visit was definitely taken; the acceptance was written, in the form of a personal letter to Queen Victoria, which the Amir handed to me in open Durbar, wrapped up in a violet silk covering, embroidered with a Persian inscription. This parcel I took back to England and ultimately transmitted to Her Majesty: and unquestionably the visit would have taken place had not the Amir learned a little later on that, had he left his country, the chances were that, in consequence of the reign of terror that prevailed under his iron hand, he would never be allowed to return, and that in his absence some less fierce and dreaded occupant would be installed upon the Afghan throne.

It was in the course of one of these public conversations that the following dialogue occurred – to understand which it should be premised that the one Englishman against whom the Amir cherished an overweening, though entirely unfounded prejudice, was Lord Roberts (then Commander-in-Chief in England), whom he was never tired of accusing of having condemned and hanged, by bought and perjured evidence, many thousands of innocent Afghans upon the arrival of the British army in Kabul after the murder of Sir L. Cavagnari in 1879. This monarch, who had not hesitated himself, as he boasted to me, to put out the eyes of thousands of his own subjects (after the Hazara rebellion), and who was utterly indifferent to human life, had no words of reprobation too strong for the British Commander, who had dared to punish a gross act of international treachery by the execution of the guilty parties; and he would constantly repeat that Roberts had killed thousands of innocent Afghan people and could never be forgiven. Hence the ensuing story.

A. 'When I come to England and to London and am received by the Queen, shall I tell you what I will do?'

C. 'Yes, Your Highness, I shall be glad to hear.'

A. 'I understand that there is in London a great Hall that is known as Westminster Hall. Is not that so?'

C. 'It is.'

A. 'There are also in London two *Mejilises* (*i.e.* Houses of Parliament). One is called the House of Lords and the other is called the House of Commons?'

C. 'It is so.'

A. 'When I come to London, I shall be received in Westminster Hall. The Queen will be seated on her throne at the end of the Hall, and the Royal Family will be around her; and on either side of the Hall will be placed the two *Mejilises* – the House of Lords on the right, and the House of Commons on the left. Is not that the case?'

C. 'It is not our usual plan; but will Your Highness proceed?'

A. 'I shall enter the Hall, and the Lords will rise on the right, and the Commons will rise on the left to greet me, and I shall advance between them up the Hall to the daïs, where will be seated the Queen upon her throne. And she will rise and will say to me, "What has Your Majesty come from Kabul to say?" And how then shall I reply?'

C. 'I am sure I do not know.'

A. 'I shall reply: "I will say nothing" – and the Queen will then ask me why I refuse to say anything; and I shall answer: "Send for Roberts. I decline to speak until Roberts comes." And then they will send for Roberts, and there will be a pause until Roberts comes, and when Roberts has come and is standing before the Queen and the two *Mejilises,* then will I speak.'

C. 'And what will Your Highness say?'

A. 'I shall tell them how Roberts paid thousands of rupees to obtain false witness at Kabul and that he slew thousands of my innocent people, and I shall ask that Roberts be punished, and when Roberts has been punished, then will I speak.'

The only person in England who failed to find the story at all amusing was Lord Roberts himself.

It was in vain that I indicated to the Amir that things in England and in London were not done exactly in that way, and that the ceremonial of his reception would hardly be of the nature described. Nothing could convince him. This was no doubt exactly the manner in which he would have managed the business in Kabul; and London meant no more to him than a larger stage and a change of scene.

When I reflected what might have happened had the visit been paid and had the Amir been confronted with the more sober realities of British official procedure, I felt almost glad that Her Majesty's Government were spared the spectacle of the Amir's disappointment and its consequences, which might have been serious; although the personal encounter between the two protagonists, had it ever taken place, could hardly have failed to be diverting.

The only person in England who, when I recounted the story, failed to find it at all amusing – and this perhaps quite pardonably – was Lord Roberts himself.

Knowing that I was a member of Parliament the Amir never spoke to me contemptuously, though often with a touch of sarcasm, about the House of Commons. But to others he was less reticent. On one occasion he told an Englishman in his service that he ought to go to the public *hammam* (Turkish Bath) in Kabul in order to see what in the Amir's opinion the British Parliament must be like. The Englishman duly went, and soon discovered what the Amir had in mind, for the place was full of men, and the high dome overhead reverberated with their calls for towels, soap, etc., and their usual loud-voiced conversations, until the meaning of any individual words and the words themselves were lost in the confusion of sounds, and only added to the general uproar.

Among other curious illustrations of the Amir's colossal, but childish vanity, I recall the following. He cherished the illusion, which was warmly encouraged by all the courtiers who were in the Durbar Hall, that he had a monopoly of all the talents and was the universal genius of Afghanistan, particularly in all matters of mechanics and the arts.

One day, as I was going to the Durbar, I passed through an antechamber in which was standing a superb Grand Piano, evidently a fresh importation from Europe, the case of which was exquisitely painted with pictorial subjects or scenes. I was told – though this was probably untrue – that the artist or designer had been no less a person than Sir E. Burne-Jones.

A. 'Did you notice the Grand Piano standing in the adjoining chamber as you came in?'

C. 'Yes, I did.'

A. 'What did you think of the painting of the case?'

C. 'I thought it magnificent.'

A. 'I painted it myself!'

The other case was this. One day I was a little late in attending the Durbar, my watch having stopped in the morning.

A. 'Why are you late to-day?'

C. 'I am sorry to say that my watch stopped this morning.'

A. 'And yours is an English watch. Send it to me, and I will put it right without difficulty. I am a professional watch-maker myself and keep right the watches of all the people of Kabul!'

I hastily explained that my watch had resumed its full and orderly functions, and accordingly was able to save it from the hands of the illustrious amateur.

I may here anticipate somewhat by giving another example of this amusing trait. After I had returned to England I married in the summer of 1895, and sent a photograph of my wife to the Amir, who responded with a handsome present. But, as the following letter will show, he could not resist, *as an expert in phrenology*, from assuring me that I had made an excellent choice. I append the translation, which he enclosed with the original letter in Persian.

'*To my wise and kind friend, the Honble. G. Curzon, M.P.*

After compliments and Persian titles and my sincere desire of seeing you again, also my great friendly expressions towards you, my very wise friend – I wish to inform you that I am greatly pleased and interested on reading the contents of your letters, dated March 15 and June 9. I beg to acknowledge the same and my reply is as follows: I was very much delighted to hear of your marriage, also delighted to receive Lady Curzon's photo. Thank God she is according to your own choice. I pray God will keep you (my own wise friend) successful in all the desires of this life.

I also congratulate you, my honest friend, that though you have only married one wife she is competent.

From my knowledge of Phrenology she is very wise and a well-wisher of yours and better than 1000 men.

'Though you have only married one wife, she is competent.'

I hope it may be God's wish, my dear friend, that you will be happy and satisfied with her always. Thanks to the Almighty you have been fortunate enough to meet with such a wife, that in the whole of England there are but a few. Faithfulness, wisdom and honesty, all these I gather from her photo and according to Phrenology. May God bless you with a goodly offspring.'

And then in a final sentence leaped forth the irresistible humour of the man:

'If she should at any time thrash you I am certain you will have done something to deserve it. – I am your sincere friend and well-wisher ABDUR RAHMAN, AMIR OF AFGHANISTAN.'

As a balance to this type of correspondence I append a single example of a more political letter, written to me while I was still a private person; but revealing many of the best-known features of the Amir's epistolary style. In the first part of the letter is a reference to a press report of something that I was alleged to have said about Afghanistan in England. The second part relates to the constant disputes between the Indian and Afghan Governments, arising out of the frontier warfare known as the Tirah Campaign, which occupied the greater part of 1897.

'May my dear, discerning friend, His most honoured Excellency, the Honourable George Curzon, Esquire, Minister of Parliament,

M.P. of the House of Commons, continue in the keeping of (God) the True Protector.

The letter of that kind friend written on December 30 A.D. 1897, corresponding to Shaban 5, A.H. 1315, reached the presence of your friend at the best of seasons. From the circumstances of your corporeal well-being joy was produced, and I rejoiced at the soundness of that dear friend's health.

As for what that kind friend wrote concerning the adverse words which have been reported to me as having been uttered by that friend, I have never had cause to complain of that kind friend's friendship, nor of his utterances concerning the State of Afghanistan; neither do I suppose any such thing. I regard you as the first of my friends, the only friend I have in the world. On this subject I have much to say, for there are many reasons for speech. When that kind friend was in Kabul, and we and you sat together in one place, and discussed our inmost thoughts about Russia and Afghanistan, and the disorder of Afghanistan, concerning the antagonism of the Russian Government, the defects of Afghanistan had still in no wise been remedied when the misconduct of a frontier contiguous to the frontier officers of the Most Glorious State of England brought about disturbance and confusion, until at length the frontier officers of that State first cast suspicion upon me for their foolish deeds and words; for they issued proclamations for a general massacre of the people of the hill-passes, and fear overtook them all, and they slew the Agents of the Most Glorious State and burned and ravaged; and several thousand men and part of the Army of the Most Glorious State died, neither did they gain anything save hostility. Alas! alas! for this nearness and proximity of Russia, and the hostility of the Afghan frontier tribes. I do not know what the end of it will be, for although I have no concern with the people of Tira and the Afridis and the peoples of Bajawar and Swat, it is now eleven months since all caravans from my dominions have been stopped, and the implements which were necessary for my engine-workshop have been detained. In proof of this I send enclosed in this packet, for your information and perusal, an Order written by the Commissioner of Peshawur for the caravan conductor (Kafila-bashi) of your friend (myself) located at Peshawur, about the detention of the oil-boxes, and I do not know what may be the reason of his (the Commissioner's) conduct. They have caused my thoughts to incline to doubt India, so that enemy and friend are passed out of my memory (*i.e.* I confuse friends and enemies). If you will again peruse the political news of India which has gone to London wherein they have said many things about (*i.e.* have cast many reflections on) my friendship, and have made (many) aspersions (you will see that) I have patiently stomached much, and by these forbearances it will be known to that kind friend that my friendship towards the Most Glorious State is very firm, for had this not been so, I too would have said something foolish; but what shall I do, or what shall I say? This much I will say that I remain the friend of the Most Glorious State and that loyalty thereunto abides in my heart, but the Agents of the Most Glorious State in India are endeavouring to bring about its overthrow. Please God it will not be overthrown on my part, though should the initiative (in hostility or provocation) be taken by the Indian Government, I do not know (what might happen): but, please God, (the initiative) will not be on my side, for my friendship towards the Most Glorious State is firmly established as a mountain. I hope from God that it may be the same on the other side, so that we may not become such as our enemies would desire.

Further you wrote "at this time (of writing) is the transition of the year and the renewal of the Christian date into 1898; therefore I send my prayers for your welfare." So also your friend (*i.e.* myself) with fullest affection, sends greetings and congratulations, (praying) that, please God, you may pass the New Year in contentment and health, and may ever remember the circumstances of your safe preservation. For the rest, good wishes. May the days of your glory and gladness be continued!

Written on Monday the 15th of the month of Ramazan the Blessed, A.H. 1315, corresponding to the 7th of February, A.D. 1898.

(Signed) AMIR ABDUR RAHMAN ZIYA'U'L-MILLATI WA'D DIN, G.C.S.I. and G.C.B.'

To return to the conversations of the Amir. Perhaps the most salient feature both of his bearing and talk was his gift of polished, but mordant sarcasm, sometimes, where his own subjects were concerned, taking the form of sardonic and fearful cruelty. I will relate four illustrations of this terrifying humour which happened during or about the time when I was at Kabul. Of one of these I was a witness. It arose during a conversation about the reputation for cruelty which the Amir had been told that he acquired in England.

A. 'What do they say about my system of government in England? Please tell me the exact truth.'

C. 'They say that Your Highness is a very powerful but a very severe ruler, and that you have repressed with great harshness all hostile movements among your turbulent and rebellious subjects.'

A. 'But they say more than that. They say that I am a cruel and bloody barbarian, and that I do not know how to govern my people or to give peace and order to my country.'

C. 'They may criticise Your Highness's methods. I do not presume to offer an opinion as to the results.'

A. (a little while later). 'Is there a paper in England called the *Standard*?'

C. 'Yes.'

A. 'Is it a good paper? Does it speak the truth?'

C. 'Broadly speaking I believe that it does.'

A. 'Is there a city in your country called Birmingham? Is it a large city? How many inhabitants has it? And is it well governed?'

C. 'Yes, it is a very large city and it has over three-quarters of a million of people, and I believe that it prides itself on its municipal

We were presently conducted to a two-horsed equipage.

When a bugle sounded, the great arena was cleared. Every seat was occupied in the vast horseshoe amphitheatre, built in imitation of the Moghul style, with Saracenic arches, and light cupolas tipped with gold. Painted a creamy white, it shone like some fairy palace of marble in the fierce light of the Indian sun.

OPPOSITE *A charger of exceptional distinction was magnanimously surrendered to me, a magnificent chestnut 'waler' well over seventeen hands in height, and of splendid appearance.*

OVERLEAF *The state elephants, all magnificently caparisoned and with their heads and trunks fantastically painted in every hue of vermilion and saffron and gamboge.*

BELOW *As the traveller looks back upon the country he has left, from his ever-increasing altitude the rich landscape widens to a vast horizon, until at length it resembles an embroidered scarf hung up against the sky.*

MAY GOD GIVE LONG LIFE TO H.E.
LORD CURZON
THE VICEROY OF INDIA
MAY YOUR CORONATION YEAR BE CROWNED WITH AN EMPIRE'S PEACE
MAY GOD BE PROPITIOUS TO THEIR MAGESTIES THE EMPEROR AND EMPRESS OF INDIA
KING EMPEROR
EDWARD
THY LOYAL SUBJECTS HEARTILY GREET THEE &.
QUEEN ALEXANDRA
WELCOME EMPEROR TO YOUR THRONE
VIVAT REX EDWARDUS
GOD BLESS OUR BELOVED EMPEROR EDWARD VII
GOD BLESS THE ROYAL FAMILY
VIVAT ALEXANDRA
O GOD, BLESS THE CROWN OF OUR KING EMPEROR EDWARD VII
GOD BLESS T.R.H. THE PRINCE & PRINCESS OF WALE'S
LONG REIGN THE EMPEROR OF INDIA
HONOUR TO OUR QUEEN EMPRESS
GOD SAVE THE H.R.H. THE DUKE & DUCHESS OF CONNAUGHT
LONG MAY THE KING REIGN
THE RATNAGIRI.
CORONATION FESTIVAL RESPECTFULLY PRESENTED TO H.H. THE LORD CURZON VICEROY OF INDIA BY MIRZA ABDOOLL LUTEEF BEG MOGUL MUNICIPAL CORPORATON AND
LOCALBOARD MEMBER RATNAGIRI
JANUARY 1

The Amir welded the Afghan tribes into a unity which they had never previously enjoyed. . . . He sought to raise his people from the squalor and apathy of their normal lives and convert them into a nation.

OPPOSITE *The Indians excel in illuminations and every form of ceremonial observance. . . . In letters, appeals and petitions, of which the Viceroy receives many scores weekly, some of the greatest triumphs are achieved.*

Reading over this chapter, as I have written it, I hope
I have not indulged in too great detail.

administration.'

A. 'Is there also another city called Manchester and is it like Birmingham?'

C. 'It is also a very large city with a very great population and is reported to be well governed.'

A. (producing a small piece of newspaper from a fold in his robe). 'Here is an extract from the *Standard*, which you say is a good paper and a truthful paper, and which says that in Manchester, which is a great and well governed city, last year there were —— murders and in Birmingham —— murders; and that many of the murderers were not captured and executed. Is that true?'

C. 'If the *Standard* is quoting official statistics, I have no doubt that it is true.'

A. (turning to his courtiers standing in a crowd at the other end of the room). 'What is the population of my country?'

Courtiers. 'Your Majesty rules over eight millions of people.'

A. 'Ah, and how many murders were committed in the whole of Afghanistan last year?'

Courtiers. 'Under Your Majesty's just and benevolent rule, where law and order are perfectly maintained, only six murders were committed in the entire country, and the guilty were caught and condemned to immediate execution.'

A. (turning to me). 'And this is the country and these are the people whom I am accused in England of not knowing how to rule, and am taunted with being barbarous and bloody and cruel. Birmingham only has one-tenth of my population and Manchester only one-fifteenth, and they are well-governed cities, and yet —— murders are committed there in the course of a year, and, as the *Standard*, which is a truthful paper, goes on to say, in a great many cases the murderers were neither caught nor executed.'

I own that I found it a little difficult to pursue, with dialectical advantage, this strain of conversation. On the other hand, the paucity of crimes of violence in Afghanistan, if it were true (as may well have been the case), was undoubtedly due, neither to respect for law nor to excellence of administration, but to the reign of terror that prevailed and to the horrible tortures inflicted upon persons suspected of murder.

One day there came running into a Durbar being held by the Amir, streaming with sweat, and in the last stage of exhaustion, a Herati Afghan, who claimed to have run all the way from Herat without stopping, in order to tell the Amir that the Russians had crossed the frontier and were advancing into Afghanistan, and he appealed for a reward from his grateful Sovereign.

A. (who did not believe the story for one moment). 'Did you see the Russians with your own eyes? And how many were they, and how many guns had they with them, and by what road are they marching?'

H. 'Your Majesty, I saw them with my own eyes, and there were 20,000 men, and they had many guns with them, and they are advancing rapidly upon the Herat–Kabul road; and they will soon be here, and I ran ahead of them without stopping, for days, in order that I might warn Your Majesty of the danger which is so near.'

A. (to his courtiers). 'This faithful man had the good fortune to be the first to see the Russian army cross the frontier near to Herat, and he has run all the way here in order to warn us of the danger. How can we sufficiently reward him? I will tell you. He also shall have the good fortune to be the first to see the Russians arrive, and we will put him in a place where he will have a better chance than any other man. Take him to the highest tree in this place, and tie him to the highest bough of the tree, and let him remain there until the Russians come – and then he shall descend from the tree and bring us the news, and he shall obtain his reward.'

And so the faithful Afghan was taken and tied up in the tree; and there he remained strung up aloft until he perished, as a warning to all other faithful Afghans whose fidelity was pursued at an unwarrantable sacrifice of the truth.

My next story is more genial in its development, though no less sinister in its consequence.

One day there was being counted out in the Durbar Hall before the Amir a great pile of gold (Bokharan *tillas*, bangles, and other coins), prior to being sent to the mint to be coined. The Afghan ministers were seated on the ground counting the *tillas*, and the Amir was looking on.

As the counting proceeded, a *harem* girl, who was dressed in man's clothes in order to act as a spy, and who was standing in the background, observed that one of the principal Afghan ministers (who we will call Suleiman Khan) was abstracting some of the gold *tillas*, and had already secreted eighteen in his worsted sock while pretending to scratch his leg. She accordingly wrote a note which she passed to one of the court attendants, who whispered in the ear of the Amir.

The Amir took no notice, and the counting continued, until all the gold had been counted or weighed. Then, following a familiar practice, he apparently forgot all about the tribute, and commenced a line of discursive reflection on an entirely different topic.

A. 'A great many people say that the Afghans are not a white-skinned people, and they say, for instance, that their skins are not so white as those of the Russians or the English. Tell me, is this true?'

Courtiers (unanimously). 'Your Majesty, there could not be a greater lie. No people have whiter skins than the Afghans, and we are convinced that no Afghan has so white a skin as Your Majesty.'

A. (much gratified). 'That is true, and to prove to you that it is the truth, I will show you my own leg!'

Thereupon the Amir – who at one of my audiences did exactly the same thing to demonstrate to me the same proposition, though in a more agreeable context – proceeded to pull his white cotton pantaloons up the calf of his leg, and to expose the colour of his skin, which (I am bound to say) was extraordinarily white, considering that his complexion was somewhat sallow, and that he had a thick growth of black or, at least, dyed hair.

A. (to his courtiers). 'There, as you see, is the calf of my leg, and you can note how white is the skin.'

Courtiers. 'Your Majesty, we never saw so white a leg, and the legs of all Russians and Englishmen are brown in comparison.'

A. 'That is true. But let me see if my people and my courtiers are as white skinned as myself, or if they are less so. (Then, turning to the throng) Haji Mohammed, let us see your leg! Ali Akbar, let us see yours! (The two legs, exhibiting various degrees of yellowish pigmentation, were then satisfactorily exposed.) Suleiman Khan, let us see your leg!'

S.K. 'Oh, Your Majesty, I beg you to excuse me. I have been suffering for some time from a severe ague in the lower part of my legs and I dare not pull down my sock.'

A. 'It will never do for my servant not to follow the example of his Sovereign, even if his skin, as may be expected, is much less white. Pull down your right sock, Suleiman Khan!'

S.K. 'I implore Your Majesty to be merciful. I am suffering the most acute agony from my ague. I must return at once to my house and have medical treatment. I entreat Your Majesty to have pity upon your faithful servant.'

A. 'Pull down your sock, Suleiman Khan.'

Thereupon the guilty sock had to be pulled down, and the fatal gold Bokharan *tillas* rolled one by one on to the floor.

The Amir, speechless with rage, threw himself back on the divan and for some time did not utter. Then he shouted, 'Take him away to the prison, strip him of all his wealth, and let him be no more seen.'

(It was told to me at Kabul, though I cannot vouch for it, that this and no less was the fate of the unhappy Suleiman Khan.)

Another incident happened soon after I left Kabul, the victim of which was an officer whom I had seen daily during my visits to the Palace. This was a dapper little figure, the Commandant of the Amir's Bodyguard, who was always in attendance, in a beautiful uniform, in the Durbar Hall. He had, when a boy, been one of the Amir's favourite *batchas* or dancing-boys (an amusement much favoured in Afghanistan), and when his master attained to power, he had been promoted stage by stage until he had reached his present eminence.

This man was believed, or found, to be guilty of some act of disloyalty or treachery to his Sovereign, and the latter heard of it before the culprit discovered that he had been detected. The scene happened in full Durbar, when one day the Amir told the story of the culprit's guilt, while he stood before him in his brilliant uniform, and thus announced the punishment:

'A *batcha* you began and a *batcha* you shall end. Go back to your house and take off your uniform and put on your petticoats (the dancing-boys in Afghanistan dance in petticoats), and come back and dance here before the Durbar.'

The wretched man, a General, and forty years of age, had to do as he was bidden, and to come and dance in the garb of a girl before the Court of Kabul. Can anything more refined in its cruelty be imagined?

I could tell many more anecdotes, some of them even more grim, of this remarkable man. One of his strangest traits was his unbounded and unconcealed contempt for his own people. Now and then he would burst out in a torrent of denunciation in open Durbar. He would say, 'The Afghans are cowards and traitors. For years they have been trying to kill me, but they cannot succeed. Either they have not the courage to shoot or they cannot shoot straight.' And then he would turn to the assembled courtiers and shout out: 'Is this not true? Are you not a craven and a miserable people?' And with one accord, with bowed heads, they would reply: 'Your Majesty, we are!'

One day he was enlarging upon this theme, and he told me two anecdotes in illustration of it. He said that when a few years before he had succeeded in defeating the rebellion of his cousin Ishak Khan, largely owing to the fact that some of the rebel regiments had deserted their leader on the battlefield (he seemed quite pleased at this, as though it showed that he himself had not won by the superior value or courage of his own troops), he had held a review at Mazar-i-Sharif in Northern Afghanistan. His loyal regiments marched past before him, and they included the battalions that had deserted from the enemy. The Amir himself was seated on a chair on a little mound, and the troops were defiling, four abreast immediately below him. As they approached, he noticed that one of his cousin's soldiers held four cartridges between his extended fingers, and, as he drew near, the man suddenly put up his rifle and fired point blank at the Amir from the distance of a few paces.

'And did he hit me?' the Amir shouted. 'Not a bit. Just at that moment I leaned aside to speak to one of my Generals and the bullet passed under my armpit and went through the leg of a slave who was standing behind me! Was not that good?' And then he burst into a roar of laughter at this admirable joke, and at the gross ineptitude of the Afghan soldier, who could not kill him even at the distance of a few feet.

Another of his stories illustrating the alleged timidity and cowardice of his people was as follows. He said that when he went to India to see Lord Dufferin, he was accorded a great military review at Rawal Pindi, and that after the review, which was held in pouring rain, he dismounted and entered the Durbar or reception tent prepared for him. There was a big table standing in the tent, and upon it was a miniature cannon. At sight of this object his terrified staff called out to him to hide, because the gun would infallibly go off and kill him.

'What did I say to them?' (he added to me). 'I said "Cowards and fools! You think that this is a real cannon. It is only a machine to cut off the end of a cigar."'

Great as was his contempt for his people, he did not mean to run any risks or to give them any opportunity of getting rid of him before his time. On one occasion he was suffering severely from toothache, and decided to have the offending tooth taken out. The surgeon prepared chloroform, whereupon the Amir asked how long he would have to remain insensible. 'About twenty minutes,' said the doctor. 'Twenty minutes!' replied the Amir. 'I cannot afford to be out of the world for twenty seconds. Take it out without chloroform!'

The Amir was very proud of his gift of ironical retort, and he furnished me with two illustrations of it, which evidently caused him the greatest satisfaction. He told me that on one occasion a Russian officer on the North-west Frontier, somewhere near Maimena or Andkui, had written him a letter to say that he proposed to exercise a force of 500 men, both cavalry and infantry, near the frontier, and he hoped that the Amir would not be alarmed, or regard this as a hostile proceeding. 'Certainly not,' replied the Amir, 'he had no objection at all, the more so as he proposed to exercise a force of 5000 Afghan troops opposite the same spot.' No more was heard of the Russian proposal.

The second occasion occurred in the course of one of our conversations. I had produced one day an extract from an English newspaper which spoke of a new British gun that could throw a projectile for a distance of 15 miles. The Amir showed neither curiosity nor surprise. But a little later he turned to the Commandant of his Artillery, who was in the Durbar room, and asked him in a casual way what was the range of the new gun which he, the Amir, had just made and sent to Herat. 'Fifty miles,' replied the Commandant, without turning a hair.

The Amir enjoyed very much talking about personal and domestic

The Amir enjoyed very much talking about personal and domestic details, and sometimes would tell me stories about the private lives of his courtiers and the secrets of the harem.

details, and sometimes would tell me stories about the private lives of his courtiers, who had to stand by looking rather sheepish while they heard the secrets of the *harem* revealed to a stranger in their presence. One day I was suffering from toothache and had a swollen face. This gave him an excuse for a dissertation on dentistry of which, as of every science, he claimed to be a master. Four things, he said, were bad for the teeth – meat, sweets, cold water, and wine. He had suffered very much from bad teeth himself, particularly when he was in Samarkand, and since the age of forty he had worn entirely false teeth. These had been put in by a dentist from Simla, and from time to time he would take out the plate while speaking. In Samarkand, however, he could put no trust in the Russian physicians, because thirty-two of his own followers fell ill and went to the Russian hospital, where every one of them died. Accordingly he studied medicine, including dentistry, himself, and ever afterwards treated both himself and his followers.

He was also much interested in the marriage laws and customs of different countries. Monogamy, as practised in England and Europe, he held to be a most pernicious system. Firstly, there being, as a rule, more women than men in European countries, monogamy meant that a large number of them remained unmarried, which was a cruel and unnatural fate. Secondly, if a man was only allowed by law to take one wife the country swarmed with 'children of God,' *i.e.* illegitimate offspring. In fact, the British Colonies, Australia, Canada, etc., were maintained as places to which to send these progeny, for whom there was no room at home. However, it was all due to our damp climate. Reared in perpetual water and mud, the English people were like rice, while the Eastern peoples, living on a dry soil, resembled wheat.

Englishmen accordingly were not strong and could not possibly manage four wives, like the Moslems. As to the late period of many English marriages (instancing my own), that was due to the fact that there were so many beautiful women in England, that a man was never satisfied, and always thought that by waiting he would get something better still.

I might, from the well-charged contents of my note-book, carefully made up every night during my stay in Afghanistan, tell many more tales of my unusual and astonishing host. Perhaps some day I may narrate some of my dealings with him, when, instead of being a visitor at his capital, I became the head of the Government of India and was called upon to correspond with him in an official capacity. He was a very difficult person to handle and a very formidable opponent to cross.

In my numerous interviews I flatter myself that I succeeded in winning the Amir's confidence, and he certainly spoke very kindly of me in his Autobiography, published by his Secretary, who acted as interpreter at our meetings. Upon me he left a profound, even if a somewhat chequered, impression. Before I left Kabul he had made and presented to me with his own hand a gold star, inlaid with rubies and diamonds, and engraved with a Persian inscription.

Seven years later, *i.e.* in October 1901, Amir Abdur Rahman Khan died at the comparatively early age of fifty-seven, though he was commonly believed to be much older. On that occasion the following Proclamation, with which I close my chapter, was issued by his son, Habibulla, who succeeded him:

> 'The blessed corpse of the august and potent king, according to his will, was carried to the Royal Taralistan with great pomp and honour, and he was interred in the ground, and placed in a place where is the real and ultimate abode of man. That august and potent monarch, that King of pleasing and praiseworthy manners, expired and sank in the depth of the kindness of God. May his abode be in Heaven!'

In summing up his character, I do not think that I can find a better description than the final verdict which was passed by the Roman biographer upon the Emperor Hadrian, the studied antitheses of which have a peculiar appropriateness in the case of the Afghan Amir: '*Severus laetus, comis gravis, lascivus cunctator, tenax liberalis, simulator simplex, saevus clemens, et semper in omnibus varius.*' ('Both stern and jovial, affable and austre, wanton and circumspect, both mean and generous, hypocritical and direct, both cruel and clement; and always – in everything – quite inconsistent.' Spartianus, *De Vita Hadriani*, 14. 11.)

He had made and presented to me with his own hand a gold star, inlaid with rubies and diamonds, and engraved with a Persian inscription.

The Mehtar of Chitral

The deep damnation of his taking-off.
SHAKESPEARE, *Macbeth*, Act I. Sc. 7.

O, my offence is rank, it smells to heaven;
It hath the primal eldest curse upon't,
A brother's murder.
SHAKESPEARE, *Hamlet*, Act III. Sc. 8.

IN another passage in this book I mention how it came about that in the autumn of 1894, after visiting the Pamirs and determining the true source of the Oxus, I crossed the main range of the Hindu Kush by the Baroghil Pass (12,460 feet) and followed the main course of the Yarkhun River in the company of Captain (now Sir Francis) Younghusband to Chitral. I was anxious to visit that little border state, because I realised its great importance, owing to its geographical position, in the scheme of frontier defence of the Indian Empire, and was convinced of the necessity of closing this small chink in the mountain palisade, which at that time Russia showed such a persistent desire to penetrate at whatever point she could find an entrance.

In this chapter I propose to relate the incidents of my journey, to describe the features and inhabitants of that remote and little-known country, and to tell how my host, the ill-starred Mehtar of Chitral, came by his doom.

Colonel Woodthorpe, Captain (afterwards Sir Edmund) Barrow, Captain Younghusband, and Lieut. Cockerill were the only Englishmen who had previously descended by this route; but my journey, made at the beginning of October, proved, as the Mehtar of Chitral afterwards told me, that though very difficult in summer, while the river is in flood and the glaciers require to be crossed, it is available from the early autumn till the late spring, when the water is sufficiently reduced to admit of the valley track being followed in or near the river-bed. Still it is not the most comfortable of experiences to be compelled, as I was on my first march, to ford a broad and rushing mountain torrent, whose force and volume nearly lift a pony from its legs, as many as twelve times in the day. In the same march I passed six glaciers, descending in snow-white cascades to the river's brink. As the evening sun shone from the glittering snow peaks behind them on to their splintered crests, and then stained crimson the jungle in the valley bottom, already reddening to the fall, I thought that I had rarely seen anything more sublime. Above Mastuj the river-bed straggled out into a respectable width, and contained a good deal of such low timber – willow, poplar, juniper, and birch. Below Mastuj it contracted and frequently assumed the conformation of a narrow and re-echoing gorge. The villages were occasional bunches of green, perched high above the torrent, upon the alluvial fan-shaped deposits that had been swept down from lateral gullies; but the general tone of the scenery was funereal and grey, the gaunt and treeless peaks rising to a height of from 10,000 feet to 14,000 feet on either side, while snow-crowned giants of 20,000 feet keep guard behind, captained by the superb Tirich Mir, a mountain monarch of nearly 25,500 feet, whose shape looms large in every Chitral landscape, and the awe of whose presence has deeply impressed the native inhabitants.

Here perhaps I should say a few preliminary words about the physical features of the region in which my experiences occurred, about its little-known people, and about the circumstances which had, in the previous decade, brought it under the notice of the Government of India, who at that time had not finally made up their minds whether to continue to take an interest in the future fortunes of the little state or to leave it severely alone.

The Yarkhun Valley and the scenery above described are not only typical of the Chitral landscape in general, but indicate the predominant physical characteristics of that state. Could the traveller mount in a balloon and float in the air from the northern to the southern confines of Chitral territory – a distance of some 200 miles – he would see below him only a sea of mountains, ridge succeeding ridge, a panorama of snow and ice and verdureless rock. It would seem to him a fearful and a forbidding country. Hardly at the bottom of the winding gorges would he discern the isolated patches, where water has converted the arid slopes into delicious parterres of green. Nor would he dream of the rich crops of fruit and grain which the strong and steady sun can win from the rugged soil, wherever the valleys widen out a little or the industry of man has carried the life-bestowing stream. Chitral, considered in its wider application as including both Yasin and Mastuj, practically consists of seven such valleys, with a general inclination from north to south, and one transverse valley, that of the Ghizar River, running from east to west.

Its northern boundary is the 'Great Snowy Mountains', as the main range of the Hindu Kush was happily designated by the early Buddhist pilgrims. On the east it is bounded by Hunza and the petty state of Punial, and further to the south by the great mountains that shut in the gorges and clans of the Indus Kohistan. On the extreme south it touches Dir territory below the Lowarai Pass, and Afghan territory near Asmar. On the west its borders run with Badakshan in the north, and lower down with the mountain haunts of the Kafirs, acknowledged since 1893 to be within the political limits of Afghanistan. The total area thus embraced is some 9000 square miles. Its population, confined for the most part to the levels between 4000 and 8000 feet, had been commonly reckoned as 70,000, but had been reduced by more careful analysis to a probable total of not more than 50,000 persons. The people themselves call their country Chitral; Kashkar is the name given to it by Pathans and Pushtu-speaking folk. Upper Chitral (*i.e.* Yasin, Ghizar, and Mastuj) – which were for long under the Khushwakt yoke – is commonly known as Khushwakto Mehtari (*i.e.* dominion), while the districts below Mastuj bear the exclusive appellation of Chitral. The situation of the country on the main and shortest line of communication between the Punjab and

Afghanistan and the Oxus, and in close proximity to the easiest passes over the Hindu Kush, had always given to Chitral an importance in excess of its intrinsic capacities. Traders, pilgrims, and warring tribesmen had passed up and down its highland tracks, which, though until a few years earlier entirely unknown to Englishmen, had been for centuries among the best trodden in Central Asia. To the Emperor Baber the country was known as Katur, from the name of its ruling family. It formed a portion of the territory obscurely described in earlier annals, with varying and often inconsistent boundaries, as Bolor.

Corresponding to the extremes of elevation are those of climate and temperature. In winter the valleys are buried in snow, and even the light-hearted national character is not impervious to the prevailing gloom. In spring and summer the sun shines gloriously, all nature breaks into song and laughter, and life is spent almost entirely in the open air. A double crop is gathered from the irrigated ground; wheat and barley in the spring; Indian corn and millet and rice (which has a great reputation in the surrounding districts) in the autumn. The holdings are very small, twenty acres being a quite exceptional property, and the average size being from one to two acres. The cultivable area, however, forms so small a proportion of the entire country that the grain supply is little more than sufficient for the needs of the population. Fruit, on the other hand, positively abounds: melons, pomegranates, apples, pears, grapes, walnuts, mulberries, apricots (which are dried and exported, and are a staple article of food); and delightful was it, at the end of a long ride under the hot sun, to dismount beneath the trees of a village orchard and, reclining on the ground, to feast on the pears and apricots and grapes that were brought in unlimited quantity on big platters by the local headman. Of flocks and herds, there are not a great many cattle, but numerous sheep and goats. Most of the ponies that I saw were said to have come from Badakshan, which is a great breeding country; but donkeys are indigenous.

The people of Chitral occupy a very distinct and unmistakable place among the Aryan tribes of the Hindu Kush. The majority speak an unwritten language of their own named Khowar, although Persian is the official and lettered tongue. Burishki is spoken in the Yasin Valley, Shina in the Ghizar Valley, and other dialects in outlying parts. But the people are extraordinarily illiterate; and Captain Younghusband told me that he did not think there were a dozen persons in the whole country who could either read or write. As regards religion, the bulk are Sunni Mohammedans of an indifferent type, this being the faith of the ruling family, but Shiahs and Maulais are also found. There is no fanaticism, however, in Chitral. Unlike the neighbouring states of Bajaur and Swat, the *mullahs* had very little influence, and would find the greatest difficulty in raising a *jehad* or religious war. In appearance the Chitralis are of fairer complexion than many of their neighbours, having occasionally even blue eyes and light hair, though the prevailing type is dark or black-haired, with the locks sometimes hanging in poetical ringlets upon the shoulders, sometimes tied up in a bunch or in curls upon either side. The

Every man of position carries his hawk upon his gloved right hand.

men are rather short of stature, but of muscular frame and wiry build.

There is something attractive, though little of real fibre, in the national character. They are a gay and impressionable race, somewhat indolent of habit, and addicted to the *dolce far niente*; simple-minded, warm-hearted, excitable, loving a jest, but possessing neither the masculine energy nor the warlike capacities that render the Hunza men the pick of the Hindu Kush tribes. The Chitralis are not natural fighters like the Pathans; and it would be quite a mistake to suppose that the skill and bravery shown in the famous siege six months after my visit had much to do with them. It was the contribution of Umra Khan's men from Bajaur, who conducted the entire operations, and infused into the Chitrali attack a spirit which it would never of itself have possessed.

Perhaps, however, the most salient Chitrali characteristic is their almost Grecian love for sport and dancing and song. Chitral is renowned for its hawks and falcons, which are caught in traps and exported to neighbouring countries, as much as from £2 to £3 being often paid for a single bird. Every man of position, as he rides forth for recreation – and very often two men will be astride of the same steed – carries his hawk upon his gloved right hand, while his attendants follow with one or two more birds; and there is for ever imprinted on the retina of my memory the sight of the Governor of the Yarkhun Valley, who rode with me for two days – a gallant old gentleman of some sixty or more years of age, with a magnificent beard stained a rich red, and enormous moustachios that protruded for several inches on either side of his face (he boasted, and probably with truth, that they were the finest in the Hindu Kush), his head wrapped round with a splendid gold and red turban, a grey velvet *choga* or cloak hanging on his shoulders, and his little boy sitting behind him on the saddle and clinging round his father's waist. This brave old sportsman rode with me hour after hour the whole day through with his hawk on his wrist, and when any quarry rose, whether quail or pigeon or duck, he let fly the bird, galloping after it to take it again on to his hand. Mehtar Nizam-ul-Mulk was also devoted to the sport, and was always attended by his hawks when we went out riding. He told me he had killed as many as thirty quail in a single day.

Not less fond are the Chitralis of dancing; and the Mehtar organised for my entertainment, while at Chitral, a nocturnal performance round an immense bonfire. Dancing is confined to the male sex, and admits if not of grace, at least of agility. One old gentleman I remember, of at least sixty years, whose bare legs were imperfectly draped by a sort of brown dressing-gown, and who pirouetted round with as much gravity, and amid as great applause, as though he had been Taglioni herself. There was also some rude but effective acting, a mimic combat taking place between some supposed Kafirs, rude half-clad fellows with wild locks, armed only with sticks, and a party of Afghans (who, as Pathans, are detested by the Chitralis), in which the Kafirs scattered and floored the Afghans amid shouts of laughter. The singing also I heard, but did not admire. One further characteristic I recall of the light-hearted, pleasure-loving Chitralis, viz. their fondness for flowers. I constantly noticed men wearing a yellow or other blossom tucked in their thick lovelocks, just as a clerk behind an English counter might carry his pen behind the ear.

The Chitrali dress is somewhat sober in colour, except upon festive occasions, but is well adapted to the extremes of climate which are encountered, and to a social condition in which wealth is rare. It consists of the brown woollen cap with rolled-up brim, common to the entire borderland, but replaced in the case of the upper classes and officials by a turban; of a *choga* or loose long coat of the same material; of white cotton drawers, and coloured worsted stockings tucked into a soft leather boot. The Mehtar gave me a *choga* faced with parti-coloured Bokharan silk. It makes an excellent dressing-gown, and I rarely put it on without thinking of that poor murdered man.

A class of hereditary nobles exists in Chitral, named Adamzadehs, to whose ranks promotion is also possible by favour of the ruler. These nobles are themselves untaxed, and are the owners of inalienable lands and villages; but their loyalty to the central power is secured by the wise custom of requiring their presence and attendance upon the Mehtar during a few months of each year at Chitral itself, where they are entertained and given presents by him. The next or middle class is called Arbab, but this is a term not in common use. The lower class, which is thought to represent the original inhabitants of the country, is named Fakir Maskin. They also are brought in touch with the capital and the ruler, each village in Chitral being bound in turn to furnish a contingent as bodyguard to the Mehtar, who arms and feeds them while in his service.

Probably, however, the respect in which the Chitralis differ most pointedly from European standards is in their unabashed disregard for the sanctity of human life. People sometimes wonder why such strange and murderous deeds should be committed in those remote regions, and how it is that instances of chivalry seem to be not inconsistent with the most revolting acts. The reason lies in the prevalent contempt for human life as such. There is neither law nor custom against the shedding of blood; and no deterrent beyond the lack of opportunity or fear of revenge restrains the would-be assassin. The existence of this unblushing code, recalling the Italy of the early Renaissance period, is fitly illustrated in the history of Chitral, which, until British influence supervened, was artistically diapered with records of intrigue, treachery, and assassination. In the narrative to which I now turn there are as many instances of cold-blooded murder, and probably more of parricide, fratricide, and the various forms of domestic crime, than could probably be found within a corresponding period in the history of any not purely barbarian state.

Up to 1889 the kingdom was divided into two parts – Lower and Upper Chitral, which were ruled by two branches of what had originally been one family, springing from a common ancestor of Persian extraction. The rulers of Chitral proper, designated by the Persian title of Mehtar (signifying 'greater'), belonged to the Katur family; those of Upper Chitral, which included Mastuj and Yasin, were of the Khushwakt stock. The two families squabbled, fought, and alternated emulous spasms of assassination with fitful intervals of reconciliation and repose. It was reserved for the Mehtar, known as Aman-ul-Mulk, a ruler who typified and reproduced in exaggerated form in his own person alike the best and worst qualities of his race, to terminate the long domestic schism by expelling his Khushwakt rivals from Upper Chitral and bringing the entire country under the Katur sway. Starting as the younger son of the ruler of less than half the modern kingdom, he ousted and killed his elder brother, who was Mehtar in about 1856. To make himself additionally secure he removed his next brother also. The next twenty years were spent in alternate conflicts and truces with the Yasin chieftains, who were successively Mir Wali (Hayward's murderer) and Pahlwan Bahadur, the two sons of the formidable and ferocious Gauhar Aman. Finally, in 1880, he conquered and expelled Pahlwan, who was the son of his (Aman-ul-Mulk's) sister, and had also married his daughter, occupied the whole of the Khushwakt country, and replaced the reigning family by his own sons, appointing Nizam-ul-Mulk, the eldest, governor of Yasin, and Afzul-ul-Mulk, the second, governor of Mastuj, with the Ghizar valley divided between them.

Aman-ul-Mulk was a ruler of no mean capacity. Unscrupulous, greedy, and deceitful, but quick-witted, imperious, and astute, he was the very man for such a state and for such times. In his declining years, when over seventy years of age, he became toothless and feeble. But for forty years of his life he was the leading figure in the Hindu Kush region. Endowed with great personal and physical vigour, the most renowned polo player, even up to an advanced age, of his time, he was the husband of many wives and the father of nearly seventy children. Perhaps in nothing did he show his shrewdness more evidently than in the clever manner in which he invoked Kashmir assistance – thereby first coming into contact with Great Britain – in order to expedite his personal and dynastic ambitions.

Formerly Chitral had been dependent upon Badakshan, and later on had paid tribute to the Amir of Kabul, after Badakshan had passed by conquest into his hands. In 1874 Aman-ul-Mulk had even gone so far as to betroth his daughter to Abdulla Jan, the heir of Amir Shir Ali Khan. In 1876, however, these arrangements having broken down, and an Afghan force threatening to advance into his country, Aman-ul-Mulk found extraneous assistance imperative, and sought the protection of Kashmir. In the same year, Captain Biddulph was the first Englishman to visit his country. Lord Lytton, who, in view of the continuous advance of Russia in Central Asia, was wisely anxious to secure an indirect control of the Hindu Kush states, advised the Maharaja of Kashmir to accept the proffered allegiance, and promised him, if by such action he became involved in military operations, to afford him countenance and military aid. In the following year an agreement was signed between Chitral and Kashmir, by which the latter undertook to protect Chitral from Afghan aggression, receiving an acknowledgement of allegiance, and a nominal tribute of horses, hawks, and hounds, and giving a subsidy of 8000 rupees in return, this being a price which Kashmir was nothing loth to pay in order to purchase immunity for Gilgit from Chitral raids. Thus strengthened, Aman-ul-Mulk made short work of his opponents, and acquired the undisputed rule of a dominion that stretched from Ishkumman almost to Asmar. It must not be supposed that any motives other than those of self-interest were responsible for the loyalty of Aman-ul-Mulk to this new connection. He was constantly trimming between the rival allegiances, and even intriguing with Afghanistan. No one, however, knew better on which side his bread was really buttered; and when Captain Biddulph (who had in the meantime been appointed British Political Officer at Gilgit) was invested by Pahlwan Bahadur at Sher Kila in Punial in 1880, he advanced to his assistance, and crushed his son-in-law and ancient foe. In 1881 he applied to be admitted to direct political relationship with the Indian Government, but was refused. The Kashmir subsidy was, however, doubled in that year.

Such was the state of affairs until the imminence of war between England and Russia in the spring of 1885 rendered it desirable that the British Government should know a little more of what was passing in those distant regions, and should exercise over the inclinations of their rulers a rather less fortuitous control. In 1881 Major Biddulph had been withdrawn from his post of observation at Gilgit. But in 1885 an imposing

Mission, consisting of Colonel (afterwards Sir W.) Lockhart, who was destined thirteen years later to be my first Commander-in-Chief in India, Colonel Woodthorpe, Captain Barrow, and Dr Giles, was dispatched to Chitral to enter into a definite agreement with Aman-ul-Mulk. The Mission met with a most friendly reception from the Mehtar, and remained at Chitral from September to November, returning again after a visit to Hunza and an exploration of the upper Oxus Valley in the spring of the ensuing year. In the agreement which was concluded Aman-ul-Mulk thus expressed himself: 'I, an eater of the salt of the English, will serve them body and soul. Should any enemy of theirs attempt to pass through this quarter I will hold the roads and passes with my loins girt until they send me help.' The Mehtar received corresponding assurances, and a present of Sniders in return. Early in 1886 he sent his eldest son, Nizam-ul-Mulk, and late in 1887 his second son, Afzul-ul-Mulk, down to India. Both young men were greatly impressed by what they saw, and carried back to their native country a very different conception of the British power from that which had hitherto prevailed. The British Mission when they retired left a native officer as British Agent at Chitral.

Colonel Lockhart had reported in favour of the acquisition of Gilgit by the Indian Government, and of the formation of a British cantonment there. As these proposals, however, were found to involve a considerable expenditure of money they were not adopted in that form; but in 1888 the late Colonel A. Durand was sent on a mission to Gilgit and Chitral to work out a plan for the re-establishment of a British Agency on a more moderate scale. The result was his own appointment as British Agent at Gilgit in the following year. The relations between the Indian Government and Chitral now assumed a more definite shape, the former henceforward sharing with the Kashmir Durbar the obligations of a suzerainty which the vassal-state was not less anxious to recognise. Visiting Aman-ul-Mulk in the same year (1889), Colonel Durand and Dr Robertson found the Mehtar very ready that roads should be made through his country, and desirous to fortify the defensive positions. A further present of Sniders was made to him, and the Kashmir subsidy was supplemented by an annual allowance of 6000 rupees from the Indian Government. Meanwhile events were marching rapidly on the Pamirs, and the trans-frontier menace, against which a policy of cismontane precaution was but an elementary safeguard, drew the two parties on the British side of the threatened border into still closer relations. In 1887 the French expedition of M. Bonvalot, after crossing the Pamirs, had made a venturous sally into Chitral, but had come to grief at Mastuj, being only rescued therefrom in a state of destitution by the courtesy of Lord Dufferin. But in August 1891 the Russian Colonel Yonoff had repeated the experiment with a body of armed men, and it was known that the ambitions of his countrymen, which had already prompted Captain Grombehevski's dalliance with the Mir of Hunza, did not exclude a similar flirtation with the Mehtar of Chitral. It was decided to strengthen the position of the latter, and in October 1891 the British contribution to

Lord Lytton, when Viceroy, was wisely anxious to secure an indirect control of the Hindu Kush states.

his subsidy was doubled, while small annual allowances were granted to the three most prominent of his sons, the condition being attached that the telegraph line should be extended from Gilgit to Chitral, and that a British officer should at an early date be permanently appointed to his Court. Some Mohammedan non-commissioned officers from the Indian army were at the same time sent to Chitral to instruct the Mehtar's troops in the use of the Snider rifle. In the same winter occurred the brilliant little Hunza-Nagar campaign.

Such was the state of affairs when, on 30 August 1892, Aman-ul-Mulk, who though more than seventy years of age, and of failing vigour, might yet have been expected to live for several years, suddenly died while in durbar. Rumours of poison were an unconscious tribute to Chitrali morality rather than an induction from established facts. Among the large family whom he left behind, three sons, of whom two have been already mentioned by name, were, by reason either of their birth or of their character, especially conspicuous. These were Nizam-ul-Mulk, the eldest legitimate son, who was Governor of Yasin, but who could not be said to have inherited his father's strength of tenacity of purpose, and who had not produced an agreeable impression upon the members of the Lockhart Mission; Afzul-ul-Mulk, his younger brother, who was Governor of Mastuj, an ambitious, reckless, and popular young man; and the son of an inferior wife, Shah-ul-Mulk, who was the most cultivated of the family. Aman-ul-Mulk had designated no heir, and the question of the succession, in a country where no fixed law prevails, had long been a source of anticipated trouble both to the Indian Government and in Chitral itself. Afzul-ul-Mulk being in Chitral when his father died, cut the knot by assuming the succession and installing himself as Mehtar at once. In true Chitrali fashion he murdered his brothers Shah-ul-Mulk and Bahram, and set off to fight his elder brother, Nizam. The latter fled in alarm to Gilgit, where he threw himself upon British protection. Afzul-ul-Mulk then wrote to the Viceroy, announcing, with a daring euphemism, that he had succeeded to the throne 'with the unanimous consent of his brothers', and asked to be recognised as Mehtar, and to have a British officer deputed to Chitral. The Indian Government, not fully acquainted with the facts, and favourably disposed towards Afzul ever since the Lockhart Mission, somewhat prematurely acceded. All seemed to have turned out well for the ambitions of the usurper.

Sher Afzul Khan established himself as Mehtar.

There happened, however, to be an elder member of the family, a brother of the late Mehtar, Sher Afzul by name, who had himself, by a judicious flight, escaped being murdered by Aman-ul-Mulk many years before, and who, having been for long an exile from the country in Kabul, was at this time in Badakshan. He had a large following in the southern part of the Chitral Valley. Collecting a band as he proceeded, and disguising them as a Badakshani caravan, he crossed the Dorah Pass, swiftly descended upon Chitral, and finding the gates of the fort open upon his arrival, on the night of 6 November, straightway entered in. Afzul-ul-Mulk, coming to the doorway of the tower to ascertain what was going on, was shot dead; and the uncle established himself as Mehtar in his place. Now, however, was the time for the rightful heir to move. Encouraged by the British representative at Gilgit, escorted by Hunza and Puniali levies, and backed by the moral support of some British-Indian troops, who were moved forward in ostensible aid to his advance, Nizam-ul-Mulk, exhibiting a courage with which no one had credited him, set out from Gilgit, marched towards Mastuj and Chitral, exchanged a few shots with the enemy at Drasan, and entered Chitral without impediment, his uncle anticipating his arrival by flight. By December the rightful heir was duly installed as Mehtar, three months having witnessed the same number of occupants of the throne. Sher Afzul retired once again to Kabul, where it was made a part of the Durand Agreement with the Amir in September 1893, that he should be kept safely interned.

Nizam's first act was to ask Colonel Durand to send him a British officer; and on 1 January 1893, Dr (afterwards Sir G.) Robertson and Captain Younghusband, with an escort of fifty Sikhs, started for Chitral. When Dr Robertson returned in May, Captain Younghusband and the Sikhs were left in order to give security to the new Mehtar. The position of the latter was for some time precarious. In Chitral the Adamzadehs were suspicious of a ruler of whose ability to maintain his position they did not feel assured. Members of the Khushwakt family threatened trouble in Yasin, and in the south a larger cloud was already gathering upon the horizon. A turbulent and formidable Pathan chieftain named Umra Khan, who, though originally only the petty chief of Jandol, had aggrandised himself at the expense of all his neighbours, fighting the Afghans, ejecting Mohammed Sherif, the Khan of Dir, and defeating both the Swatis and the Mohmands, had also upon the death of Aman-ul-Mulk (one of whose daughters he had married) advanced into Chitral territory and seized Narsat Fort, only forty miles from Chitral. With him was Amir-ul-Mulk, his wife's brother, and half-brother of Nizam; and the two were understood to be intriguing against the new Mehtar in that quarter. In these circumstances Nizam, conscious of the moral weight that his position derived from the avowed protection and backing of the Indian Government, requested, in May 1893, that 'two or three British officers, with one hundred or more or less number of Sepoys, should remain permanently in Chitral, and should build a cantonment wherever they desired', and that the telegraph wire should be extended to Chitral. The Indian Government doubled the number of the escort, but withdrew Captain Younghusband to Mastuj, being apparently of opinion that whilst at that distance (66 miles) a British officer could give to the Mehtar the requisite encouragement and support, he would escape the entanglements that might ensue from a too close propinquity to an unstable *régime*. Lord Kimberley, however, then Secretary of State for India, while admitting that 'the near prospect of the Russian occupation of the Pamirs extending to the north bank of the Panja, which is less than a day's march from the Chitral frontier, renders it a matter of importance to us to be able to control the external affairs of Chitral', only sanctioned the retention of Captain Younghusband as a temporary measure; and in

January 1894 instructions were sent to Kashmir that he should be withdrawn at the close of the winter. In June, however, of the same year, the Pamir difficulty with Russia not being yet disposed of, the demarcation of the Chitrali-Afghan frontier, under the Durand Agreement (which had been concluded in the previous autumn) not having taken place, and Umra Khan still causing trouble in the south, the withdrawal of Captain Younghusband, though still maintained in principle, was postponed for another year. The Mehtar's repeated appeals that the officer should be stationed, not at Mastuj, where in an emergency he would be helpless and useless, but at Chitral, which had not previously produced much effect, were thought 'to be supported by weighty reasons, and to deserve consideration' by Sir H. Fowler, who had become Secretary of State in 1894. But no action had been taken in this direction; neither had any one dared to tell the Mehtar of the impending total withdrawal, when I rode down to Chitral in 1894, the first Englishman, not on official duty, who had so far proceeded to that remote but interesting spot. (The previous visitors were Biddulph in 1878, the Lockhart Mission in 1885-6, Ney Elias in 1886, Durand and Robertson in 1888 and onwards, Captain Tyler in 1890, Younghusband, Bruce, and Gordon in 1898. Alexander Gardner alleged that he went to Chitral, and he probably did so, although from the MS. of his travels, written down from memory in the later years of his life, other travellers who have seen it as well as myself have been unable to trace the steps of his journey.)

I have narrated these proceedings at some length because they are typical of the steps by which the Indian Government has often been compelled, with genuine reluctance, to extend its responsibilities, and because they were the prelude to the bloody drama which was to be enacted so soon after my visit, and the later and peaceful sequel to which I was myself as Viceroy to supervise.

After three days' marching down the Yarkhun Valley from the Baroghil Pass, I was met at a distance of some miles from Mastuj by Captain Younghusband, and we rode in together to that place. Here the valley broadened out, and its bottom was filled by a big flat plain, much of which was swamp, and the rest coarse grass. In the distance the magnificent cone of Tirich Mir closed the valley, and soared grandly into the air. On a sloping plateau or fan above the valley-bottom were situated the tiny village and dilapidated fort of Mastuj, where the British escort of a hundred Sikhs were stationed under the command of Lieutenant Harley, who afterwards so greatly distinguished himself and won the DSO at Chitral. The governor, Bahadur Khan, Mehtar Jao (*i.e.* a Mehtar's son), being a younger brother of Aman-ul-Mulk, a pleasant old gentleman, with henna-dyed beard, came out to greet me, and we rode in to the music of the village band and dismounted under an immense solitary *chenar* (plane) outside the fort. Mastuj, from its position at the confluence of the Yarkhun and Laspur rivers, has always been a place of some importance. The Emperor Timur passed several times this way in his campaigns in Kafiristan and Chitral. The place also endured a seven months' siege from the Chinese during the reign of Shah Khush Ahmed.

Mastuj Fort was a typical Chitrali structure, consisting of a walled enclosure fifty yards square, the curtain being about twenty feet in height, with four square towers fifteen feet higher at the angles, and a lower tower over the gateway. The whole was built of stones, timber, and mud. The place illustrated both the discomforts of Chitrali existence and the artistic aptitudes of the people. For whilst to get to my room, which was the principal one in the building, and had been occupied by Afzul-ul-Mulk when Governor, I had to crawl along a low tunnel and climb a rickety ladder, the room itself contained a good deal of old wood-carving on the pillars and cornice. The light was admitted and smoke escaped by a hole in the roof. The British officers camped in tents in the garden (which was inside the walls), and the mess-room was a sort of elevated loggia overlooking the latter, and adorned with rude frescoes by Afzul's men. In this fort a force of 46 Sikhs and 250 Kashmir troops, under Captain Bretherton and Lieutenant Moberly, was invested for eighteen days in March and April of the following year, until relieved by Colonel Kelly's column from Chitral.

From Mastuj I rode down to Chitral with Captain Younghusband in two days, the first being on the right and the remainder on the left bank of the river, which is crossed half a mile below Mastuj by a rope bridge, and a mile above Buni, where the stream is narrower, by a rope and twig bridge. This was my first experience of crossing a rope bridge or *jhūla*, which, however, is a misnomer, seeing that the bridge is not made of a rope at all, but of birch or willow twigs twisted together into a stout cable. Three of these cables, somewhat loosely tied together, constitute the foot-rope, which hangs in a deep curve across the river or gorge that requires to be bridged. The breadth of the combined strands is from six to eight inches, but as the withes by which they are held together are continually breaking, it frequently happens that one cable sags more than its fellow, and the passenger has to be careful of his footing. The usual plan is to go across slowly, planting the feet, turned outwards, one immediately in front of the other. At a distance of from two to three feet above the foot-rope are suspended on either side two side-cables, similarly composed, to act as hand-rails. These are attached to the foot-rope by a succession of V-shaped ties, and are sometimes held apart from each other at the top by cross-sticks, over which the passenger has, in addition to his other perils, to step. All three cables are securely lashed at the land ends round heavy logs which are buried on the two banks in big hummocks of stones. At the start, therefore, both foot and side ropes are almost in the same plane, and one has to scramble down upon the rope almost upon one's back. In the middle of the dip the weight of the passenger bellies down the foot-rope, and his hands are sometimes nearly as high as his armpits. As he gets to the other side he has again to scramble forward with his hands down to his knees. The entire structure, though stoutly made, looks very frail, and has a detestable habit of swinging, particularly in at all a high wind, that takes the heart out of some people. On the present occasion nothing would induce one of my companions, Lieut. Harley, who was shortly to win the DSO for conspicuous bravery,

The British officers camped in tents in the garden.

The entire structure has a detestable habit of swinging that takes the heart out of some people.

to cross the rope bridge below Mastuj, and he preferred to swim the river, which was very swift and full, on horseback at a spot lower down where there was a so-called but very dangerous ford. The most remarkable lady traveller of my knowledge once came to a Tibetan river spanned by one of these bridges after a journey of uncommon hardship and exposure. She absolutely declined to cross it, and preferred to be taken over on an improvised raft of inflated goat-skins, upon which she ran a very excellent risk of being drowned. On the other hand, the majority of persons soon get used to the *jhula*, and experience no alarm. I did not cross many myself, but I confess that I did not find these either difficult or terrifying. If the bridge is in good condition, and the cables are intact, it is almost impossible – unless a man completely loses his head – to fall in. The main difficulties arise from the swaying of the ropes and the dizzy rush of the torrent, which is sometimes only a few inches below one's feet in mid-stream (though elsewhere, in the case of deep gorges, from 100 to 200 feet underneath), and from the sharp ends and twigs that project from the hand-rails and catch in one's sleeves or gloves. The natives often cross these bridges in parties of from six to a dozen at a time, and will even carry other men or animals over on their backs; though should the bridge break, as it is apt to do when so presumed upon, the whole of those upon it are in all probability drowned. At about six miles below Mastuj I remember riding along a stony place on the right bank, that descended in a long slope from the foot of the mountains to the river. The latter at this point flowed right up against the left cliff-wall of the valley, which was from side to side about a mile in width. There was nothing to indicate that the sloping plain was anything but continuous, until suddenly we came upon a prodigious cleft or *nullah*, with perpendicular walls, cut like a gash to the depth of some 250 feet through the plain down to the level of the river, into which flowed a stream that trickled at its bottom. The track zigzagged steeply down one wall of this astonishing cañon, and clambered up the other. I thought this a most remarkable natural phenomenon, and learned that it was known as the Nisa Gol, and was famous for the fights which had often taken place there, and for its supposed impregnability. Six months later it was held in strength against the English, with *sangars* on the lip of the *nullah*, by the Chitrali army which had withdrawn from Mastuj, but was taken with the utmost gallantry by Colonel Kelly's force on 30 April 1895. The main body with the guns advanced across the plain and shelled the *sangars*, while the enemy's flank was turned and their position rendered untenable by the action of the Hunza and Puniali levies, who scaled the mountain heights to the right.

At more than one other place I passed over ground that was destined half a year later to become historic. Six miles below Buni, on the left bank, is the tiny hamlet of Koragh, and between this and Reshun the valley is contracted into a narrow ravine, where the track crosses steep shaly slopes of detritus, or skirts the cliffs that descend sharply to the water's edge. It is a rough and trying stage, and it told so severely on the pony I was riding, which had been a gift from the Mehtar to Younghusband, that it began to spit blood, and I had to dismount and lead it into Reshun, where it died in the course of the night. This was the spot where Captain Ross (whom I had met at Gilgit), starting with a detachment of Sikhs to the relief of Lieutenants Fowler and Edwardes, who, with a party of sappers and Bengal infantry, were believed to be in danger at Reshun, suddenly found himself cut off in front and behind, the enemy hurling rocks down the steep shoots and firing from *sangars* on both banks of the river. After a gallant resistance and repeated attempts to cut his way through, Ross and forty-six of the Sikhs and nine camp-followers were killed, and Lieutenant Jones and fourteen Sikhs, of whom ten were wounded, managed, under heavy fire, to get back to Buni. This happened on March 10, 1895.

At Reshun, Younghusband and I camped under the trees of a delightful orchard bordering on the polo ground. Adjoining this were a number of houses, in which, while Ross and Jones were fruitlessly struggling to their rescue, Edwardes and Fowler, with sixty-two men, for five days held out against an overwhelming force of the enemy, until, on March 15, an armistice having been declared, they were captured by treachery on the polo ground, and were carried off first to Chitral and afterwards by Umra Khan to his fort at Barwa in Jandol. (Umra Khan treated both officers well, hoping by their ultimate release, which took place a month later, to stave off the retribution which awaited him from the relieving force of General Low.) More serious, however, even than this catastrophe was the capture by the enemy of no fewer than 34,000 rounds of ammunition in the British camp. A few hours later these were in the hands of the beleaguering force that was hard pressing Robertson and his brave 500 in the fort at Chitral; and who knows how many a British bullet found its billet there among the heroic defenders of the British flag?

As we descended the valley the scenery became prettier and more romantic, if the defile did not itself become less rugged than in its higher portions. On each alluvial fan to which water could be brought from the hills above was planted a village with its orchard trees and well-cultivated plots; and the dark green patches stood out as sharply from the gaunt background as does a Persian plain village against the stark desolation of the desert. Where there was no water, all was lifeless and grim as death itself. Fans would be seen with soil not less favourable or more obdurate than that of their neighbours, but either no streams descended from the mountains, or such as did had bored a furrow from 100 to 150 feet in depth – as at the Nisa Gol – right through the soft heart of the slope, and, there being no water-wheels or pumps in Chitral, splashed aimlessly into the river. On the mountains no timber was to be seen till we neared Chitral. In some places the river was contracted to a breadth of a few yards – admitting of being bridged – between confronting cliffs. Elsewhere it spread out in the valley-bottom as broad as the Thames at Oxford.

On the morning of the second day we were met outside the village of Barnas by the young Shuja-ul-Mulk, a good-looking boy of about twelve years of age, a son of the old Mehtar, and half-brother accordingly of

Nizam. He lived at Barnas with his foster-father, an Adamzadeh. The boy was brought out to meet us clad in a green velvet tunic, and was lifted on to his pony. His long black hair hung in ringlets on either side of his face, and was matched in colour by a pair of very large and piercing eyes, the lower eyelids of which were pencilled with henna. His mouth and teeth were prominent, and were said to resemble greatly the early pictures of his father, Aman-ul-Mulk. The lad wore an intelligent expression, but had nothing to say. We consumed apricots and pears together in an orchard; but little did either of us think that in less than six months he would be elevated to the *musnud* of Chitral.

The next stage was Koghazi, where the village headman, a forbidding-looking individual, with black hair in curls, a big stomach, and a round fat face like that of a mediaeval abbot, entertained us with the luscious small seedless grapes of the country. Pressing on, we found that the road had been specially repaired for us by order of the Mehtar, and that new galleries had been built out where the *paris* were particularly stiff. Soon we were met by some of Nizam's ministers, who gave me friendly greeting, and escorted us to a spot where, in a narrow and rocky defile by the river's edge, the Mehtar was seen approaching at the head of a cavalcade. This was about four miles from Chitral. Nizam dismounted and I did the same, and we met and saluted each other on foot. His appearance and build were singularly unlike those of the average Chitrali. Indeed, his light curly hair, moustache, and beard might have adorned the face of any Englishman. An irresolute, amiable expression pervaded his features, and his manner and movements, until he recovered confidence, were timid and almost cringing. But this shyness wore off completely as we became better acquainted, and although of weak character and debauched habits, he never in any situation looked anything but a gentleman. On this occasion he wore a smart green velvet suit, the tunic and trousers of which were decorated by broad gold braid, the production of his Kokandi court tailor. Nizam-al-Mulk was at this time thirty-three or thirty-four years of age; but the Nemesis of his country and his race was already hovering unsuspected above his head, and he was never to see another birthday.

Having cleared the defile, we were met by a party of some hundred mounted men, and the whole cavalcade streamed amid clouds of dust along the open plain, across the fields, and over the low stone walls. Soon we came to a place where shooting from horseback at full gallop at a gourd filled with ashes, swinging from the top of a pole, was performed for my entertainment. This is one of the favourite national sports. Resuming our way, we crossed the river by the Chitral Bridge, a single-span timber structure, built on the cantilever principle, forty-five yards long by four feet wide, and guarded by a gatehouse on the near side, and by two stone towers on the opposite bank. We dismounted, the Mehtar, according to the polite fashion of the country in escorting a guest, holding me by the hand. As we drew near to the fort, which is about half a mile below the bridge, the entire population turned out to meet us; two brass six-pounders, the gift of the Indian Government, boomed a formal salute,

Thirteen players took part and the game lasted an hour.

and – a most picturesque and novel spectacle – the crest of the hills was lined for over a quarter of a mile by several hundred men, who with matchlocks fired a noisy *feu de joie* into the air. The men of the Mehtar's bodyguard, a hundred strong, in white drawers and old scarlet tunics, purchased at Peshawur, were drawn up outside the fort. Leaving the latter below us to the left, we mounted somewhat higher up the hill, passed through Chitral *serai* – an enclosure surrounded by low mud houses, where the Peshawri and Badakshani merchants deposit their goods, and which was the only semblance of a bazaar in the entire region of the Hindu Kush – crossed a *nullah*, down which trickled a scanty stream, and reached a house and grounds that had been prepared for my reception. In the garden were pitched a tent and *shamiana* that had been presented by Sir W. Lockhart to Aman-ul-Mulk when he left Chitral.

These quarters were those that had been placed at the disposal of the British Agent when at Chitral. Subsequently during the siege they were occupied by our arch-enemy, the meteoric uncle, Sher Afzul; but again, when the siege was over, they became the headquarters of the British officers. Immediately behind the garden enclosure was the burial-ground of the reigning family of Chitral. By far the largest grave, in deference I imagine to his great reputation, was that of Aman-ul-Mulk, which was a lofty rectangular mound, faced on all sides with stone; and with the two curving isolated stones that are usually planted on the top of Chitrali tombs fixed in the ground at the head and foot. Afzul-ul-Mulk's was a smaller grave, with no marks of distinction. Adjoining the graveyard was the Jumma Musjid or town mosque of Chitral, an unpretentious building.

During my stay in Chitral I was shown such sights as the place contained or admitted of. A game of polo was organised; but it struck me that, though better mounted, the players did not touch quite the same level of excellence that I had seen at Hunza. Thirteen took part, and the game lasted an hour. The Mehtar was one of the best players, if not the best. Whenever he got a goal and struck off, galloping down three-quarters of the ground, all the spectators shouted loudly; and I also remember a short, black-bearded man, whom, as the head of the armed forces of Chitral, we dubbed the commander-in-chief, clad in blue trousers and a purple velvet tunic, who rode like a demon and shouted like a boy. The ground at Chitral was peculiarly shaped. It was on the slope of a hill, and on the upper side had a big bay or extension, with an old *chenar* tree in the middle.

The ground was of turf, but was somewhat cut up and dusty. Elsewhere in this volume I have described the game of polo as it is, or then was, played in the mountain fastnesses of the Hindu Kush.

Chitral Fort which six months later was to be the scene of one of the most heroic exploits that ever adorned the page of British history.

I made a careful inspection of the fort, where the Mehtar was residing, and which six months later was to be the scene of one of the most heroic exploits that have ever adorned the page of British history. The fort was a very picturesque structure, rising almost from the river's edge, with its tall angle-towers projecting from the lower walls, the whole from a little distance being embosomed in a wealth of *chenars*, walnuts, and orchard

LXXII.

trees. But for purposes of defence it could scarcely have been placed in a worse position, the immediate surroundings affording every opportunity for close-range firing and for sheltered approach, and the interior being commanded from nearly all sides by Martini-fire from the hills. Like all Chitral forts that I saw, the building consisted of a square enclosure quite eighty yards on each face, with walls about twenty-five feet in height, built of unhewn stones held together by transverse tiers and by mud. At each corner was a square tower twenty feet higher, the immense amount of woodwork in these towers, particularly at their outer angles, explaining the constant attempts made by the enemy during the siege to set fire to them. The tower nearest to the *serai* and to Sher Afzul's house was that from which the improvised Union Jack was flown that infused such heart into the defenders. On the north or river face was a waterway running down to the river for a distance of forty yards, protected half-way down by a fifth or water-tower. The efforts of the besiegers to cut off or to render untenable this waterway, and of the garrison to protect it from a never-ending assault, were among the most thrilling episodes of the subsequent siege. On the east and west faces of the fort were magnificent groves of *chenars*, extending almost up to the walls. Of these the enemy did not fail to make good use. Beneath the clump on the western side was a big open-air terrace, with platforms for the large durbars, overlooking the bend of the river, and in full view of the tutelary presence of Tirich Mir. On its southern and eastern face the fort was surrounded by a garden within a lower wall.

The main entrance was on the western face, nearest to the Chitral Bridge. I passed through a heavy wooden gateway, with a small trap-gate opening in it for use after dark, into a narrow passage where the guard were stationed. This led into the main interior court, entirely surrounded by buildings. On the left hand was a new mosque, an unpretentious open structure with wooden pillars, and with the *kibleh* on the back or west wall, which was being built by the Mehtar; also a new durbar hall with some simple but effective wood-carving. On the opposite side was the tower at the door of which Afzul-ul-Mulk as he came out was shot through the head by Sher Afzul's men. Under a shed were a few guns, including the two mountain-guns that had banged off on the occasion of my arrival. On the right or southern side latticed windows looked down from an upper storey on to the court and betrayed the women's quarters. On the river side, in the direction of the water-tower, were the stables. These were the main features of the interior as I remember them. For an acount of the purposes to which they were put, and of the part which they played in the history of the siege, I must refer my readers to the published accounts of the latter.

It will, however, still be remembered that among its most brilliant incidents was the sally led by my companion, Lieutenant Harley, which resulted in the blowing up of a mine that was being dug by the besiegers towards the gun-tower, at the south-east angle of the fort. This mine led from a summer-house, distant about forty yards from the walls; and in the mouth of the excavation, which was inside this building, thirty-five of the enemy were bayoneted by the Sikhs as they came up from the death-trap, little thinking of their doom. I vividly recollect that garden-house; for in it the Mehtar entertained Captain Younghusband and myself to lunch during our stay. The entrance was laid with stripes of silk and *kincob*, and the meal took place in a room with a veranda round it open to the sky. There were pictures from the English illustrated papers hanging on the walls, among which I detected a portrait of my friend Margot Asquith, who had married her eminent husband a few months before. Which of us then thought that those papers would before long be illustrating the room itself?

More interesting, however, at that time than any sight or scene of Chitral was the interview in which the Mehtar, accompanied by his principal ministers, discussed with me the condition and the prospects of his state. We sat in the open air in front of the *shamiana*, in the compound of the British Agent's house, and for over two hours I was kept an attentive listener to their pleadings, their anxieties, and their fears. One might have expected from these remote and inexperienced natives, whose entire life had been spent in isolation from the great hum of the outer world, a want of *savoir faire* or a narrowness of vision in harmony with the restricted outlook of their existence. But there was a certain natural dignity in the speech and bearing of those untutored men; and I have rarely heard an argument more fluently expressed or more cogently sustained. The Mehtar was nervous about the external and internal fortune of his state. Conscious of the manifest insecurity of his own position, and alarmed at the peril that threatened his rule from the turbulent ambitions of neighbouring chieftains, he petitioned earnestly for a more emphatic definition of British responsibilities in connection with Chitral. He asked that the British officer attached to his court and the Indian escort should be stationed, not, as then, at the mistaken post of Mastuj, but at Chitral itself. Had this course been adopted at an earlier date, it is conceivable, in my judgement, that some, at any rate, of the subsequent disasters need never have occurred. He was anxious that roads should be made and the telegraph wire extended through his country. He wanted to raise a large body of native levies to be trained by British officers. Like his father before him, when Sir W. Lockhart visited Chitral in 1885, he pleaded for a *Sanad* or document recognising the hereditary right of himself and his family to the Mehtarship. In Umra Khan, with prophetic accuracy, he recognised his most dangerous foe; and he urged that he should be allowed to join with Mohammed Sherif Khan, the evicted ruler of Dir, in expelling the Jandoli chieftain from that state, and at the same time in recovering for himself Narsat, which had been similarly filched from Chitral. Finally, he declared that it was the duty of the Indian Government, on its own account, to crush the pretensions of Umra Khan – a task which, before six months had passed, the consequences of his own assassination were forcibly to impress upon that Government.

On another occasion Younghusband and I saw the Mehtar and his court in a more festive vein; for with such scanty fare as our resources could produce, consisting of tinned soup, army rations, *pilau*, chicken, stewed pears, two bottles of beer and two of whisky and of ginger-wine, we entertained the whole party to dinner. The Mehtar sat with us at a table in one of the raised recesses of the room; the rest of the court squatted or lounged on the floor below. They tried our heterogeneous drinks with shouts of delighted laughter, and regaled us with their own music and story. The whisky and the ginger-wine were mixed together – I am not sure that a little beer was not added – and I can recall the sight of one Chitrali nobleman pouring this amazing concoction down the throat of another, at the same time that he held him by the nose. Among the guests was a blind scion of the old ruling family of Badakshan, who came in and twanged a primitive guitar. Professional Chitrali singers and dancers, all males, added to the prevailing din. One of the Mehtar's brothers, Isfendiar by name, was invited as a musician of more than ordinary repute, and entertained us with a peculiarly lugubrious chant.

But the spectacle that chiefly lingers in my memory was this. I have previously mentioned Amir-ul-Mulk, half-brother and next heir of Nizam, who had already conspired against him, but whom, weakly ignoring the bloody but immutable prescriptions of his family, and regarding him as a semi-idiot, he had invited back to Chitral a few months before from exile with the arch-foe Umra Khan. The Mehtar had specially asked me if I would invite this youth, who was only nineteen years of age, to the banquet, and I had naturally concurred. I observed him standing in the background of the room, a sullen and repulsive figure, with long black locks and a look of gloom. Two months later the Mehtar perished at his fratricidal hands.

On these and on other occasions during my stay, I had opportunities of studying both the character of Nizam, and the position and authority of the Mehtar. Nizam was amiable, good-tempered, and intelligent; but he was not the man either for his people or the times. Both of the latter demanded a ruler cast in the stern and truculent mould of old Aman-ul-Mulk: a tyrant with open manners and no scruples. Nizam was avaricious, which made him unpopular, and of depraved habits, being addicted to drunkenness and unnatural vices whereby he shocked a not too sensitive public opinion. Nevertheless, it was evident that, quite apart from the personality of its occupant, the position of Mehtar in Chitral was encompassed with a great and traditional respect, apparent in every act and deed. The Mehtar was the centre of every scene, the leader of every proceeding in which he took part; and no subject interfered or participated except at his invitation. The Chitralis are a people tenaciously attached to old observance and custom, including fidelity to the ruling house as such, though not necessarily to its individual members; and they look with a suspicious horror, not upon crime, but upon innovation.

Hence it will readily be understood that the government of Chitral was almost exclusively a personal government. The Mehtar was supreme. He alone had the power of life and death. Theoretically, the whole property of the country belonged to him, and, in more than theory, he actually disposed of the persons and possessions of his subjects. For instance, he might and did give away men's wives. I even heard of a case in which the original husband having condoned his offence, the Mehtar took the wife away from the second husband to whom she had been assigned, and restored her to her former spouse. As Mehtar, he was supreme in judicial as well as in executive authority. Certain penalties, determined by custom, were assigned to particular crimes. For example, in cases of adultery the injured husband was entitled, and was even bound, to kill both the offending wife and the lover. He was then protected by the Mehtar. But should he kill the wife and not the lover, he was sued as a murderer by the wife's relations. A story was told me of the pursuit of an unfaithful wife and her lover by the husband, in the course of which the lover escaped, while the woman tumbled into the river and was drowned. Upon appeal to the Mehtar, the husband had to pay compensation. In ordinary cases, murder was compounded by a fine to the family of the victim (in all these countries human life has not its actuarial value as here, contingent upon health and probable duration, but its mathematical value, determined by sex, position, and substance), with a *douceur* to the Mehtar thrown in. If the fines were not paid, the culprit might be put to death either by the family or by the Mehtar. In these and in all similar exercises of authority the Mehtar was assisted by a Diwan-begi or Chief Minister, and by two or three *wazirs* or councillors, who were constantly in his company. There were usually also two *aksakals* (*lit.* white-beards) or elders in personal attendance upon him, and a number of chief men from outlying villages who visited the court in relays, and took turns of 'waiting' upon the Mehtar.

A real and very efficient check upon any abuse (according to Chitrali standards) of the authority thus created was furnished by the publicity with which government and justice were alike administered. Did the Mehtar dispose of wives, or confiscate property, or assess fines, or sentence to death, in any sort of secluded Star Chamber, the system could not endure. But all was done *coram populo* in open durbar, in the presence of the people, or of as many of them as chose to attend, and in the light of heaven. Chitral, in fact, had its Parliament and its democratic constitution. For, just as the British House of Commons is an assembly in which nominally all members take an equal part, but where in reality the two front benches to a large extent conduct the business, under the eyes and subject to the possible animadversion of the remainder, so in Chitral, the Mehtar, seated on a higher platform, and hedged about with a certain dignity, dispensed justice or law in sight of some hundreds of his subjects, who heard the arguments, watched the process of debate, and by their attitude in the main decided the issue. Such durbars were held on most days of the week in Chitral, very often twice in the day, in the morning and again at night. Justice compels me to add that the speeches were less long and the general demeanour more decorous than in some western assemblies.

Chitral consisted at the time of my visit of the fort and cluster of neighbouring hamlets on both banks of the river, with a population of about 1500 persons, that collectively bore the local name; the Chitral District, under the immediate control of the Mehtar, comprising the main valley of the Chitral river, with a population in its villages of some 10,000; and, finally, of the outlying valleys included within the confines of the state. The name has been applied in this country, with insufficient distinction, to all three. The total revenue (the whole of which went into the hands of the Mehtar) was almost incapable of estimate, being largely paid in kind, but its main constituents were as follows: House-tax and land-tax, not assessed (for no land settlement had ever been made in Chitral), but roughly paid in contributions of *ghi*, *atta*, barley, firewood, etc., either to the Mehtar or to servants of the Mehtar, when on duty; octroi on caravans and trade; mineral resources, consisting of a little gold dust, of orpiment, and of lead; the timber monopoly, belonging to the Mehtar, and estimated at Rs.20,000 a year, the material consisting of deodar logs, cut down on the mountain-sides, tumbled in to the river, and floated down with the floods; and the subsidy from the Indian and Kashmir Governments, which in 1894 was Rs.30,000. In former days an additional and lucrative source of revenue was the slave-trade, Chitrali girls having an exceptional reputation for beauty in the surrounding countries. The closing of the Kabul slave-market by Amir Abdur Rahman Khan, and the civilising agency of Russian advance towards and across the Pamirs, had already considerably reduced the extent and value of this traffic, when the British appeared upon the scene and finally put a stop to it, a sentence of absolute prohibition being the first sequel of the siege and subsequent *régime*.

When I rode away from Chitral in October 1894, Nizam-ul-Mulk accompanying me on horseback for some distance, with a dear little boy, the youngest of his half-brothers, seated on his horse behind him and clinging around his waist, though my own goodbye to him was probably a final one (since one does not go twice in a lifetime, except on duty, to Chitral), no one could have anticipated his imminent doom. In the middle of December the annual subsidy from Kashmir and India reached Chitral, and the treasury was known to be full. On January 1 Nizam went out hawking with the sinister half-brother, Amir-ul-Mulk. He had dismounted, and was having his turban tied round his head by an attendant, when he was shot from behind at a signal from the traitor, and left to die, the rest of the party, with the murderer, galloping off to secure the fort and the treasure. There can be little doubt that the crime was planned in advance, and that Amir-ul-Mulk was acting in connivance with, although in reality the puppet of, his brother-in-law, Umra Khan.

Then ensued the fateful series of events culminating in the siege and defence, and finally in the relief of Chitral, which, during the months of February, March, and April of 1895, sent a thrill, first of apprehension, and later of pride and congratulation, throughout the British-speaking world. I shall not here recapitulate a story which found at the time accomplished and veracious chroniclers among its own heroes. The following were the leading episodes: On 1 February Sir G. Robertson, the British Resident at Gilgit, arrived at Chitral after a difficult but

A bridge was built over the Panjkora River.

unopposed march across the mountains in the dead of winter. On 9 February Umra Khan, who immediately upon the assassination of Nizam had advanced from the south, captured Kila Drosh, a Chitrali fort twenty-five miles south of Chitral. On 20 February Sher Afzul, the meteoric uncle, who had either escaped or been let loose from Kabul, reappeared upon the scene, and added to the dynastic and political complications. On 1 March Robertson retired into the fort with five other British officers, 99 Sikhs, over 300 Kashmiri Imperial Service troops, and a large number of servants, camp-followers, and Chitralis, making a total of some 550 persons. On 14 March an ultimatum was sent by the Indian Government to Umra Khan; a proclamation was made to the tribes, and the advance of a force of 14,000 men under Sir Robert Low was ordered from Peshawur. On 23 March Colonel Kelly, in command of the Northern Relief Column, 600 strong, started from Gilgit. On 1 April General Low's army crossed the frontier; on 3 April the Malakand was stormed; on 7 April the Swat River crossed; on 12 April a bridge was built over the Panjkora River, and on 17 April the Janbatai Pass was crossed. Meanwhile Kelly was advancing under circumstances of exceptional severity from the north. On 9 April he relieved Mastuj, which had been beleaguered for eighteen days; on 13 April occurred the fight at Nisa Gol, and on 20 April he reached Chitral. But meanwhile the news of the twofold advance had already produced its effect at that place. There for nearly seven weeks the garrison had endured with unbroken spirit and amazing resource the perils and anxieties of a daily and nightly siege. On 2 March the murderer Amir-ul-Mulk was taken into custody, and his half-brother Shuja-ul-Mulk, whom I had met at Barnas, and who had been brought in by the British, was made provisional Mehtar. On 3 March took place the disastrous reconnaissance in which Captain Baird, with whom I rode down to Gilgit, lost his life, and the Dogra general and major were killed. On 4 March the siege began. On 7 March Sher Afzul arrived outside Chitral, and assumed the conduct of operations. On 8 and 14 March attempts were made to fire the water-tower. From 16 to 23 March there was a truce and unsuccessful negotiations. On 29 March a Union Jack, having been patched together in the fort, was hoisted on the south-west tower. On 5 April the enemy occupied the summer-house where I had lunched with Nizam, and commenced a series of attacks upon the gun-tower, as well as a subterranean mine. On 11 April there was a general attack upon the fort, which ended in failure. On 17 April Lieutenant Harley made his gallant sortie, blew up the mine, and killed sixty of the enemy. On 18 April a voice was heard shouting important news in the night: Sher Afzul and the Chitralis had fled, and the siege was raised. Even in this skeleton summary of events as they occurred, if it be studied in relation to the locality as already described in this chapter, ample evidence will be forthcoming of the magnitude of the peril endured and the glory of the triumph won. Chitral, whatever else may befall it, can never lose the place it then gained in the records of Indian bravery and British heroism.

From Chitral Fort Younghusband and I rode back to Gilgit, a distance by the route that we followed of somewhat over 200 miles. Here I need only record one or two incidents of that journey. We crossed the watershed between the Yarkhun and the Ghizar Valley by the Shandur Pass (13,500 feet). A *dak* had come in while we were at Mastuj, and had brought with it a copy of my book, *Problems of the Far East*, which had appeared in England since my departure, and which I had not before seen in its published guise. With it came a stout bundle of newspaper reviews; and any author can sympathise with my emotions of pleasure as, with the reins thrown on the neck of my horse, I rode up the steep and stony ascent that leads to the pass, reading the too favourable notices of my book, and stuffing them into my holsters as I proceeded.

At a distance of about 70 miles from Mastuj we came to the junction of the Yasin with the Ghizar River, and a little below this saw the then new fort of Gupis, built of stone and mud by the Kashmir Imperial Service Troops. As we arrived the British officer in command rode out to greet me and offered us the modest hospitality of the fort. This was a Captain Townshend, who was subsequently to attain fame as the defender of Kut in the Mesopotamian campaign of the Great War. In his company I visited the lines inside the fort, the keep, containing the officers' quarters, the dispensary, hospital, school, stores, and magazine; and I saw a brass six-pounder, which had once done service in the Abyssinian campaign, fired from the roof of the gun-tower at a range of 900 yards. A Union Jack had just arrived and been hoisted, and was for the first time

A series of events which sent a thrill, first of apprehension, and later of pride and congratulation, through the English-speaking world.

The storms of warfare that burst upon Chitral.

fluttering merrily in the breeze. As for the men, of whom there were 250 in the fort, half Dogras and half Gurkhas, and who went through manual and bayonet exercise for my inspection, they were the smartest of any of the Kashmiri troops whom I had encountered on the frontier. The Dogra colonel and major took me down the ranks, and the men were given a holiday in honour of the visit of a British Member of Parliament, an individual whose identity was probably to them a complete conundrum.

Even more vividly, however, than the inspection of the garrison do I remember the night spent with my somewhat unusual host. He combined with an absorbing interest in military science and an equal familiarity with the writings of Hamley and Clausewitz, and the strategy of Hannibal, Marlborough, and the Emperor Napoleon, an interest in the gayer side of existence, of which Paris was to him the hub and symbol. On the walls of his mud dwelling were pinned somewhat daring coloured illustrations from Parisian journals of the lighter type; and he regaled us through a long evening with French songs to the accompaniment of a banjo.

Through the little state of Punial I was accompanied by the Raja, Akbar Khan, a big-lipped, fat, and comfortable-looking personage, who had been to India and who discoursed to me about the history of his state, from the chiefship of which he had at a later date to be removed. Riding with me through a chill and savage gorge, he spied upon the opposite cliff a herd of markhor, whereupon he announced his intention of slaying one of their number with a Martini carbine which he carried. I showed some incredulity, as the distance across the ravine was at least 400 yards; but the old Raja dismounted, took a long aim, and fired, with the unquestionable result that one of the markhor fell. I have no doubt that he 'browned' the lot, and made a lucky hit; but he was overjoyed at his prowess, with which I had luckily abstained from competing. The track over the *paris* in the Gakuch and Punial districts was formerly of the most villainous description, the descent of one very steep place being only accomplished by the aid of a sort of fixed pole with projections, very much like the pole in the bear's den in the Zoological Gardens. But the Kashmir sappers had recently been hard at work, and I have no doubt that there is now something more worth of the name of a road.

Raja Akbar Khan's residence was at Cher (or Sher) Kila, *i.e.* Rock Fort, a village and fort with a good many fruit trees, situated upon a large alluvial fan on the left bank of the river. The fort was a large quadrangular structure, with many towers and bastions, on the water's edge, one side of it being built on a cliff that rose sharply from the river. Here was a very long rope bridge, 340 feet in length. Though it was in excellent repair, I confess I was rather glad that I was not called upon to cross it. The Raja told me that a few years before it had snapped with fourteen men upon it, all of whom had been swept away and had perished. On the tenth morning after leaving Chitral, I rode back again into civilisation at Gilgit. There I heard that the Tsar was dying, and that the Amir of Afghanistan, whom I hoped to visit, was lying dangerously ill at Kabul. At the same time, though I did not know it, it was being announced in the English

A difficult but unopposed march across the mountains.

newspapers that I had disappeared from view, and that the gravest doubts were entertained as to my safety.

Here my readers may perhaps ask what became of the little country of Chitral when the storms of warfare that burst upon it in 1895 had subsided and peace was restored. It is a tale from which I may extract a certain amount of modest satisfaction, since I staked much upon a solution which was denounced and derided by the Pacifist school at the time, but which has since been attended with unbroken success. After my return to England early in 1895, there ensued a correspondence in the *Times* newspaper, between the months of March and June 1895, in which I fought the battle of the retention of Chitral against the combined forces of General Sir John Adye, Sir James Lyall (ex-Lieutenant-Governor of the Punjab), Field-Marshal Sir Neville Chamberlain, and the first Lord Chelmsford. I urged that we should not abandon our position in Chitral; that we should appoint a Political Officer to the state; and above all that we should keep open the road from the South; thereby reducing our line of communication with British India from 700 to less than 300 miles. The Retreatists would not have these proposals at any price. Such a policy, they said, would involve a ruinous outlay, an immense garrison, and the eternal and implacable hostility of the tribes. Sir N. Chamberlain in particular wrote:

The tribesmen will only be kept quiet by our retaining at a great annual cost a sufficient force to overawe them.

> 'If we remain in Chitral, Bajaur, and Swat, the tribesmen will only be kept quiet by our retaining at a great annual cost a sufficient force in the Valley to overawe them. Reduce or withdraw that force and they will rise again. No British force or British Agent can be in those valleys with the good will of the great mass of the people. . . . Mr Curzon's policy is bound to lead to further annexation with a largely increased expenditure as assuredly as the night follows the day.'

These views had prevailed with the Liberal Secretary of State, Sir Henry Fowler (afterwards Lord Wolverhampton), and with Lord Rosebery's Government when, in a fortunate hour, that Government fell, in the summer of 1895, and was succeeded by a Ministry of which Lord Salisbury was the chief.

At his request I wrote a Minute for the Cabinet, of which I may quote the concluding paragraph:

> 'The road from Peshawur has already been half constructed during the recent campaign. Why should not an effort be made, by placing detachments at fixed distances upon it (if necessary), and by subsidising the tribes, to keep it open? No one can say that it will be a failure until the experiment has been tried. There is no need for permanent military occupation or annexation, nor for interference with native customs or administration. The roads along the entire Gilgit frontier are already so maintained and policed. The same prevails in the mountain border between the Indus and Afghanistan. Local levies can be raised, as in Beluchistan and Hunza, from the tribes themselves. They will make excellent soldiers, and will gladly serve for an assured pay. What the poorer classes fear and dislike is the *corvée*, and being

obliged to carry loads as coolies. If they are secured from these burdens they will soon acquiesce in the new condition; *vide* the former and present state of the Gilgit road. As regards Chitral itself, it is the corollary of this argument that, while not interfering (any more than we did before) with native institutions or customs, a British Political Officer should still be maintained at or near to Chitral itself, with an escort adequate to secure his safety; and that British suzerainty should continue to be paramount along the entire Hindu Kush frontier. For a time more men may be required, and greater expense may be incurred than hitherto in the setting up of this new order. Later on the tension will be relaxed, and reduction will be possible. In any case even increased outlay will be a cheap insurance against the future troubles and expenditure that present evacuation will some day involve.'

These arguments were accepted by the Cabinet. The young Mehtar was confirmed on the *gadi*; Chitral was detached from the Gilgit Agency; Captain Gurdon, a very capable young officer, was appointed Political Officer; and it was decided to complete and keep open the southern road. The siege having demonstrated what was already obvious, viz. that the old Chitral Fort was planted in the very worst position for military defence, it was handed back as a residence to the Mehtar, while the British Political Officer and his escort were stationed in a new fort, built at a slight distance on a more defensible site. Such was the success of these arrangements that, during the serious outbreak that set the entire Indian frontier ablaze from Swat to Samana in the autumn of 1897, uninterrupted tranquillity prevailed in Chitral. In the ensuing year I became Viceroy, and had the pleasure of carrying to completion the arrangements which I had foreshadowed four years before. Refusing the proposal of the military authorities for a large fort at Chitral, I provided for a small garrison at Drosh, at the southern end of the valley, made a telegraph line to Chitral, and started the formation of the corps of native levies or scouts which I had advocated. The British garrison was reduced to one Indian battalion, and the yearly reliefs were carried out during my term of office, 1899-1905, without the firing of a single shot. The young Mehtar proved to be a loyal and capable ruler, and, along with his brother chieftains of the Hindu Kush border, subsequently paid me a visit at Calcutta.

After I had left India, this happy condition of affairs continued, and has never since been disturbed. Chitral is now under the North-west Frontier Province, which I was instrumental in creating, and a single Political Officer, under the Chief Commissioner, acts for the three states of Dir, Swat, and Chitral, whose inhabitants according to Sir Neville Chamberlain ought to be in a state of chronic and embittered revolt. When the war with Afghanistan broke out in 1919 and the rest of the Frontier Militia broke, and when the Afghans actually invaded Chitral, the little state and its ruler stood firm as a rock. So peaceful is the scene that the Chitral garrison, with the exception of a single Indian company, is concentrated entirely at Drosh; the relays take place biennially without a hitch, and the Chitrali Scouts, service in which is exceedingly popular, have now (1925) reached a total of nearly 1000 men, with 2 British officers.

Reading over this chapter, as I have written it, I hope I have not indulged in too great detail. If I have it has been not without some purpose. For I have sought to draw an accurate picture of a small patch of the world's surface, almost unknown except to a few Indian politicals or Indian soldiers, of a people who, embedded in this remote and ancient ethnological stratum, have retained an individuality of their own for centuries; of events in the history of those parts which, though now wellnigh forgotten, made a great and resounding reverberation at the time; and of a political problem which, for more than a century, has been enacted and re-enacted on the Indian stage as the pressure of internal forces, or the fear of aggression from without, has driven the ploughshare of the Indian Government through the stony furrows of the border mountains right up to the outer pale of the British protectorate. Chitral is, in my view, an illustration of how that problem, by the exercise of some initial firmness and by wise administration afterwards, may be satisfactorily solved. Just as a small stone cast into the water may produce a big ripple, that widens out into larger and larger circles before the commotion dies, so it came about that little Chitral for a short space shook the quiet of the great world and will have its place in the history of the Asiatic continent, while, now that it has again relapsed into obscurity, it remains both a lesson and a type.

Kashmir to Gilgit

We, we have chosen our path –
Path to a clear-purposed goal,
Path of advance! – but it leads,
A long, steep journey, through sunk
Gorges, o'er mountains in snow.
MATTHEW ARNOLD, *Rugby Chapel.*

As the traveller leaves the plains of India, and, ascending the lower foot-slopes of the Himalayas, looks back upon the country he has left, and as from his ever-increasing altitude the rich landscape widens to a vast horizon, until at length it resembles an embroidered scarf hung up against the sky, he can appreciate the fascination which those verdant plains, that fair and almost illimitable expanse, with its teeming population, its great cities, its agricultural wealth, its capacities for luxury and ease, must have exercised upon the hardier and more penurious peoples of the north, when, bursting through their mountain barriers on the tide of rapine or conquest, they first caught sight of that enchanted vision and pressed forward to so desirable a goal. Such were the emotions of Timur and Baber, of Mahmud of Ghuzni and of Nadir Shah. Such must have been the feelings of an earlier and a greater conqueror, Alexander of Macedon. It is with sensations not essentially dissimilar that Hindustan is still regarded by the races whose habitat is confined to northern latitudes and less favoured climes. As, in their forward march across the sandy steppes of Central Asia, these have found themselves arrested by the turbulent ferocity of the Afghans or by the snows and glaciers of the Pamirs, adventurous spirits among them have not unnaturally projected their gaze across the intervening barriers to the sunny regions which a superior fortune has conferred upon Great Britain, and which have always carried with them the dominion of the East. Hence it is that, in no spirit of challenge or provocation, but in deference to the imperious necessities of self-defence, the Indian Government has for more than three-quarters of a century been obliged, as the gap between the advancing frontiers has steadily narrowed, to look with such anxious concern to its north-western border, and to provide by every means that military science or political statecraft can suggest against the possibility of invasion or attack.

Among the territories that lie between the inner and outer mountain barriers of Hindustan, none has been more qualified to excite a conqueror's desire, and none in the amplitude of its beauty and resources affords a sharper contrast to the severe and sterile region by which it is bounded, than the Vale of Kashmir. When the traveller from the declivities of either the northern or the southern hills beholds it outspread at his feet – 100 miles of agricultural fatness and wealth – he grasps the appositeness of the designation, the Happy Valley. 'It lies deep-meadow'd, happy, fair with orchard-lawns and bowery hollows.'

Already from hearsay or reading the principal landmarks are familiar to his view. He sees the shining expanse of the Wular Lake lying at the base of the hills that conceal the zigzags of the Gilgit road. Into it on the one side flow the sluggish coils of the Jhelum river, brown with the dirt and drainage of Srinagar. Emerging on the other side, they again meander over the plain until the sliding loops are contracted and tortured into foam as they enter the Baramula gorge, and commence their roaring descent to the distant Indus. Away to the south-east in the centre of the plain, though nearer to the base of the northern hills, rise the twin elevations of the Hari Parbat, crowned with the Emperor Akbar's fort, and the Takht-i-Suleiman, or Solomon's Throne, culminating in the ruins of an ancient temple. Between the two, the traveller knows that Srinagar, the City of the Sun, lines both banks of the twisting stream. These are the main interior landmarks. The surface of the plain is carpeted with the green of rice crops and maize, and with scattered clumps of timber. Its successive levels, or *karewas*, as the natural terraces are called, indicate the bed of the lake with which the entire basin was once filled. Over their surface the water is conducted in tiny channels from streams that furrow a stony track from the mountains.

The framework of this idyllic scene is supplied by a panorama of heights as noble as any in the world. The lower spurs are wooded up to an elevation of from 8000 feet to 10,000 feet with the deodar or Himalayan cedar, with English timber, and with various pines. Then comes a bleaker zone of scant herbage and stones, frequently veiled in mist wreaths or drowned in lakes of aërial foam. Above and beyond rise the white eternal crests of the Himalayan peaks; Haramuk, with his soaring dome, and Nanga Parbat, one of the most beautiful of mountains, with a jagged edge that appears to pierce the zenith. In this Elysian valley English flowers and fruits abound, English ladies move to and fro without escort, English children bloom. In the surrounding gorges and ravines young English officers find a yearly training-ground for their muscles and a grateful vacation from duty in the pursuit of wild deer, ibex, and goat; and the 'race for the *nullahs*' which ensues, as soon as the season of leave commences, is a tribute at once to the emulation of the sportsman and the hospitality of the state.

A metropolitan city affords no inadequate criterion of the customs and aptitudes, of the religious feeling and social conditions, of the inhabitants of a state. In its palaces we see the splendour or insignificance of its sovereigns; in its temples is displayed the dominion or the decay of religion; in its shops and bazaars we may appraise the extent and quality of its commerce; in its private habitations, from the mansion of the nobleman or merchant to the coolie's hut of mud or reeds, we may bridge the interval between the comfort that springs from aristocratic birth or official dignity or successful trade, and the squalor that is the immemorial portion of the Asiatic peasant and artisan. Srinagar is rich in the grounds for such an induction. Let me say at once that the city, picturesque, and even romantic as in some respect it is, appeared to me, as I saw it more than thirty years ago, to have been altogether extrava-

gantly praised. Being situated on both banks of a river, from which diverge a certain number of canals, it has sometimes been compared to Bangkok, the capital of Siam, while both cities have been compared to Venice. Srinagar was about as much like Bangkok, and both were as much like Venice, as a hansom cab is like a gondola. Srinagar was essentially tumbledown, slatternly, ignoble, unregenerate. It had in it nothing of the grandiose, or even imposing. Its colour was a uniform and dirty drab; its picturesqueness was that of decrepitude; its romance, if any, was that of decay.

Srinagar was as much like Venice as a hansom cab is like a gondola.

Imagine a river from 90 to 150 yards in normal width, with banks from 15 to 30 feet in height, which for over two miles of its serpentine course is fringed on either side by an irregular line of two- or even three-storeyed buildings. Nearly all these buildings are of a crude, dust-coloured brick, held together by layers of mud. Many of them are in a state of extreme dilapidation; though a certain comeliness is lent to the more pretentious by the balconies and lattices of pierced woodwork that overlook the stream. They are precariously saved from the ravages of the floods, either by being elevated upon long wooden piles or upon a crumbling masonry embankment, among whose stones may be seen embedded the capitals and cornices of ancient Hindu temples – a significant testimony to the indifference with which successive dynasties in Kashmir have treated the cult of their predecessors, and which finds an additional illustration in the contrast between the ancient mosques, attesting the religion of the majority of the people, and the Hindu temples with pyramidal cupolas coated over with tin plates (mostly the sides of broken-up oil-cans) that reflect the pagan zeal of the Dogras or ruling race.

In spite of the precautions above alluded to, the Jhelum is apt to rise above the embankment and the piles, and to assail the rickety structures on their summit. In 1893 the flood, which was the biggest known for fifty years, had inundated the European quarter known as the Munshi Bagh, stood several feet deep in the ground-floor of the houses, and swept clean away six of the seven wooden bridges that spanned the stream. They were afterwards restored on the former model, whch was said to have an antiquity of 400 years. It is well adapted both to the aesthetic and to the more material aspects of Srinagar. A wooden platform with hand-rail is laid upon three immense stacks or piers in the bed of the stream, which have the appearance of scaffoldings from a distance, but in reality consist of a superstructure of deodar logs laid roughly across each other upon a foundation of piles, and packed with loose stones. In former days there were rows of shops on the top of two at least of the bridges, as upon old London Bridge, and upon the Ponte Vecchio at Florence. But on the newer fabric these had disappeared. Between the piers the fish leap from the muddy water, and boatmen are constantly letting down and drawing up immense nets. One of the features of the river is the number of wooden bathing-boxes or platforms that are moored near to the sides for the ablutions either of daily life or of religious observance.

This chapter is not intended to be a guide-book of Srinagar, and therefore I will say nothing about the mosques or public buildings, the palaces or bazaars, of the town. It is better indeed and fairer to Srinagar not to leave its aquatic highway at all, for there is concentrated whatever it possesses of individuality or charm. Out of a total population estimated in 1894 at 132,000, some 10,000 had their habitation on the river. Thereon might be seen the several varieties of Kashmir boat – the *bahat*, a big grain barge, slowly propelled by poles; the *dunga*, or ordinary passenger boat, which was used both for residence and for journeys, and which had a sloping roof of mats or reeds; the *shikara*, or light craft, the Srinagar equivalent to the caïque of Stamboul, which was swiftly urged along by boatmen wielding heart-shaped paddles of wood; and the *parinda*, or ceremonial barge, where the occupant sits beneath a canopy near the bows, while behind him thirty or forty men sitting in two rows drive the boat with frantic energy through the water. European taste had been responsible for the recent introduction of house-boats, built very much upon the lines of an Oxford College Barge. Herein many of the foreign residents lived permanently, the interior being decorated by Kashmiri workmen with elegant panelling, and supplied with all the comforts of an exotic civilisation.

The environs of the city are beautified by magnificent clumps of *chenar*, the Oriental plane. Among the many contributions of the Moghul emperors of Agra and Delhi to the embellishment of the Kashmir capital, which was their favourite summer retreat, for none have later generations more reasons to be grateful than for the artistic forethought which originated in so many places, avenues, or groves of these stately trees, and which even imposed upon the native villages as a yearly duty the plantation of a stipulated number. Later dynasties have responded by an almost equally abundant introduction of poplars, and the long lines and avenues of the latter are among the delights of suburban Srinagar.

No visitor goes away without diverging from the river by one of the lateral canals and spending a morning in his boat in furrowing the glassy surface of the Dal Lake, immediately behind the city, and in inspecting the pleasure gardens and pavilions around its shores that were erected for the diversion or the dalliance of the Moghul sovereigns. The floating gardens of the lake are famous; great lotus leaves and water-lilies quiver idly upon the pellucid surface; wild-fowl of every description dart in and out of the rushes, and kingfishers flash like streaks of blue flame amid the trees. Perhaps our destination is the Nasim Bagh, or Garden of Soft Breezes, or the Nishat Bagh, or Garden of Bliss, or the Shalamar Bagh – the two latter the creation of the Emperor Jehangir more than three centuries gone by. There the water still descends from terrace to terrace and ripples in deftly constructed cascades; it still spurts from the Moghul fountains, and splashes in the decaying and deserted pools. The gardens, once so trim and neat, though little tended, are still bright with flowers. In the pavilions that are built above the waters one may lie at ease on the very spot where the emperors and their sultanas played and quarrelled and were reconciled. The eye wanders over the terraces and cascades and pools, and across the blue levels of the lake, to where the Takht-i-Suleiman and the Hari Parbat, like two grim sentinels, keep watch at the gates of the invisible city at their feet, and at such a moment, and from this agreeable distance, the beauty of Srinagar becomes crystallised into a positive sensation.

To the traveller, however, and in a scarcely less degree to the sportsman, Srinagar is only the gateway to regions possessing an even more potent fascination beyond. The young subaltern halts there on his way to shoot ibex or markhor in the *nullahs* of the Hindu Kush or amid the crags of Baltistan. The explorer or the voyager takes it in his stride on the march to Gilgit, or the Pamirs. It was as a member of the second class that in 1904 I passed through on my way to the outer frontier of the Indian Empire. I afterwards wrote a book about the latter, which though it was already in print and had been sold for a substantial sum to an enterprising publisher, I was never allowed to bring out; for, when I had actually corrected the final proofs and my photographs had been engraved, I was appointed Viceroy of India; and the Prime Minister, Lord Salisbury, declared with, I believe, a quite unnecessary punctilio, that a new Viceroy ought not to publish anything about the country which he was soon to rule. So my plates were put away, the cheque was returned, and my proof sheets reposed, as they have done ever since, in a tin box from which they will now never emerge – not indeed from any pedantry or spleen, but because I find them to be superfluous and out of date. The

Pamir Question has been settled, at any rate for the time being; the majority of the little mountain republics have not the political interest or strategical importance that they once possessed; and what was then all but virgin ground has since been frequently trodden and described. Here I will only give a slight sketch of the region in question, in its relation to the frontier problem as a whole.

The frontier pass of Gilgit is situated 230 miles north of Srinagar, and is separated from it by the main Himilayan range. A glance at the map will indicate the importance which, owing to its geographical situation, the place has always possessed in the military and dynastic contests of the Hindu Kush region. Planted on a fertile oasis, at a slight distance above the junction of the Hunza River – which runs down through the valley of that name from the watershed separating India from the Eastern Pamirs – and the Gilgit River, which flows in from the borders of Chitral on the west, receiving in its course tributaries from Yasin and Ishkumman, it has always been the point from which connection with or control over the neighbouring states south of the great ranges could most effectively be maintained; while its position in relation to the main valley of the Indus, into which the Gilgit River flows thirty miles lower down, rendered it the northern key of that mysterious mountain fastness, variously known as the Kohistan or Highlands, and Yaghistan or Outlawland, where for hundreds of years, either in the main valley of the Indus or in the lateral ravines, lawless and savage communities have retained, and still retain, an independent existence, a scourge to each other and a terror to their neighbours. Thus Gilgit, from its central position, has always been of great importance for controlling the tribes of the north, and for coercing and keeping in check the tribes of the south.

The Kashmir government nominated a governor to Gilgit.

At one time ruled by a Hindu dynasty that united under its sway the petty neighbouring states from Hunza to Gurais, and from Chilas to Chitral, in later days it became the sport of warring tribes, being alternately conquered and held by Punial, Nagar, and Yasin. At length, some eighty years ago, it was taken by the Sikhs, and in 1846 passed, with the remainder of the splendid heritage that we so lightly bartered to Golab Singh, into the hands of the Dogra chief. Since then Gilgit has been taken and lost and retaken, but has for the most part remained in the hands of Kashmir. The price, however, that required to be paid for the all but barren glory of possession was ruinous both in money and men. A garrison, at one time amounting to 6000 men, was maintained by the Maharaja's Government in the neighbourhood; ill looked after, undisciplined and unpaid, they abominated their service, and deserted when they could. The *begar* or *corvée* that was enforced, both to fill their ranks and to supply them with provisions, decimated the mountain peoples and entailed fearful misery and oppression. The villages along the line of route from Kashmir were abandoned by their inhabitants, who either fled into the hills or paid extravagant sums in blackmail to escape from the military inquisition. Those who were successfully impressed received no mercy at the hands of their captors, but were driven like beasts of burden under their loads, and when worn out were brutally left to perish by the way. At the end of the time the Gilgit garrison profited little by these exactions, for, owing to the universal embezzlement in high places, but few of the supplies contracted for reached their destination; and the Dogra troops were in almost as much danger from starvation as they were from the assaults of an exasperated foe. Though maintaining a titular Raja, connected with the old ruling family, the Kashmir Government nominated a governor to Gilgit in addition to the general commanding the forces; and as late as 1885 the annual charge on the Kashmir treasury for maintaining this isolated post alone amounted to £7000.

It was a fortunate day when the misgovernment of the Kashmir State and contemporary events in Central Asia compelled the Indian Government to look more closely into and eventually to make itself responsible for the border defences of Kashmir.

In 1878 the first British Agent or Political Officer was appointed to reside at Gilgit. In one of the customary waves of political reaction he was presently withdrawn. But the intrigues of Russia, then in her most Chauvinistic temper, on and beyond the outer frontier, compelled the Indian Government to reconsider its decision, and the post was revived and made permanent in 1889. Simultaneously the duty of providing the frontier garrisons was withdrawn from the Kashmir Durbar, and was entrusted to the newly constituted Kashmir Imperial Service troops, commanded by British officers, in whose hands it has ever since remained. Thus it was that, almost unwittingly to start with – as is the way with British Governments – but not too soon, Great Britain made herself accountable for the adequate defence of what are the natural boundaries, not of a feudatory state, but of the Indian Empire itself, and assumed a task which has ever since been invested not with a local, but with an imperial significance.

The country between the Kashmir Valley and Gilgit consists of an intricate maze of mountains, seldom presenting a mile of level ground, and requiring to be crossed by passes, the highest of which is 13,450 feet above the sea. In former days the road that connected the two places was only a mountain track, precariously skirting immense precipices and threading profound ravines. Its defects of construction caused appalling loss of life, both to baggage animals and to men. The first desideratum of effective and economic defence was therefore the provision of a proper military road. The work was begun in 1890 and completed two years later, being interrupted and severely strained by the Hunza-Nagar campaign of the winter of 1891.

At the time of my visit, less than three years later, the number of British and Kashmir troops stationed on the frontier was still over 3000 men – a total long since reduced to an almost insignificant quota – and the entire food-supply for this considerable force during the winter had to be conveyed across the mountain passes before these were blocked by snow. Communication by baggage animals was then liable to be suspended for over seven months, so that the entire work of the year must be accomplished in the remaining four to five, the dates between which the passes were regarded as really passable being from 1 July to 10 October. For this work there were being employed in the autumn of 1894 no fewer than 15,000 animals – 7500 ponies, 6700 bullocks, 250 mules, 250 donkeys, and 800 camels, supplied by Pathan tribesmen, mostly Mohmand refugees.

My own journey on pony back to Gilgit was made in nine days; but this was due to special facilities in the provision of relays, the demands upon all available resources being so severe that, except with special permission, which was then rarely given, no private travellers were allowed by the Indian Government to proceed upon the military road. The camp-following with which I went up, and which included four Europeans, consisted of twenty-six animals and thirty-five men. We slept in tents or in bungalows, a certain number of the latter having been erected for the accommodation of travellers along the road, consisting of a building with rough stone walls, divided into two compartments, but containing so far neither furniture, flooring, nor, in some cases, doors. The regularity and comparative absence of friction with which this laborious system of transport operated in a country singularly poor in supplies, and in face of the most capricious vicissitudes of nature, reflected the greatest credit upon the officers engaged. To the inhabitants of the localities traversed the certainty of paid employment and of a fair wage came as a pleasant relief from the horrors of the old *corvée*; while the villages north of Astor and in the Indus Valley for the first time tasted security from the raids of the dreaded freebooters of Chilas. The agricultural resources of the surrounding districts had been heavily taxed for the provision of supplies, and husbandry had been compelled to yield to the superior necessities of transport. But, as time passed by, matters had righted themselves, and the diminution in the strain had removed the temporary deterrent to cultivation.

I need not describe the stages of this journey, for which my readers may be referred to the accounts in the excellent books of Mr E. F. Knight and Sir M. Conway, and to later publications; but I may, in passing, sum up the more general impressions. As regards the scenery of the road, its main characteristic is the almost total absence of horizonal lines. The track itself winds up and down, now along the roaring bed or a snow-grey torrent, anon 2000 feet above the yellow riband that hums faintly in the deep gorge below. It scales with mathematical zigzags precipices upon which the foot of man could not otherwise rest. Again it plunges into the shade of Alpine pine forests, or follows the sterile sinuations of sombre ravines. I can only recall one level valley-bottom in the entire journey, and that, at Gurais, is the bed of an ancient lake. The nearest mountains, with their stony buttresses and forbidding peaks, as a rule shut out the snowy giants behind; but here and there through gaps, or at the head of lateral *nullahs*, glimpses are caught of summits more than 20,000 feet high; while from the passes is obtained in fine weather a superb retrospect towards the Kashmir Valley (the white clouds resting in the hollows like cotton-wool), or a bewildering outlook over the tumult of Himalayan peaks. Nanga Parbat, 26,620 feet, is the monarch among the loftier summits, and the sight of his imperial form, as seen from the Indus

As regards the scenery of the road, its main characteristic is the almost total absence of horizontal lines.

Valley at Bunji – a sheer 22,000 feet in height from the spectator's level to his topmost crown – is one of the glories of Kashmir. It was on this great mountain that the well-known Alpine climber, Mr A. Mummery, lost his life, it is supposed from an avalanche, in August 1895.

On the whole, however, I found the scenery of the roads more impressive than beautiful, more sullen than joyous, more rugged than picturesque. It may be divided into three sections. The first is that from Bandipur to Minimerg, a distance of sixty miles. This is the prettiest part of the journey, for the track winds through Alpine pine woods and skirts romantic glens. It contains, however, one pass, the Tragbal or Rajdiangan, 11,800 feet high, which is greatly feared in winter because of its long, bald summit, across which the snow-laden gales shriek their accents of death to animal and man. A loftier and more famous, or infamous, pass occurs in the second section, which is relatively treeless and barren, and which stretches (with certain agreeable interludes) for ninety miles from Minimerg to the Indus at Ramghat. This is the Burzil, which I crossed as early as the first week of September in a snowstorm, with the thermometer at only one degree above freezing-point; and the height of which I registered by boiling-point thermometer and aneroid as 13,450 feet. Countless are the tales which actual suffering no less than superstitious horror has associated with the five or six miles of barren *couloir*, culminating in a desolate plateau, in which are concentrated the main dangers of the pass. Here I was shown a rock under which five men crouched to eat their supper, and were found frozen to death in the morning. There some similar casualty occurred. In October 1891 over a hundred men of a British Indian regiment, marching up to Gilgit for the campaign, had been frost-bitten in a single night, and some had died. One of our men assured us that he had been present when a coolie, walking the hindmost in a string, was forcibly seized and thrown into a neighbouring gully by a monstrous *jin* or demon, as tall as from the earth to the sky, and covered with hair over a foot long. In this repellent and treeless region, heaps of detritus, loosened by the snow, continually slide down the rocky slopes, and mud avalanches, carrying boulders as large as a cottage, creep down the side ravines. The cultivated terraces and orchards of Astor, where were stationed 800 men of a Sikh regiment (destined, at no distant date, to form a portion of Colonel Kelly's famous relief expedition to Chitral), supply a welcome oasis of verdure and comfort in the midst of the surrounding desolation. A wooden hand-rail around a modest grave there marks the last resting-place of one of the most promising among the gallant young band of English officers whom frontier warfare or exploration in India had shown in recent years to possess the same stubborn grit as of old. This was Lieutenant Davison, who was arrested by the Russians at the same time as Captain Younghusband on the Pamirs in 1891, and expelled by them from non-Russian territory. In 1893 he died of dysentery near Astor.

In descending the Hatu Pir to Ramghat, a vision was disclosed of a new landscape, opening to the eye the last section of our march through the valleys of the Indus and its confluent the Gilgit River. It was certainly a strange, and even impressive, spectacle. Mountains brown and grey and blue and purple, according to the perspective in which they were seen or to the light that fell upon them, but uniformly devoid of the faintest speck of verdure, descend to the Tartarean trough in which the Indus rolls its turbid and inky volume towards the remote Indian plains. Its valley is here composed of shingle slopes and boulder-strewn wastes and minutely pulverised sand, the sand and stones refracting with merciless ferocity the unfeeling glare of the sun. The ride to Gilgit was unredeemed by any solace save that which was afforded by the small oasis of Bunji and the hospitality of the little knot of British officers there collected, to the entertainment offered by whom I have paid tribute in an earlier chapter; and it was with sensations of profound relief that the traveller saw outstretched before him the richer and greener slopes of Minawar and Gilgit, where a more abundant verdure is extracted from the mountain detritus spread out in the geological formation known as an alluvial fan.

Throughout the journey a practical reminder of civilisation was furnished by the telegraph wire, constructed partly by the Indian, partly by the Kashmir Government, but entirely maintained, on imperial grounds, by the former. It ran in close proximity to the military road. Whole slices of forest had required to be cut down to safeguard the wire from falling timber in winter, and the hardships to which the snowed-up telegraph clerks, who then looked after the maintenance of communications, were exposed were not the least disagreeable of its resultant obligations. As soon as the snow began to fall and the winter set in, they were cut off from all connection, except such as the wire could give, with the outer world. Indoors their lives might be sufficiently comfortable, even if monotonous. But the moment they learned, by the periodical testing of the wires, that an interruption had taken place, out they must sally, at all hazards and in all weathers, from the two stations on either side of the fault, to repair the fracture. This, as a rule, would have resulted from one of the many avalanches that, at nearly all seasons, but most of all in winter, come leaping down the mountain-sides in platoons, and almost in squadrons, and that might be as dangerous to the repair-party as they had previously proved to be to the poles and wires. The instances were not rare of risks run and acts of heroism performed by the telegraph clerks and their native linemen on this isolated strand of Great Britain's world-embracing cable of Empire, as great as any of those recorded on the battlefield or at the cannon's mouth.

The character of the scattered native villages passed *en route* is adapted to the same climatic conditions. They consist of small clusters of log-huts, built of roughly hewn pine logs laid transversely upon each other and packed with mud and stones. A small door, some two feet in height, about half-way up the side, indicates the level at which the snow is wont to lie. A square hole in the flat mud roof affords the sole passage for either light to enter or smoke to issue. At Gurais, Astor, and other places are native forts, crazy structures of mud and stones, loopholed for musketry, and sometimes containing an elevated bastion with embrasures for a gun. They no doubt served their purpose as a place of refuge from the raids of ill-armed highland clans, and are sometimes planted in situations of natural strength. They could, however, almost invariably be shelled from neighbouring heights, and a few well-directed shots would probably knock the ramshackle old relics to pieces.

Polo is the national past-time.

South of the Burzil the people appeared to belong to the same race as in the Kashmir plain; but northward we encountered a new type, of which we afterwards met with numerous specimens as we proceeded to Astor and Gilgit and passed on to Hunza and Nagar. These belong to the race to whom, for convenience sake, the name Dard, which they do not themselves either know or acknowledge, has been applied; and who, though speaking different languages and emanating from different stocks, illustrate, with greater or less uniformity, a primitive Aryan type. A cloth cap upon the head, rolled up to form a sort of brim, and a brown *choga*, or loose woollen dressing-gown, woven by themselves, are the differentiating articles of costume. Strong, clearly marked features, black curling locks, sometimes varied by chestnut hair and blue eyes, and a masculine bearing are the salient characteristics of external appearance. Hardy mountaineers they are, and such also is their deportment. Polo is the

Gilgit afforded an agreeable contrast to the villages hitherto passed.

national pastime of these highland tribes, and several polo grounds are passed upon the march. I have said something about the Hindu Kush variety of the game in another chapter. Very little animal life was visible from the road. Carrion crows, a few vultures, pigeons, and occasional *chikor* (the counterpart of the red-legged partridge) were seen. No big game showed itself; but between Doian and Bunji, and again between Bunji and Gilgit, open out the famous *nullahs*, where markhor, and ibex, and oorial abound; and there was not an officer then ordered to Gilgit who did not feel the penance of exile assuaged in advance by the anticipation of *shikar* in those once prolific but now, I fear, depleted ravines. The measurement of horns had assumed a scientific exactitude, and woe betide the luckless sportsman who, with a too hasty or ignorant rifle, infringed the unwritten law of Gilgit.

It was with sincere pleasure that the English visitor, at that period, rode into this distant outpost of British arms, and received the warm welcome that was always extended to strangers by the little band of officers who were there upholding the honour of the British flag.

Gilgit itself, both in the extent of its cultivated area (over two square miles), in the richness and frequency of its orchard clumps, and in the size and comparative strength of its fort upon the river-bank, afforded an agreeable contrast to the villages hitherto passed. The British Agency, a cool and comfortable bungalow, owed its construction and its lawn-tennis ground to Colonel Biddulph twenty years before. The modern importance of the place and the improved appearance of affairs were, however, mainly the work of Colonel Algernon Durand. A light suspension bridge had replaced the old rope bridge across the river, and at every turn were evidences of increasing security and of British occupation.

Outside the Agency at Gilgit, in a grove of trees, lies the grave of the first British pioneer of frontier exploration on this part of the border. This was Mr G.W. Hayward, who, having been sent out by the Royal Geographical Society in 1868 to explore the Pamirs from Yarkand, and having failed in that direction, determined to try his fortune from another quarter, and to penetrate to the forbidden region by way of Yasin and the passes over the Hindu Kush. The story of his murder in Dakot, in July 1870, by Mir Wali, the treacherous ruler of Yasin, acting, it is sometimes said, under the instructions of his father-in-law, Aman-ul-Mulk of Chitral, was told in his great work on Kashmir by Mr Drew, who was at that time in the service of the Maharaja, and who recovered both the papers and the body of the murdered man. When at Dakot in August 1885, as a member of Sir William Lockhart's Chitral mission, the late Colonel Woodthorpe met an eye-witness of the tragedy fifteen years earlier, and as this account has never yet been given to the public, it may be permissible to reproduce it here.

The British Agency, a cool and comfortable bungalow, owed its construction and its lawn tennis ground to Colonel Biddulph.

'It is just before dawn in the valley of Dakot. Not far from a grove of pollard willows stands a single tent, through the open door of which the light falls upon the ground in front. In this tent sits a solitary weary man; by his side, on the table at which he is writing, lie a rifle and a

pistol loaded. He has been warned by one whose word he cannot doubt, that Mir Wali is seeking his life that night, and he knows that from among those dark trees men are eagerly watching for a moment of unwariness on his part to rush forward across that patch of light-illumined ground and seize him. All night he has been writing to keep himself from a sleep which he knows would be fatal; but as the first rays of dawn appear over the eternal snows, exhausted nature gives way; his eyes close, and his head sinks – only for a moment; but in that moment his ever-watchful and crafty enemies rush forward, and before he can seize his weapons and defend himself, he is a prisoner, and is dragged forth to death. He makes one request – it is to be allowed to ascend a low mound, and take one last glance at the earth and sky he will never look upon again. His prayer is granted; he is unbound, and as he stands up there, tall against the morning sky, with the rising sun lighting up his fair hair as a glory, he is beautiful to look upon. He glances at the sky, at those lofty snow-clad peaks and mighty glaciers reaching down into the very valley, at the valley itself, with its straggling hamlets half-hidden among the willow groves, whence rises the smoke of newly kindled fires; he hears the noise of life beginning again, the voices of women, and the laugh of happy children, and then with firm step he comes down, back to his savage foes, and calmly says, "I am ready." He is instantly cut down by one of Mir Wali's men, and as he falls he receives his death-stroke from the sword of his treacherous friend, whose honoured guest he had so lately been.'

This scene has been made the subject of a poem by Sir H. Newbolt in the publication entitled *Admirals All*. Mir Wali was subsequently killed by order of Aman-ul-Mulk, who was anxious to ingratiate himself with the British authorities. One of the actual murderers was always believed to be Mohammed Rafi Khan, who, at the time of my visit to the frontier, was, in spite of his many iniquities, still Hakim or Governor of the Laspur district in Chitral. Six months later, when the rebellion broke out, and the British force was beleaguered in Chitral Fort, the old scoundrel justified both his reputation and his career by openly joining the enemy. Meanwhile the brave young Hayward sleeps under the orchard trees at Gilgit, a type of British pluck and an inspiration to his successors.

Meanwhile the brave young Hayward sleeps under the orchard trees, a type of British pluck and an inspiration to his successors.

KASHMIR TO GILGIT

SIR HENRY NEWBOLT

He fell among Thieves

'Ye have robb'd,' said he, 'ye have slaughter'd and
made an end,
Take your ill-got plunder, and bury the dead:
What will ye more of your guest and sometime friend?'
'Blood for our blood,' they said.

He laugh'd: 'If one may settle the score for five,
I am ready; but let the reckoning stand till day:
I have loved the sunlight as dearly as any alive.'
'You shall die at dawn,' said they.

He flung his empty revolver down the slope,
He climb'd alone to the Eastward edge of the trees;
All night long in a dream untroubled of hope
He brooded, clasping his knees.

He did not hear the monotonous roar that fills
The ravine where the Yassin river sullenly flows;
He did not see the starlight on the Laspur hills,
Or the far Afghan snows.

He saw the April noon on his books aglow,
The wistaria trailing in at the window wide;
He heard his father's voice from the terrace below
Calling him down to ride.

He saw the gray little church across the park,
The mounds that hid the loved and honour'd dead;
The Norman arch, the chancel softly dark,
The brasses black and red.

He saw the School Close, sunny and green,
The runner beside him, the stand by the parapet wall,
The distant tape, and the crowd roaring between,
His own name over all.

He saw the dark wainscot and timber'd roof,
The long tables, and the faces merry and keen;
The College Eight and their trainer dining aloof,
The Dons on the daïs serene.

He watch'd the liner's stem ploughing the foam,
He felt her trembling speed and the thrash of her screw;
He heard the passengers' voices talking of home,
He saw the flag she flew.

And now it was dawn. He rose strong on his feet,
And strode to his ruin'd camp below the wood;
He drank the breath of the morning cool and sweet:
His murderers round him stood.

Light on the Laspur hills was broadening fast,
The blood-red snow-peaks chill'd to a dazzling white;
He turn'd, and saw the golden circle at last,
Cut by the Eastern height.

'O glorious Life, Who dwellest in earth and sun,
I have lived, I praise and adore Thee.'
A sword swept.
Over the pass the voices one by one
Faded, and the hill slept.

From Gilgit to the Pamirs

On every side now rose
Rocks, which, in unimaginable forms,
Lifted their black and barren pinnacles
In the light of evening, and, its precipice
Obscuring the ravine, disclosed above,
'Mid toppling stones, black gulfs, and yawning caves,
Whose windings gave ten thousand various tongues
To the loud stream.

SHELLEY, *Alastor*.

The Yashin Valley, looking towards the Darkot pass, a route to the extreme confines of the Indian Empire.

FFOM Gilgit two routes are available to the extreme confines of the Indian Empire and the passes of the Hindu Kush. In a country which consists perhaps of the most stupendous mountain network that anywhere exists, it is not surprising to learn that the only avenues of exit or entrance are provided by the river gorges, which are hewn like deep, irregular gashes in the heart of the mountainous mass. On the eastern side the Hunza River, furrowing a rugged channel down the Hunza-Nagar Valley, opens up such a passage to the western extremity of the Mustagh or Ice-range – the physical prolongation of the Karakoram Mountains – which at this point, abutting on the Taghdumbash Pamir, merges in the main range of the Hindu Kush. On the west the Gilgit River flows down from Yashin, and may be followed up towards the Darkot and Baroghil Passes across the true Hindu Kush, whence a descent is made into the valley of the Upper Oxus and Wakhan. It was by the former route that I rode and marched, through some of the most wonderful surroundings and over some of the most inaccessible ground in the world, from Gilgit to the Kilik Pass, a distance of 140 miles.

I hesitate to say whether the Hunza Valley is more remarkable for its political and human interest or for its scenery, and in this chapter I shall have something to say about both. Perhaps, as its natural features may appeal to a wider audience – for the grandeur of peak and spire, of glacier and gorge, will affect those who may be indifferent to the ethnology or history of so petty a branch of the human family as is hidden away in this chink of the world's surface – I may deal first with them. In the Hunza Valley and its immediate environs, within a radius of fifty miles of its capital, Baltit, are congregated some of the most striking physical phenomena in the universe. Here a tumult of the highest known peaks lift their unscaled pinnacles above the deepest valleys, the most sombre ravines. Within a range of seventy miles there are eight crests with an elevation of over 24,000 feet, while the little state of Hunza alone is said to contain more summits of over 20,000 feet than there are of over 10,000 feet in the entire Alps. The longest glaciers on the globe outside of the Arctic Circle pour their frozen cataracts down the river and tortured hollows of the mountains. Great rivers foam and thunder in flood-time

The Mir of Hunza (third from left) at the Fort of Baltit, the chief place of Hunza.

along the resounding gorges, though sometimes reduced in winter – the season of low waters – to errant threads. Avalanches of snow, and – still more remarkable – of mud, come plunging down the long slopes, and distort the face of Nature as though by some lamentable disease. In this great workshop of primeval forces, wherever the imprisoned energies are not still at work, they have left their indelible traces in the stormy outline of the crags, in the watermarks of lakes that have burst their bounds and have fled, in the artificial structure of the alluvial terraces, in the deep scouring of the impetuous streams. In the valley of the Hunza River, up which my track lay, Nature would seem to have exerted her supreme energy, and in one chord to have comprised almost every note in her vast and majestic diapason of sound. For there she shows herself in the same moment both tender and savage, both radiant and appalling, the relentless spirit that hovers above the ice-towers and the gentle patroness of the field and orchard, the tutelary deity of the haunts of men.

Never can I forget the abruptness and splendour of the surprise when, shortly after leaving the fort of Chalt, thirty miles beyond Gilgit, there soared into view the lordly apparition of the great mountain Rakapushi, lifting above the boulder-strewn or forest-clad declivities of his lower stature 18,000 feet of unsullied ice and snow to a total height of 25,550 feet above the sea. Next to the sight of Kangchenjunga from beyond Darjiling, this is the finest mountain spectacle that I have seen. Rakapushi is one of the most superbly modelled of mountains. Everywhere visible as we ascend the valley, he keeps watch over the lower summits and over the smiling belts of green and the orchard plots below that owe their existence to his glacial bounty. But up above, where no raiment but the royal ermine clothes his shoulders, his true majesty is best revealed. There enormous and shining glaciers fill the hollows of his sides, the ice-fields stretch for mile on mile of breadth and height, and only upon the needle-point of his highest crest is the snow unable to settle. In that remote empyrean we visualise an age beyond the boundaries of human thought, a silence as from the dawn of time. As we gaze at Rakapushi we find an unconscious answer to the poet's query –

> What pleasure lives in height (the shepherd sang) –
> In height and cold, the splendour of the hills?

For there, in more than fancy, we can

> Walk
> With Death and Morning on the silver horns.

Before us are

> The firths of ice
> That huddling slant in furrow-cloven falls
> To roll the torrent out of dusky doors.

And though the eye, aching with the dazzling vision, may seek a transient solace in the restful verdure of the lower and terraced slopes, may wander over the cultivated surface of the alluvial fans, and may even dip into the deep gorge where the river hums 1000 feet below our feet, yet it cannot

The Hunza valley where Nature would seem to have exerted her supreme energy.

As we gaze at Rakapushi, we find an unconscious answer to the poet's query.

for long resist the enchantment of those glimmering peaks, and ever hankers for the fascination of the summit. Rakapushi stands there and will stand as long as this orb endures, under the heavenly vault, under the eternal stars, ancestral, godlike, sublime, tremendous.

This remote mountain valley has an importance for Englishmen which its geographical isolation would lead few to suspect. It is one of the northern gates of India, through which a would-be invader must advance if he advance at all. It is further inhabited by a people of whom till thirty years ago very little was known, but whose reputation for warlike ferocity had combined with the natural strength of their mountain lair to produce in the minds of their neighbours an impression of terror – in their own, one of absolute invincibility. Hunza or Kanjut, as it is called by the people living to the north of the Hindu Kush, with whom the Hunza men have ethnological and other connections, is the state on the right or northern bank of the river to which it gives its name. Nagar is the state on the left or the southern bank. The confines of the former extend to the crests that are the watershed between the Indus and Oxus basins. The barriers of Nagar are the great glaciers that fill the troughs of the main Himalayan range. The larger part of the surface, however, of both states is given up to snow and ice, and the cultivable and inhabited areas, which are co-extensive, are limited to a few hundred square miles, supporting in the case of Hunza a population of about 6500, and in that of Nagar of 7000.

Both peoples claim a similar origin, and undoubtedly belong to the same stock. Whether this is a primitive Aryan type, whose characteristics have been preserved by their isolation in these mountain retreats, or whether they are of Turanian descent, but have been Aryanised by Hindu immigration and conquest from the south, I will not here pause to discuss. The weight of argument seems, on the whole, to be in favour of the former hypothesis. Yeshkin is the name of the tribal caste to which the majority claim to belong, and Burishki or Burishaski is the dialect which they speak. It belongs to the Scythian as distinguished from the Iranian group. They call themselves Birchik, which is identical with Warshik, the name borne by the cognate peoples of the Upper Yasin Valley.

Both peoples are also Mohammedans of a sort. The Nagar men are indifferent Shiahs; the Hunza folk are Maulais, or adherents of the sect sometimes known as Ismailis, whose spiritual head is the Aga Khan at Bombay. Religion, however, sits very lightly on the conscience of the men of Hunza. I could not ascertain that any of them feel it incumbent upon them to proceed on pilgrimage to Bombay; and the Aga is only represented among them by certain *pirs*, or holy men, who extract a sort of Peter's pence from the people. Their scriptures are contained in a book entitled *Kalam-i-pr*. The Hunza mosques appear to be invested with no particular sanctity, and to be regarded with very scant reverence. One of them was even occupied, when I passed through, by a company of traders. The superstitious fear of spirits has a far stronger hold than veneration for the prophet, and nearly every man carries a number of charms attached to some part of his dress or person. I even saw them affixed to the leg of a horse. Before the advent of Europeans these and similar superstitions prevailed to an almost grotesque degree. Even now they are but dubiously thawing beneath the mild rays of civilisation.

The men of both peoples are of a robust, hardy, masculine type, and frequently of more than the average stature. The most strongly marked feature is the nose, which is large and prominent. They wear their hair, which is almost always black, shaven on the top of the crown and down the middle of the back of the head; but it is suffered to grow upon the temples, and falls in a thick bunch, or sometimes in a cluster of ringlets, behind either ear. They are very vain of these lovelocks, which are greatly admired by the opposite sex. A devoted lover will sometimes go so far as to cut off his curls and present them to the object of his attachment as a pledge of his affection. The common dress is a rolled woollen cap, a brown or grey woollen *choga* or dressing-gown, loose white pantaloons, and stockings stuck into flexible leather top-boots; while the poorer orders have their feet either bare or sandalled with leather *pabus*, made of ibex-skin. Following the Mussulman practice, the women of the higher classes, though unveiled, are kept carefully concealed. There is no law against polygamy or concubinage, but the narrowness of means is found to be a strong practical argument in favour of a single establishment.

The Hunzakuts or Kanjutis enjoy the reputation of being the finer and more virile race; and during the inter-tribal warfare which was always more or less going on, except on the occasions when the two states combined their forces against a common foe, Sikh, Dogra, or British, they were invariably victorious. Their most notable characteristic, however, was their raiding and slave-hunting proclivity. Apologists for Hunza explain that the insufficiency of the cultivated area of the state to sustain the excessive population naturally drove the superfluous manhood to this source of mingled exercise and subsistence. However this may be, the Kanjutis were the scourge of the entire frontier, and might have been styled the Turkomans of the Hindu Kush. By a clandestine arrangement with China, to whom they paid some sort of allegiance, the caravans between Yarkand and Leh were recognised as their special perquisite. Marching swiftly by difficult mountain tracks, they burst upon the defenceless lines of animals and men, appropriated the former and sold the latter into slavery in Chinese Turkestan. The Shingshal Pass, which is one of great difficulty and elevation (14,719 feet), was one of their favourite lines of advance and retreat; and they pushed their daring forays as far as Kulanuldi in the upper valley of the Yarkand river, and even to Shahidula on the main caravan road from Leh. Up to 1890 there was many a victim of their forays still an exile in Kashgaria; but largely owing to the exertions of the British representative in Kashgar, over 2000 slaves, one-fourth of whom were reported to be of Indian origin, were afterwards released; while in 1897 the sale or tenure of slaves was finally prohibited throughout Chinese Turkestan by proclamation of the Taotai. For this, if for no other reason, the subjugation by England of the Hunza man-hunters was an incalculable service to the whole mountain border, which groaned under their cruel rapine.

The whole mountain border groaned under the cruel Hunza rapine.

Both states are, and have long been, ruled by a line of chieftains, said to have originally sprung from a common ancestor, and constantly blended by intermarriage. These rulers are styled Thum (pronounced Tum) in the language of the country, and Mir by the peoples living beyond the Hindu Kush. The Thums of Hunza and Nagar were looked upon as very big personages by their own peoples and by the entire neighbourhood, and were, in fact, excellent types of the petty but truculent Asiatic independent monarch; until, in an evil day for themselves, their propensity for fratricide, parricide, and other domestic escapades, coupled with the man-hunting tastes and the political intrigues to which I shall presently allude, brought them into sharp collision with the British power.

The history of the connection of Hunza-Nagar, first with Kashmir, and then with the Indian Government, affords indeed a synopsis in miniature of the same problem that is perpetually in course of evolution along the entire frontier. It is a history whose successive stages are independence, breaking into lawlessness and outrage, open hostility, bringing defeat, and final control, resulting in contented allegiance.

Eighty years ago, when Golab Singh, the Raja of Jummu, to whom the

British Government had just given, or rather sold, Kashmir, was endeavouring to subjugate and define the outlying and Trans-Indus portions of his new possession, and when neither he nor the Indian Government knew very clearly where that border was, we catch a glimpse of the Hunza-Nagar states that is prophetic of later experiences. Lieutenants Vans-Agnew and Young were sent in 1847 to the Gilgit frontier in the Hunza Valley, which was at that time at Chaprot, and at this point asked leave of Ghazanfur Khan, the Raja of Hunza, to visit his territory. This request was contemptuously refused, and a long spell of hostilities ensued between the two tribes and the Dogra forces, in which both were alternately victorious, but throughout which the Hunza and Nagar territories, though occasionally invaded, remained practically inviolate. Nevertheless the two rulers were at length impelled to recognise the suzerainty of Kashmir, to whom nagar from the year 1868, and Hunza from the following year, paid an annual tribute of gold-dust (extracted by washing from the Hunza River), fruit, horses, and hounds. Later on this tribute was more than compensated by small annual subsidies paid to the two chiefs by the Kashmir Government.

Major Biddulph, the first British Agent at Gilgit, was the first Englishman to visit Hunza, in 1876. Ghazan Khan, the son and successor of Shah Ghazanfur, was then upon the throne. He was still the ruler when, ten years later, in April 1886, Sir W. Lockhart's Mission passed through Hunza on its way to the Pamirs. The old Raja, who as yet knew very little of the British, and who was swollen with his own importance, was not the man to lose so excellent an opportunity of asserting his power. He refused to allow the Mission to proceed upon its journey unless Colonel Lockhart would promise to restore to him Chaprot, which had long been a bone of contention between the Hunza and Nagar chiefs, and which was at that time, under an arrangement made by the Kashmir Government, held in *jagir* by a younger son of the Nagar Raja, while a Kashmir garrison occupied the fort. It was only with much difficulty and by astute diplomacy that Colonel Lockhart got through. Later in the same year old Ghazan Khan was murdered by his son Safdar Ali Khan, a peculiarly bloodthirsty ruffian, who at the same time poisoned his mother, threw two of his brothers down a precipice and made away with a third – a proceeding which did not excite any particular astonishment in that country, and which its perpetrator announced in the following euphemistic terms to his suzerain, the Maharaja of Kashmir:

> 'By the will of God and the decree of fate, my late father and I recently fell out. I took the initiative and settled the matter, and have placed myself on the throne of my ancestors.'

In 1888 Captain Grombchevski and his Cossacks appeared upon the scene, and executed that private sally across the Hindu Kush into Hunza whose immediate result was still further to inflate the truculent Raja with his own importance, but whose ulterior consequences were to prove so little favourable to its originators' designs. What was the exact nature of the intercourse between the two parties has never been divulged, but that some sort of agreement was arrived at was subsequently admitted by the Thum himself. From this time forward Safdar Ali Khan began to speak of the White Monarch, as he called the Tsar of Russia, as his friend, and in his correspondence and conversation to allude to himself as the equal of that Sovereign, of the Emperor of China, and of the Empress of India – a quartet of potentates who, in his opinion, divided the globe. In the same year the combined forces of Hunza and Nagar marched down the valley and expelled the Kashmir garrison from the fort of Chalt, which had long been within the Kashmir border. It was, however, recovered by the Kashmiris before the end of the year.

Matters having reached this stage, it was considered desirable by the Indian Government to intervene, with a view, if possible, to anticipating any larger trouble that might threaten to occur. Captain (afterwards Colonel) A. Durand, who had been appointed to the post from which, nine years earlier, Major Biddulph had been withdrawn, was dispatched by the Indian Government to Hunza and Nagar to enter into negotiations with the rulers of those states. Conditions were formulated, and an agreement was signed with both, by which the Rajas acknowledged the suzerainty of Great Britain (as the overlord of Kashmir), and opened their territories to the free passage of officers deputed by the British Government; while the Hunza chieftain further undertook to desist form the raiding upon which he and his people had hitherto thrived. In return, substantial subsidies – in addition to the allowance already made by the Kashmir Durbar – were to be given by the Indian Government. Safdar Ali Khan, though boorish and at times insolent, appeared to be satisfied with this arrangement, from which, he wrote to Colonel Durand, 'he would never deviate as long as he lived'; and later in the same year he gave a civil reception to Captain Younghusband, who returned *via* Hunza to Gilgit from his exploration of the Mustagh mountains.

So matters remained until 1891, when news arrived tht Uzar Khan, the heir-apparent of Nagar, seemingly fired by emulation of the earlier exploits of the Hunza chief, had also murdered two of his brothers and announced his intention, if he could catch him, of doing the same to a third. Simultaneously the two Rajas made combined preparations once again to seize the forts of Chalt and Chaprot – a design in which they were cleverly baulked by a rapid move on the part of Colonel Durand. In this summer, and just at this time, there appeared upon the Pamirs the first of the famous Russian 'hunting expeditions' of Colonel Yonoff. Safdar Ali Khan was ascertained to be in communication with them, and an embassy from him arrived at Marghilan in August to interview Baron Vrevsky, the Russian Governor-General of Turkestan, who was making a tour upon the Alai. Safdar Ali's next step was to intercept and decline to forward the correspondence to the Indian Government of Captain Younghusband himself. Meanwhile, as early as 1890, the time-honoured raiding had again been resumed. Thus in every particular the agreement of 1889 was being or had been systematically violated by the signatory chiefs.

It was in these circumstances that, Colonel Durand's scanty force at

Gilgit having been reinforced by officers, men, and guns from India, it was decided to send an ultimatum to the recalcitrant rulers, informing them that a new fort was to be built at Chalt and that a military road would be constructed to Hunza on one side of the river and to Nagar on the other, so as to give freedom of access to the frontier, which the Indian Government had determined to hold. The chiefs, who had already burned their boats, began at once to collect their forces, ill-used Colonel Durand's messenger, and returned an insolent answer to the ultimatum. Safdar Ali, who excelled in this sort of correspondence, declared in one letter that 'he cared nothing for the womanly English, as he hung upon the skirts of the manly Russians, and had given orders to his followers to bring him the Gilgit Agent's head on a platter'. In another letter he wrote: 'I will withstand you even though I have to use bullets of gold. We will cut off your head, Colonel Durand, and then report you to the Indian Government.'

Then followed the brief but memorable campaign of December 1891, by which, in less than three weeks, these illusions were abruptly dispelled, the two chieftains were humbled and crushed, the two states subdued, and the British flag carried by a few hundred native soldiers, under the leading of a handful of British officers, to the crest of the Hindu Kush. On December 2, 1891, the advance was begun, with a force numbering a little over 1000 men. Nilt Fort was carried by storm, with a loss of six killed and twenty-seven wounded. After a stoppage of eighteen days, the cliff beyond was stormed and carried on December 20. On December 21 the Khan of Nagar made submission, the Khan of Hunza and his Wazir having already fled. On December 30 the pursuing party reached the Kilik Pass and the Hindu Kush.

The narrative of this campaign, which added no fewer than three names to the proud roll of the Victoria Cross, has been admirably told by Mr Knight, who himself took part in it, in his book, *Where Three Empires Meet*, and I should display but a poor regard for my readers were I by a later and inferior reptition of his narrative to qualify the pleasure which they must already have derived from the perusal of his work. Travelling over the ground as I did less than three years after the fighting, I was able to see how the conquerors had in the interval utilised their fortune, and by what steps and how surely this nest of mountain-wasps, who stung and worried upon the frontier, and made Simla quake, had been converted into a useful and reliable outpost on the extreme ramparts of our Indian Empire.

The entire Hunza Valley, from Gilgit to the crest of the Kilik Pass, may be divided into two sections, the first extending for a little over sixty miles from the confluence of the Hunza River with the Gilgit River, three miles below the Gilgit Fort, as far as the two capitals, Baltit and Nagar; the second section following the upper waters of the same stream from that point for eighty miles to the Chinese frontier on the Taghdumbash Pamir. A good deal of traffic to and fro had taken place on the former section since the war, and something in the nature of a road had been constructed or hewn out of the mountain-side. Before that time the road, if it could be so called without a grim jest, consisted in many parts of rocky and ladder-like tracks up the sides of the cliffs, and of narrow galleries built out with timbers round the edges of the precipices.

As I started from Gilgit upon the first stage to Nomal, I rode into a dust-storm that raged for two hours, and rendered even more dolorous the sorrowful sterility of the scene. A pitiless wind drove a scud of dust and gravel into eyes, nostrils, ears, and mouth, and rendered it almost impossible to see one's horse's head. Our men, who had been sent on in advance with the baggage mules, took eight hours to cover the eighteen miles. Sullenness is the main characteristic of the scenery. The river, with a rushing coffee-coloured flood from 50 to 100 yards in width, has cut for itself a deep trench through the ends of the alluvial fans that have poured down from the side valleys, or through the terminal moraines pushed forward by gigantic glaciers behind. Sometimes its vertical walls are 300 feet high, while the slope of the upper cliff may rise for another 3000. The alluvial fans, which are exactly so shaped, the handle being towards the gorge from which they issue, and the broad end abutting upon the river, support a scanty growth of trees or scrub. Sometimes they slope to the water's edge, at others they terminate in gravelly cliffs. The road or track runs at one moment over the sand or amid boulders in the river-bed; at another it climbs a *pari* or steep cliff 1000 feet above. The mountains look as if they had passed through a seven-times-heated furnace, and had had all life scorched out of their veins. Scarcely a sign of vegetation was encountered, except at Nomal, until we reached the oasis of Chalt, where is a fort that had been the frontier outpost of Kashmir arms prior to the campaign of 1891, and was now occupied by seventy men of the Imperial Service troops. The inhabitants, who had been scared away in former days by the terror of Hunza raids, were returning, and the cultivated area had already considerably increased. There I was met by the Raja of Chalt and Chaprot, a grandson of old Jafar Khan, the Thum of Nagar. He was a Jewish-looking lad, with prominent nose, black hair curling behind his ears, and a brown rolled cap on his head, with an amulet containing a text from the Koran affixed to it.

Below the fort of Chalt we crossed by a light suspension bridge, built at the time of the campaign, to the left or Nagar bank of the river, and presently ascended a *kotal* or ridge which the natives, who might have utilised it for a very serious resistance, foolishly abandoned to the advancing British force on 1 December, 1891. The troops had then to climb to the summit by steep zigzags along the side of the mountain; but the road is now carried round the rocks overhanging the river. It is at this point that Rakapushi bursts, with all his splendour, upon the traveller's vision; which, indeed, he never quits until after we have left Baltit. Happy should be the people from whose eyes such a spectacle is never absent; and had poetry, instead of rapine, been the particular aptitude of the men of Hunza, Rakapushi must have created a folk-lore or inspired a legend.

At about the fortieth mile up the valley we come to the broken-down fort of Nilt, which was the scene of the two most brilliant achievements of the '91 campaign. Everyone who is familiar with its incidents will remember that this was the spot at which the Hunza-Nagar men had concentrated the whole of their defensive strength; that Colonel Durand, in command of the expedition, was wounded here on the first day of fighting; that the gate of the fort was blown up with gun-cotton, at the imminent risk of his life, by Captain Aylmer, and the fort itself carried by storm; that the advance was then delayed for nearly three weeks by the strong *sangars*, or stone breastworks, that had been constructed and filled with their best sharpshooters by the enemy on the opposite side of the deep *nullah* beyond, completely blocking the way up the valley; that this position was eventually taken by Lieutenants Manners Smith and Taylor and their Gurkhas and Dogras, who scaled the vertical cliff-wall, over 1000 feet in height, below the uppermost *sangar*, and surprised and put to the sword its defenders; that all resistance then collapsed, and the surrender and occupation of the two capitals speedily ensued. With all these details I was already familiar; but I confess to having been surprised at the extraordinary natural strength of the position, and to having underestimated the bravery involved in its capture. The fort, although a rickety old place in itself, occupied the entire space between the base of the mountain and the edge of the deep gorge in which the river flows several hundred feet below. The small and sloping piece of ground up which the British were compelled to march to the assault was completely swept by rifle-fire from its walls. Captain Aylmer ought to have been killed several times over while creeping twice along the wall to ignite the fuse in the gate. Finally, the terriffic cliff which Lieutenant Manners Smith scaled would not suggest that form of approach any more than would Shakespeare's cliff at Dover. The inhabitants of the place had developed into eager cicerones, and were apparently as proud of the manner in which their fort had been taken as could possibly be the intrepid handful of heroes who added this brilliant chapter to the records of British military prowess. I had the further advantage of travelling in the company of, and going over the ground with, Sir H. Lennard, who had served as a volunteer in the campaign.

The white Wolseley helmet worn by Lieutenant Manners Smith who scaled the vertical cliff-wall, over 1000 feet in height.

From Nilt on the Nagar bank and from Maiun on the opposite or Hunza side of the valley commences a series of charming oases or belts of cultivation, belonging to the respective states. In these a walled fort, containing or surrounded by a rabbit-warren of mud hovels, commonly rises in the midst of carefully terraced fields, planted with millet, wheat, barley, buckwheat, or lucerne, and of orchard clumps, producing a rich spoil of apricots, walnuts, apples, pears, melons, mulberries, peaches, and grapes. Delicious rills of water, issuing from glacier sources, trickle through the cultivated plots. On the Nagar bank the green spots are more frequent and more gracious, for they have a superior supply. Finally, on both banks the cultivation merges in a broad and continuous strip, towards the upper end of which the two capitals – if, indeed, these fort-villages are worthy of such a name – are situated. Nagar – which I was unable to visit, the rope bridge across the river having broken down – is planted on the bank of the Maiatsil or Hispar River, a confluent of the

Hunza River, into which it flows five miles below the fort and town. Baltit, the chief place of Hunza (there being no town or village of the latter name), crowns a loftier and more picturesque elevation at a little distance from the right bank of the Hunza River, and takes its title, as does its neighbour Altit, from the Baltis of Baltistan, by a contingent of whom the two castles were built, as a wedding-present to the daughter of a Balti ruler, who, long years ago, wedded a former Mir of Hunza.

After crossing the river back again to the Hunza bank by a suspension bridge, replacing the old rope bridge, we came to Aliabad, a fort-village, where were the barracks for the Kashmir troops of the Hunza garrison. We next passed two small villages built on the top of rocky mounds, and named respectively Hyderabad and Chamar Kun (*i.e.* Iron Fort), and were presently met, at a short distance outside Baltit, by the Raja, Mohammed Nazim Khan, by his brother, Nafiz Khan, and his Wazir, Humaiun Beg, who rode with us to the bungalow of Lieutenant Gurdon, at that time acting as Political Officer in Hunza, and afterwards Political Officer at Chitral. The Raja was attired in a bright yellow velvet tunic covering white pantaloons that were tucked into long leather boots. The Wazir was in purple velvet.

After the flight of the murderous Safdar Ali Khan at the end of 1891, Humaiun Beg, who belonged to the hereditary family of Wazirs of Hunza, and had occupied that post under old Ghazan Khan, but who had been ejected by Safdar Ali, and had taken refuge in Chitral, was installed by the British as temporary Governor of the petty state pending the decision of the Government of India as to the new ruler. When Mohammed Nazim was appointed, Humaiun resumed his former post of Wazir, which he long occupied with the greatest advantage to the state. He was a man of uncommon shrewdness and ability, and on more than one occasion later, notably in the Chitral campaign of 1895, proved his absolute loyalty to the British. For this and other services he was in 1898 appointed a Khan Bahadur. Travelling, as I did, in his company for several days, I formed a high regard for this unusual man, who struck me as the most agreeable and capable personality whom I met in the Hindu Kush States. He was about forty-five years of age, though his hard life had greyed his beard and made him look older. In his earlier and unregenerate days he had been a great leader of raids, and had conducted one of the most renowned and successful of the Hunza forays far into the territory of Yarkand. When Safdar Ali Khan started upon his debauch of general assassination, Humaiun was fortunately absent from Hunza, and succeeded in effecting his escape. His two children, however, were at Baltit, and fell into the hands of the Thum, who, reluctant to belie his homicidal reputation, fully intended to put them to death. After the success, however, of the British at Nilt, he was in such a hurry to escape the Sahibs that he had not time to carry out his resolve. He retained sufficient presence of mind to carry off Humaiun's wife, who was reputed to be the best-looking woman in Hunza; but she was subsequently restored to her husband from Yarkand. All these details I learned in the course of my numerous conversations with the Wazir.

Mohammed Nazim Khan, the Thum (left), possessed good features and an amiable expression.

Mohammed Nazim Khan, the Thum, who was to be my host, had fortunately been ill at the time of Safdar Ali's family clearance, and had accordingly escaped the fate of his brothers, being supposed to be not worth the killing. He was the son of Ghazan Khan by another wife. At the time of my visit he was about twenty-eight years of age, and his conduct as ruler had fully justified the choice made by the Indian Government. He possessed good features and an amiable expression, particularly when he smiled and disclosed a row of singularly good teeth. His black hair was cut close on the forehead and in the middle of the head; but hung in very long locks behind his ears upon either shoulder. He usually wore a white turban wound round a conical skull-cap and the costume which I have previously described. He had two wives, by whom he was the father of one son and two daughters.

I visited him in the so-called castle of Baltit, a most picturesque five-storeyed edifice – the model of a feudal baron's stronghold – that rises to a considerable height above the low buildings of the town. The streets or alleys of Baltit are almost as steep as staircases, and the fort is planted at the very top of the town, which contained a population of about

1300 souls. At the gate I was received by the Raja, and we climbed together to the upper storey by wooden ladders conducting through hatchways in the floor, until we emerged upon an open space on the roof, adorned with rude mural decorations and a little native wood-carving. Here the Russian explorer, Captain Grombchevski, had been received, and had opened negotiations with Safdar Ali Khan in 1888. A small chamber opens on to this terrace, spread out with carpets, and furnished with a low divan, upon which we took our seats. From the terrace there is a wide and glorious outlook over the flat-roofed cubes of the town, each with a square orifice in its mud ceiling for light and smoke; over the cultivated fields and orchards beyond, all aglow in the afternoon sun; down to the deep grey gorge, with the silken thread of the river whispering many hundreds of feet below; and up to the eternal snows and the glistening spear-point of Rakapushi. Not less remarkable than this panorama, though in a different sense, is the view in the opposite or northern direction, immediately behind the town. Right above it towers a great mountain mass, and this again is backed by a fantastic grouping of needle-spires. The town of Baltit, in addition to its situation, is also distinguished for an artificial cutting right through and round the side of the hill below which it stands, this arduous work having been accomplished with the most primitive wooden implements and with curved ibex-horns by the inhabitants, in order to conduct to the lower levels the waters of a glacier stream behind.

The sister, formerly the rival, state of Nagar I was unable, as I have explained, to visit, but I subsequently made the acquaintance of the ruling Thum, Sikandar Khan, a splendid polo player, and a man of singularly fine appearance, whose features would have not belied the Hellenic descent that is claimed by many of the mountain tribes of the Himalayas and Hindu Kush, and that was typified by his Christian name.

Of the two peoples the Hunza men have always been the more warlike. They are also excellent mountaineers, their whole lives being spent among rocks and crags. In the various expeditions in which their levies have since fought under British officers, they have more than once been employed in turning an enemy's flank by scaling almost inaccessible heights, and have acquitted themselves right well. No doubt they were great rascals in their freebooter days, but slave-hunting being now out of vogue, they turned the same energies with cheerful alacrity to less questionable pursuits. I learned to like those of them in whose company I marched, and at the end of my journey I voted them the manliest and most attractive of the Aryan tribes of the Hindu Kush. The Nagar people also accepted their beating with dignity, and have never since given any trouble. Safdar Ali successfully escaped the long hand of the British *raj*, and being regarded by the Chinese in some sort as a tributary or subject, was detained by them at Urumchi, in the New Dominion. Uzar Khan, his fellow-fratricide of Nagar, who could claim no similar refuge or consideration, was surrendered and immured in the state prison of Hari Parbat at Srinagar. Old Jafar Khan, his father, though suspected, managed to escape positive incrimination, and was left undisturbed at

Nagar, where he continued, a senile phantom, to survive. The younger son, Sikandar Khan, wisely sided with the English, accompanied Colonel Durand's force, and received his reward in being recognised as ruler.

The only external difference in the political status of the two communities arising from the new order was that they were no longer permitted to fight each other, to enslave their neighbours, or to coquet with the foreigner, but were obliged to conform their political relations to the views of the Indian Government. I know of no case in history where conquest was so rapidly followed by contentment, or where the beaten party so soon became the fellow-combatants and allies of their victors. When the Chitral crisis occurred in 1895, the two Mirs furnished at their own request 300 levies and 600 coolies for Colonel Keey's relief expedition, in addition to the permanent body of levies raised from both states; and both chiefs appeared in person at Gilgit at the head of their men. Tranquil in the assured enjoyment of their independence, and in the undisturbed cultivation of their lands, and yet eager to fight for a suzerain whom they respect, the Hunza-Nagar tribes have thus been a living answer to those persons who contended in 1891-92 that we should inflict an irreparable injury upon them and heap up certain trouble for ourselves, by interfering with their liberty, which, as interpreted by their chiefs, was merely the liberty to harry and plunder and slay their less masculine or warlike neighbours. The people themselves extracted very little from the raids, the proceeds of which were commonly pocketed by the *khans*, and there was quite as much satisfaction within as without the borders of Hunza when the embargo was finally declared. As a further illustration of the peace that was already settling down upon the land, I may mention that in May 1895, for the first time in history, the Mir of Hunza visited the once rival state of Nagar. In bringing about these results, and in teaching the tribesmen that England is their friend as well as master, too much credit can scarcely be given to the series of young British officers – as a rule, only subalterns in rank – who successively filled the post of British Agent in the Hunza Valley.

Less than ten years afterwards, when I was Viceroy, I invited the whole of these border chieftains down to Calcutta as the guests of Government, and we there renewed the friendly contact of 1894. Among my possessions is a photograph of the chiefs that was taken on that occasion, and bears their signatures. We gave them an evening party at Government House, where they particularly enjoyed the ices, which they had never seen or tasted before; and I can recall the picture of the old Raja of Astor, who was not much accustomed to the use of a chair, seated on the marble floor, wearing an immense white turban, and stuffing a strawberry ice with his fingers into his mouth.

At intervals since we have exchanged salutations from a great distance, and I can never forget those manly and genial highlanders of the Hindu Kush.

From Baltit Lennard and I commenced our march upon the second stage of the Hunza Valley road to the Pamirs. The distance to the Kilik

Pass is about eighty-two miles, over one of the worst tracks in the world. At a little beyond Baltit the valley of the Hunza River, which from Chalt has pursued an easterly course, turns due north, and the river cuts a deep gash or furrows an uproarious channel along its bottom on its descent from the watershed of the Pamirs. The scenery also changes. In place of the richly cultivated terraces and the abounding orchards of both the Hunza and the Nagar slopes in the lower valley, we find only rare villages and still rarer cultivation, and are in a region of rock and stones. Big glaciers propel their petrified cascades to the very edge of the river. In many places this requires to be forded. Sometimes the road is only conducted round the edge of the precipices that overhang the torrent by artificial ladders and ledges, built out from the cliff with stones loosely laid upon supports of brushwood and timber jammed into the interstices of the rock. This sounds very dreadful, but in practice is much less alarming, the galleries, though only lasting for a few days, being sufficiently strong at the beginning, and being slightly inclined inwards toward the face of the cliff.

Over this vile stretch of country there are two tracks, the upper or summer track, which avoids the river-bed, then filled with a fierce and swirling torrent, and climbs to the summit of the cliffs, several thousand feet above the water; and the lower or winter track, which can only be pursued when, the melting of the snow by the hot summer suns being over, the current dwindles to a number of fordable channels, across and amid the boulder-piled fringes of which the traveller picks his way. The second track is not commonly available till the beginning of October; but a few cloudy days had sensibly lowered the river, and it was thought that, with the aid of the Thum's people, who accompanied us in large numbers, the route might be found practicable, except in a few places where, to avoid the still swollen stream, we should require to scale the heights. The whole of our baggage, tents, etc., had to be carried on the backs of men, the route being quite impracticable for baggage-animals. We had riding-horses ourselves, but there were many places where these had to be abandoned and swum across the river; while in others we were compelled to ford it on their backs. This was the least agreeable experience of our march, the current being swift, and the glacier-grey water being icy cold. The Hunza men, however, besides being strong and willing, proved to be fearless swimmers. Stripping, they plunged into the water and swam on either side of our ponies, holding them up and preventing them from being swept down. In order to reward them we offered prizes for a swimming contest across the river and back. Their style is a hand-over-hand swimming, and many of the men were carried down at least 300 yards before they succeeded in getting out on the farther bank. They also swam with *mussuks*, or inflated goat-skins, lying with their stomachs on the skins, the hinder legs of which they tied round their thighs, and propelling themselves with their hands and feet. By this method in flood-time they bring their women across the river, strapping the lady on to a *mussuk* and swimming at its side themselves.

From Bulji Das onwards the valley is called Little Guhjal, its inhabitants being Wakhis, who originally emigrated from Big Guhjal, or Wakhan, and who still speak the Wakhi language. On the second day, soon after we had passed the fort at Gulmit – where, as at all the villages, travelling in the company of the Raja, we were met and played in by the village band – a cliff was pointed out to us where the amiable Safdar Ali, in the course of his flight in December 1891, had thrown down and killed one more of his brothers. On this day we crossed the snout of three glaciers; one of which, the great Pasu glacier, comes striding down to the river's edge with a wilderness of *séracs* and icetowers, and terminates in a prodigious moraine. On the third day we crossed the Batur galcier, which is a long twisting ice-flood over twenty miles in length. Its surface was split up with lofty pinnacles and crevasses, and we picked our way across in a little over an hour, over ice-hills sprinkled with a black gravelly debris. The retrospect was a frozen strait of choppy waves, ridge upon ridge of ice, some snow-white, others as black as soot. This glacier is constantly changing its track, and is sometimes quite impassable. In this neighbourhood, also, we observed gold-washing on the banks of the river: a man crouching with a wooden trough on a heap of stones by the water's edge, shovelling into it a pile of soil, and then laboriously washing and sifting it out with the aid of a bowl made from a gourd. In this way a few grain are penuriously extracted, and are bought by the Mir with grain, being used by him to pay his annual tribute of twenty ounces of gold-dust to the Kashmir Government, as well as the few *tolas* of gold which he is still allowed to pay to China.

On the fourth day we passed on the right or west bank of the river the *nullah* that conducts to the diffficult Irshad Pass leading to Sarhad, in Wakhan, as well as to the Chilinji Pass, which conducts into the Karumbar valley of Yasin. According to the presence or absence of snow on a particular peak in this part of the main valley do the Hunza people know whether the Irshad Pass is or is not open. A little later we crossed, on the east bank, the deep and narrow gorge down which the Khunjerab River flows from the Khunjerab Pass, leading on to the Taghdumbash Pamir. On the fifth day, following up the valley, which gradually rose, and was filled with clumps of willow and birch in the river's bed, we reached Murkush, just below the junction of the two *nullahs* that conduct respectively to the Kilik and Mintaka Passes, leading on to the same Pamir. Pursuing the former or left-hand of these, we camped at an elevation of 13,360 feet (having risen 5400 feet since leaving Baltit), at a few miles from the foot of the Kilik Pass. On the morrow we crossed the latter. I took the elevation on the summit with a boiling-point thermometer, ordinary thermometer, and aneroid, and found it to be 15,870 feet. The top of the Kilik is a long flattish plateau, covered with stones and interspersed with grassy swamps and standing water. There was no snow on the pass itself, though the snow-line was but little above us on the surrounding mountains, which were draped in white. This is the pass of which Captain Grombchevski, who crossed it in August 1888, penned the somewhat hyperbolic report that it is 'exceedingly easy, so that a cart with a full team of horses could follow it'. Here we bade good-bye to the

I took the elevation on the summit with a boiling-point thermometer, ordinary thermometer, and aneroid, and found it to be 15,870 feet. Then I sat down and completed a letter to the Times.

Thum of Hunza and his men, the limits of whose jurisdiction we had reached, and were met by Kasim Beg, the Kirghiz chief of the Taghdumbash Pamir, who was a Chinese subject, and who had received instructions to attend upon us while in Chinese territory.

I sat down on a rock at the top of the pass and completed a letter to the *Times*, as whose special correspondent I was acting. The letter would go southwards with the streams that flow into the Indus and so into the great Indian Ocean. My own face was turned towards the north, where at my feet I could see the springs whose waters, running eastwards, were ultimately to lose themselves in the great Tibetan depression of Lob Nor; while within a few miles of me, on the other side, the rills were trickling westwards that would presently merge in the mighty Oxus, and wend their way through the heart of Central Asia to their distant home in the Aral Sea. I stood, therefore, literally upon the water-parting, the Great Divide of the Asiatic Continent. India, with all its accumulated treasures, lay behind me, ring-fenced by the terrific barriers through and across which I had laboriously climbed. Central Asia, with its rival domination and its mysterious destinies, lay before me. I was on the southern eave of the 'Roof of the World'. Before me, in the language of Milton,

> A frozen continent
> Lies dark and wild, beat with perpetual storms
> Of whirlwind and dire hail, which on firm land
> Thaws not, but gathers heap, and ruin seems
> Of ancient pile: all else deep snow and ice.

But the Pamirs are another story, which I cannot tell here.

The Cradle of Polo

Soon as the Lord of Heaven had sprung his horse
Over horizon into the blue field,
Salâman kindled with the wine of sleep
Mounted a barb of fire for the Maidán;
He and a troop of Princes – Kings in blood,
Kings in the kingdom-troubling tribe of beauty,
All young in years and courage, bat in hand,
Galloped afield, tossed down the golden ball
And chased, so many crescent Moons a full;
And, all alike intent upon the Game,
Salámán still would carry from them all
The prize, and shouting 'Hal!' drive home the ball.
(From the *Salámán and Absal of Jamia*; translated by E. FitzGerald.)

Let other people play at other things:
The king of games is still the game of Kings.
J.K. STEPHEN.

EVERY one knows that the game of polo had its origin in remote times, centuries before the Christian era, in the sport-loving East. Under the name of *changan* (which was really the name of the stick) it was played at the Court and in the capitals of successive dynasties of Persian kings; and to this day the Great Square or Piazza of Ispahan contains the stone pillars, 9 feet high and 24 feet apart, which marked the goals, and the open stand from which the game was watched by the Court. From Persia the game spread westwards to Constantinople and eastwards as far as China; commencing everywhere by being the favourite pastime of princes and nobles, but developing whenever the ponies and the means were forthcoming, into the popular recreation of the people.

It was played by the monarchs who fought the Crusaders, but not apparently by the Crusaders themselves, who amid the hundred things, good and bad, which they brought back from the Orient, appear strangely to have altogether omitted polo. Tamerlane is said to have encouraged his courtiers to play the game with the heads of their slaughtered enemies – a form of the sport which cannot have been provocative of either swift or scientific play. The great Akbar was so fond of it that he could not desist at sundown, but must play with luminous balls at night. More than one prince was killed on the polo ground. The game was illustrated by the Court painters and extolled in the verses of the most famous bards.

Then, somehow or other, polo vanished altogether from sight, and in the fall of dynasties, or amid the tumult and confusion that marked the eighteenth century in Asia, it ceased to be played, and remained a tradition in local chronicles or in the pages of poets and historians.

Suddenly, in the middle of the last century, it was discovered simultaneously, and by an absolutely fortuitous coincidence, to have survived in the two extreme corners of the Indian peninsula; hidden away, on the one side in the mighty mountains of the Hindu Kush that separate British India from the Central Asian *massif*, and at the other end, in the tangle of the hills that divide the watersheds of Burma and Assam. Reports came from the north-west that the game was still played in the little principalities or communities of Dardistan, Baltistan, and Ladakh; from the north-east, that it had been rediscovered in the tiny highland state of Manipur. How exactly it got to those places and was preserved there – like some unknown or forgotten animal type in a mid-African forest – no one seemed precisely to know. Doubtless it was a legacy to the Hindu Kush communities from the Central Asian Court of the descendants of the Moghuls. To Manipur it must have come from China.

There seems to be some dispute as to the exact dates at which the discovery was first made, and as to the individual pioneers who 'brought the good news from Ghent', and introduced the game that was destined ere long to become the favourite sport of the Englishman in India. But there can be no doubt that the precedence belongs to Manipur. Somewhere about 1854 or a little later, English planters in Cachar (Assam) learned the game from Manipuri settlers and exiles who had carried it thither from their own valley: a European polo club was formed at Silchar in 1859; in 1862 it was brought down to Calcutta, and from there enthusiastic officers took it up-country to the principal cantonments of Northern India as far as Peshawur.

Almost simultaneously, or possibly a little later, young British officers on leave in Kashmir saw the game played by some troops of the Maharaja at Srinagar, and became its sponsors on returning to their stations in the Punjab; although whether its first introduction there was due to their initiative, or to the Manipuri wave which by this time had flowed in a north-westerly direction as far as Lahore, is not quite certain. Anyhow, just as Grotefend and Rawlinson succeeded, by quite independent labours, in deciphering the cuneiform script in the first half of the nineteenth century, so, early in the second half, the immortal game burst upon India and the world like two almost simultaneous thunder-claps from the clear sky of the border ranges, whence no one had expected any particular good ever to come.

I imagine that there are but few persons who have been enabled by the accident of service or of travel, to see and to compare the native game as it is still played, or was played only a few years ago, in both those remote localities. As I happen to be one of that number, it may be worth while to set down the exact features of the two varieties of the game, as practised in Manipur and in the Hindu Kush states, so that polo lovers in England may realise how much or how little of the two Indian prototypes has survived in the process of immigration to Europe; and in what manner the game is pursued – unless it has since been anglicised out of all recognition – by the wild tribesmen of the Indian border.

Young British officers on leave in Kashmir became the game's sponsors.

I first saw it played in the course of my visit to the Pamirs in 1894. On my way northward from Srinagar, I came across the polo grounds of Astor, Gilgit, Hunza, Nagar, Mastuj, Reshun, and Chitral; there is also a ground at Yasin. Farther to the east, in Baltistan, there are polo grounds

The immortal game burst upon India and the world like two almost simultaneous thunder-claps from the clear sky of the border ranges.

at Shigar, Rondu, and Shardu. Yet more to the east, the game is played in Ladakh, and the principal arena used to be the main street of Leh.

There are slight differences in these various forms of the game, but the similarity is sufficiently great to admit of their being classified as a single genus.

It is from this quarter that the name, as we know it, takes its rise: for polo or *pulu* is the Tibetan word for the willow root, of which the ball is commonly made. The polo grounds vary greatly in size and shape, according to the space available. The Astor ground was 150 yards long by 20 yards wide. Other grounds were from 200 to 250 yards in length – I measured one as 280 yards – and from 30 to 40 in width. The ground is sometimes of grass but quite as often of *put* or sandy earth, beaten to a hard consistency by galloping hoofs, and is usually surrounded by a low wall of rough stones, upon which the spectators take their seats, and from which the ball rebounds into play. The goals are low white stones fixed in the ground. At Hunza they were only about seven feet apart, but elsewhere I found the distance between them to be from twenty to thirty feet. The game is commonly played to the music of a band, who are seated on the wall above the middle of the ground. Their instruments were, as a rule, a big drum, a couple of kettledrums, and two or three clarionets with a note very much like a bagpipe. These instruments discoursed a steady but somewhat discordant music, which rose into a frantic din when a goal was scored. The performers were drawn from a special and very low caste, called *Dom*, who were also the leather-workers of the community.

There appeared to be no limit to the number of players who might take part, but the number ordinarily ranged from four to twelve or more a side. The ponies which they bestrode were country bred, and as a rule came from Badakshan on the one side and Baltistan on the other, being from twelve to thirteen hands in height, sometimes rather less, exceedingly strong, wiry, and active. The players rode them with a plain snaffle and a single rein, frequently of rope; the saddles were of rather a primitive description, being sometimes little more than a rough pile or pad of thick cloth, though the better-equipped players used a saddle with a very high pummel and heavy crupper. None of them wore spurs, but they wielded a short whip suspended from the wrist. Owing, no doubt, to the small size of the ponies, a much shorter polo stick was employed than is common in England, the length being little more than three feet. The handle was of almond wood or wild cherry or bamboo, and sometimes of hazel or ash, and was fitted into a heavy plane or willow-wood head, which was apt to be curved in shape. The ball was of willow wood and very heavy, until the British officers, who habitually joined in the native game, introduced the lighter English ball of bamboo root. As far as I could ascertain there were no particular rules until the British players appeared on the scene: the hooking of sticks was freely indulged in; no scruple was entertained about 'off-side' and 'crossing'; and the most glorious scuffles with indiscriminate banging and whacking took place, in which players and ponies were equally belaboured, but which neither appeared in the least to mind. The men rode with the utmost impetuosity and without a symptom of fear, and performed feats of horsemanship

The game is commonly played to the music of a band.

which, considering their primitive mounts, were truly astounding. They would charge at full speed right against the rough stone wall, being often as nearly as possible precipitated from their steeds with the violence of the impact.

By far the prettiest sight, however, excelling in speed and grace anything seen on an English polo ground, was the fashion in which the game was opened, or resumed after a goal had been scored. Instead of the ball being thrown by an umpire into the middle of the ground, the opener of the game (or the winner of the last goal) started off at a full gallop from one corner of the ground, with the whole of the rest of the field behind him, shouting as they raced. In his hand he held the ball, and, when he came to the centre of the field, he threw it into the air and struck it a mighty blow with his polo stick as it fell, the ball describing a parabola in the air before it finally touched the ground, when not infrequently – such was the skill of the best players and the force of the stroke – it sped between the opposing goalposts and scored a goal. There was a well-known Nagar player at the time of my visit, who might usually be counted on for a goal in this fashion. The knack was sometimes, but rarely, acquired by the English players. I never saw one accomplish the feat.

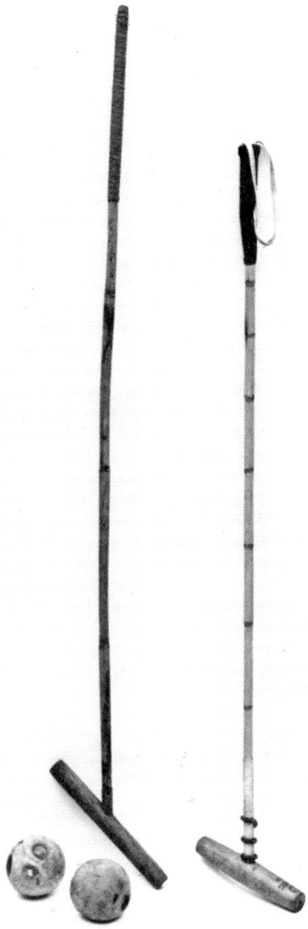

The polo stick common in England.

Already, however, in 1894, the picturesque practice which I have described was falling into desuetude; for, as pointed out by the British officers, it gave little or no opportunity to the defending side to save their goal. Accordingly at Baltit, the capital of Hunza, the victorious captain (usually the Raja), better mounted and more richly clad than the remainder, only galloped down one-quarter of the distance before striking off, while his adversaries, awaiting him in the centre, had a chance of intercepting the ball.

There was another respect in which the local practice had already undergone a notable modification. In the native game, a goal was not scored until one of the victorious side had dismounted from his pony and picked up the ball, the result being a fearful *mêlée*, very much like a 'scrum' or 'bully' at football, in which, however, horses were mingled with human beings in the struggle, often at considerable risk to both. This rule had already been abandoned, and the goal was counted as soon as the ball had passed between the posts.

Of course, our European game is more orthodox: the ground is more even, the riders are better mounted, the rules more precise, the strokes more scientific, and the play more brilliant. But I shall never forget the spectacle of that galloping crowd of shouting men: the brightly clad Raja thundering in front; the swing of his upright polo stick; the crack as the head of the mallet unfailingly hit the falling ball; and the whiz of the latter as it flew through the air towards the enemy goal.

At Chitral, and I dare say elsewhere, the beaten side had to dance to the victors; and it was the particular pleasure of the Mehtar (afterwards, as is elsewhere related, unhappily murdered) to select as captain of the opposite team to himself, which was invariably beaten, an old gentleman who had previously made an unsuccessful attempt upon his life, and upon whom it amused him to wreak this playful revenge. The dancing that I saw at Hunza and elsewhere was not exactly what we should describe by that name in England. The dancers conducted a sort of running monologue with the members of the band, who gesticulated in reply, and followed their movements with encouraging shouts and yells. The dancing was not confined to the young; and I remember one performer, a grave and elderly individual in top-boots, with a floating brown *choga* or dressing-gown, who hopped about, and postured, and spun round amid the rapt admiration of the crowd. There was also a sort of sword-dance, performed by a man from Nagar with two swords.

Seven years later I saw the game played at Manipur, when I rode overland from Assam to Burma – the only Viceroy to visit that little state which ten years earlier had been the scene of one of the most frightful and inexplicable tragedies in Anglo-Indian history.

Polo in Manipur presented many similarities to the Hindu Kush game, but some remarkable contrasts. The capital being situated on a level plain in the middle of a broad valley, there was scope for a level ground of much larger dimensions than in the mountains of the mighty Hindu Kush. Accordingly, the Manipur ground was 225 yards long by 110 broad, and was covered with very fair turf. But its most striking feature was that it had no goalposts, the ground being surrounded by a low bank about two feet high, the striking of the ball across which at either end was the Manipuri equivalent of a goal. On the western side was a stand reserved for members of the Raja's family, most of whom were good players, being well mounted and having been trained to the game from childhood. The number of players was indeterminate, the correct number being from seven to nine a side, though there was no limit. The game that I saw was one of ten a side, and it was preceded and followed by a ceremonial which undesignedly illustrated the Chinese origin of the local game and the earliest Chinese connections of the state. Before the play began, the ten players lined up in front of me, as representative of the King-Emperor in India, and prostrated themselves at full length on the ground, twice striking the soil with their foreheads; the same homage was repeated at the close of the encounter.

Unlike the practice of the Hindu Kush border, the ball was thrown into the midst of the players when the terminal lines had been crossed, or when the ball went out; but it was not rolled along the ground when thrown in, but tossed in the air, the players being at liberty to strike it before it reached the earth.

The ponies were, I thought, smaller than those which I had seen at the other end of the Indian frontier, varying from ten or eleven to twelve hands in height, but they were caparisoned in quite a peculiar manner. Big round balls of soft white cotton were suspended from their heads and backs to protect them from the blows of the polo sticks; while the legs of the players were similarly defended by a shield or flap of hard leather in front of the stirrups. In the latter, which were broad and heavy, the rider placed neither the ball nor the arch of his sole, but his naked toes. On his legs were worsted gaiters or leggings, reaching from the ankle to the knee. Round the loins he wore the native *dhoti* of white cotton or silk, the upper part of the body being clothed in a short jacket, or left bare. The players either coiled their long black hair in a knot behind the head or allowed it to stream over their shoulders with high projecting pummel and cantle. What with the rattling of the leather flaps and the flying hither and thither of the cotton balls, and the cries of the players, the scene was one of uncommon excitement and commotion. In the days before the catastrophe to which I have referred, Sunday evening was the favourite time of play, and then the *serapati* in his coloured jacket and silk drawers was the hero of the scene. When the princes played, a stake was offered in the shape of muslin cloths or turbans, hung up at the end of the ground, and these became the prize of the winning side, the losers having to pay the cost.

The implements of the game were less heavy than those which I have before described – perhaps owing to British influence: the ball being of bamboo root, large and light; the head of the polo club was of heavy wood, but the handle was commonly of well-seasoned cane, the upper end being covered with red or blue cloth. There were no *chukkers*, as in our game, the players being at liberty to change their ponies whenever they pleased; and there was the same delightful absence of rules on which I have already commented.

I do not in the least agree with those who have said either of the Hindu Kush or the Manipur polo, or of both, that the game was a dribbling game, played at an easy canter, without any hard hitting; slow to take part in, and slower to watch. On the contrary it seemed to me, in both localities, to consist mainly of hard galloping and tremendously hard hitting. I saw in both places difficult or fancy strokes which it would baffle any Englishman or American to attempt; there was one Manipuri stroke in which the player caught the ball in the air, tossed it up, and throwing his reins on the pony's neck, hit the ball with the stick held in both hands.

I do not pretend to compare either of these rather primitive types of the game with the highly finished variety that may be seen at Hurlingham or Meadowbank – any more than one would compare village cricket with a Test Match at Lord's, or rounders with baseball. But the higher types would never have been produced or evolved had it not been for these hardy mountaineers, preserving the tradition and maintaining the glorious spirit of the game throughout the centuries.